PARTY WALL
LAW AND PRACTICE

Second edition

PARTY WALLS
LAW AND PRACTICE

Second Edition

Stephen Bickford-Smith BA, FCIArb,
*Barrister and Chartered Arbitrator,
Landmark Chambers*

and

Colin Sydenham MA
Barrister

JORDANS
2004

Published by
Jordan Publishing Limited
21 St Thomas Street
Bristol BS1 6JS

© Jordan Publishing Limited 2004

All rights reserved. No part of this publication may be reproduced, stored in a retrieval system, or transmitted in any way or by any means, including photocopying or recording, without the written permission of the copyright holder, application for which should be addressed to the publisher.

British Library Cataloguing-in-Publication Data
A catalogue record for this book is available from the British Library.

ISBN 0 85308 799 7

Typeset by MFK-Mendip, Frome, Somerset
Printed in Great Britain by MPG Books, Bodmin, Cornwall

PREFACE TO THE FIRST EDITION

'Nam tua res agitur paries cum proximus ardet.'
(For it is your business if your neighbour's party wall catches fire.)
(Horace Epistles I, xviii, 84)

The words of Horace attest the antiquity of concerns about party walls. And no wonder, since man is an intensely territorial animal, and party walls demarcate the boundaries between adjoining private territories. Two millennia after Horace, Robert Frost's neighbour observed that 'Good fences make good neighbours', yet the common law, with its insistence on the sanctity of each neighbour's property rights, will often frustrate the good neighbour who wishes to repair, rebuild or improve (let alone develop) a party wall.

As a result, local statutory regimes have been enacted which establish summary procedures enabling party walls to be dealt with in ways which are approved by a panel of surveyors. The best known of these regimes is in Inner London, where its origins can be traced back to the years immediately after the Great Fire. A succession of London Building Acts culminated in that of 1939, which still owed much to its predecessor of 1894. Now, for the first time, this metropolitan regime, with relatively minor modifications, is to be extended to the whole of England and Wales by the Party Wall etc Act 1996.

The relaxation of the common law straitjacket is welcome. So is the unique and expeditious procedure for the resolution of disputes. The system has worked well in London, and this is demonstrated by the fact that only a handful of cases on it have reached the law reports this century. Partly this success must be attributable to a corps of experienced surveyors who are familiar with the legislation: partly also, no doubt, to ignorance of the legislation on the part of the public, coupled with neighbourly forbearance.

Whether the system will work well on a countrywide scale remains to be seen. The Law Society opposed the Bill, partly on the ground that the costs of the dispute resolution procedure will be out of proportion to the modest value of many of the properties which will now be affected. There are technical reservations too. The Act is by no means emancipated from its nineteenth century parentage. It imposes contingent liabilities on owners of land, but it is a stranger to the techniques of registration which have been with us since 1925. It does not recognise the existence of successors in title. It is harsh to occupiers who do not satisfy its definition of 'owner'. These points are elaborated in the text.

Halsbury apart, there is no book on party walls written by and for practising lawyers, and there are many professionals throughout the country, surveyors and land agents as well as lawyers, who will now need to familiarise themselves with the workings of the 1996 Act. This book is intended for them. We have endeavoured not only to provide an introduction to the Act, but to set the legislation in its conveyancing and property law context. The appendices include the text of the 1996 Act and of Part VI of the 1939 Act, a checklist of the notices that are required by the 1996 Act, and a set of precedents. We hope that these will all be of practical use. We have not thought it necessary to include the text of the 1894 Act, but in preparing this book we have had frequent recourse to the commentary on that Act written by A.R. Rudall and published, as it happens, by Jordan & Sons Ltd in 1922. It is appropriate that this book should be published under the successor imprint. We record our grateful thanks to the professional team who have helped us through the pains of authorship. The authors and publishers are grateful to The Stationery Office for giving their kind permission to reproduce the statutory materials in this book.

STEPHEN BICKFORD-SMITH
COLIN SYDENHAM
December 1996

PREFACE TO THE SECOND EDITION

The Act has given rise to relatively few reported cases in the 6½ years since it came into force, and even the tally of cases decided on its predecessor, part 6 of the London Building Acts (Amendment) Act 1939 is not long. This is probably due more to the pragmatic way in which experienced surveyors and lawyers have approached disputes which have threatened to get out of hand than to any lack of scope for argument afforded by the often obscure provisions of the statute itself. Various suggestions for reform have been advanced but it is unlikely that any amending legislation will be brought forward in the near future.

In this new edition we have taken account of developments not only directly related to party walls but also in other areas of the law which are relevant to this field, notably the coming into force of the Civil Procedure Rules 1998 and the Human Rights Act of the same year. The opportunity has been taken to revise and expand the text to include fuller discussion of points of difficulty, without, it is hoped, sacrificing conciseness unduly.

The law is stated as at 1 December 2003.

STEPHEN BICKFORD-SMITH
COLIN SYDENHAM
December 2003

CONTENTS

Preface to the First Edition	v
Preface to the Second Edition	vii
Table of Cases	xv
Table of Statutes	xxiii
Table of Statutory Instruments	xxix
Table of European Legislation	xxxi

Chapter 1	INTRODUCTION TO THE ACT		1
	1.1	Sources of Current Law	1
	1.2	Antecedents	1
	1.3	The 1939 Act	2
	1.4	Operation of the Act	2
	1.5	Structure of the Book	3
	1.6	Application	5
	1.7	Commencement and Transitional Provisions	5
Chapter 2	APPLICATION OF THE ACT		7
	2.1	Definitions	7
	2.2	Party Wall	7
	2.3	Party Fence Wall	9
	2.4	Party Structure	9
	2.5	Owner	10
	2.6	Other Expressions	11
	2.7	Extent	12
	2.8	Multiple Owners	12
	2.9	Flats	13
Chapter 3	RIGHTS OF BUILDING OWNER		15
	3.1	Introduction	15
	3.2	Boundary Not Built on: Section 1	15
	3.3	Building on the Boundary	17
	3.4	Building Wholly on Building Owner's Land	19
	3.5	Disputes	20
	3.6	Boundary Already Built on: Section 2	21
	3.7	Rights Under Section 2	21
	3.8	Party Structure Notice	24
	3.9	Counter-notice: Section 4	26
	3.10	Disputes: Section 5	27
Chapter 4	ADJACENT EXCAVATION AND CONSTRUCTION		29
	4.1	Introduction	29
	4.2	Distances	29

4.3	Measurements	30
4.4	Meaning of 'Excavation'	32
4.5	Meaning of 'Building or Structure'	33
4.6	Bottom of the Foundations	34
4.7	Section 6(3)	34
4.8	Notices	34
4.9	Scope of Dispute	35
4.10	Lapse of Notice	35
4.11	Plans	36
4.12	Common Law Liability	36
4.13	Further References	37

Chapter 5	SPECIAL FOUNDATIONS	39
5.1	Introduction	39
5.2	Definition	39
5.3	General Principle	39
5.4	Sections 1 and 2	39
5.5	Party Structure Notice	40
5.6	Counter-notice	40
5.7	Consent in Writing	41
5.8	Expenses	41

Chapter 6	ANCILLARY RIGHTS AND OBLIGATIONS	45
6.1	Introduction	45
6.2	Section 7	45
6.3	Section 7(5): What Work may be Carried Out	45
6.4	Section 7(1): Unnecessary Inconvenience	46
6.5	Section 7(3) and 11(6): Premises Laid Open	47
6.6	Section 7(2): Compensation	48
6.7	Relation of Section 7(2) to other Compensatory Provisions	51
6.8	Enforcement	52
6.9	Duty to Make Good	53
6.10	Section 11(8): Payment in Lieu	54

Chapter 7	RIGHTS OF ENTRY	55
7.1	Introduction	55
7.2	Right of Building Owner	55
7.3	Right of Surveyors	56
7.4	Notice Before Entry	56
7.5	Usual Working Hours	57
7.6	Civil Remedy	57
7.7	Occupiers	58
7.8	Human Rights Aspects	58

Chapter 8	**THE AWARD – PROCEDURE AND SCOPE**		59
	8.1	Introduction	59
	8.2	Dispute	59
	8.3	Qualification and Independence of Surveyors	60
	8.4	Machinery of Appointment	61
	8.5	Methods of Appointment and Selection	62
	8.6	Secondary Methods	62
	8.7	Death and Incapacity of Surveyors	63
	8.8	Refusal and Neglect by Surveyors	64
	8.9	Refusal and Neglect by Parties' Surveyors	64
	8.10	Making the Award	66
	8.11	Service of the Award	67
	8.12	Scope of Award: Surveyors' Jurisdiction	67
	8.13	Limits of Jurisdiction	68
	8.14	Preliminary Determination of Jurisdiction	69
	8.15	Successive Awards	70
	8.16	Retrospective Awards	70
	8.17	Multiple Parties	71
	8.18	Procedure and Form of Award	71
	8.19	Surveyors as Arbitrators	72
	8.20	Immunity of Surveyors	72
Chapter 9	**THE AWARD – EFFECT AND ENFORCEMENT**		75
	9.1	Introduction	75
	9.2	Effect	75
	9.3	Estoppel	75
	9.4	Enforcement: Action on the Award	76
	9.5	Enforcement: Action outside the Award	79
	9.6	Adjoining Occupiers	80
	9.7	Interest	81
	9.8	Venue	81
	9.9	Procedure	82
	9.10	Limitation	82
Chapter 10	**RIGHTS OF APPEAL**		85
	10.1	Introduction	85
	10.2	Extent of Matters which can be Raised on Appeal, and Mode of Appeal	85
	10.3	Venue	89
	10.4	Appeal to the Court of Appeal	90
	10.5	Time-limits	91
	10.6	Effect of Appeal	91
	10.7	Other Methods of Challenging an Award	92
	10.8	Severability	92

Chapter 11	FINANCIAL MATTERS		93
	11.1	Introduction	93
	11.2	The Meaning of 'Costs' and 'Expenses'	93
	11.3	Expenses: General Rule	94
	11.4	Liabilities of Adjoining Owner	95
	11.5	Costs	96
	11.6	Other Liabilities of Building Owner	97
	11.7	Recovering Expenses from Adjoining Owner	98
	11.8	Section 14	98
Chapter 12	SECURITY FOR EXPENSES		101
	12.1	Introduction	101
	12.2	Security by the Building Owner	102
	12.3	Factors	102
	12.4	Amount	103
	12.5	Manner of giving Security	104
	12.6	Security by Adjoining Owner	104
	12.7	Procedure: Time Limit	105
	12.8	Failure to Respond or Comply	106
Chapter 13	SERVICE OF NOTICES		109
	13.1	Introduction	109
	13.2	Formal Requirements of Notices	109
	13.3	Amendment of Notice	110
	13.4	Mode of Service	110
	13.5	Other Methods of Service	112
	13.6	Service on the Owner of Premises	112
	13.7	Persons on Whom Notices Must be Served	112
	13.8	Joint Owners	113
	13.9	Failure to Serve Notices	113
	13.10	Waiver of Time-limits or Irregularities in Notices	113
Chapter 14	SUCCESSORS IN TITLE		115
	14.1	Introduction	115
	14.2	Definitions	115
	14.3	Assignability: Benefit and Burden	116
	14.4	Before Award: Dispute Procedure	116
	14.5	Agreement	117
	14.6	Dispute	117
	14.7	Dissenting Successor	118
	14.8	After Award	118
	14.9	Immediate Rights and Liabilities	119
	14.10	Contingent Rights and Liabilities	119
	14.11	Conveyancing Implications	122

	14.12	Liabilities Affecting a Purchaser	122
	14.13	Registration as Land Charge	122
	14.14	Action for Conveyancers	124
	14.15	Shortcomings	126
Chapter 15	**RELATIONSHIP WITH OTHER AREAS OF LAW**		127
	15.1	Introduction	127
	15.2	Common Law Rights in Party Walls	127
	15.3	Section 9	128
	15.4	Right to Light	129
	15.5	Right of Support	130
	15.6	Protection from the Weather	131
	15.7	Negligence	132
	15.8	Nuisance	132
	15.9	Trespass	134
	15.10	Breach of Statutory Duty	134
	15.11	Access to Neighbouring Land Act 1992	136
	15.12	Other Statutory Requirements	137
	15.13	Human Rights Act 1988	138
Chapter 16	**CRIMINAL OFFENCES**		141
	16.1	Section 16(1): Refusal of Entry	141
	16.2	Vicarious Liability	141
	16.3	Refusal	142
	16.4	Reasonable Cause	142
	16.5	Entry Pursuant to the Act	142
	16.6	Occupiers	143
	16.7	Section 16(2): Hindering Entry	143
	16.8	Procedure	143
Chapter 17	**REFORM**		145
	17.1	Introduction	145
	17.2	ODPM Review	145
	17.3	Pyramus and Thisbe Club	146
	17.4	Authors' Views	148
Appendix 1	Party Wall etc Act 1996 with Commentary		151
Appendix 2	London Building Acts (Amendment) Act 1939, Part VI		171
Appendix 3	Checklists of Notices		185
Appendix 4	Precedents		189
Appendix 5	Party Wall etc Bill in Parliament		225
Appendix 6	Errors and Inconsistences		227
Index			229

TABLE OF CASES

References in the right-hand column are to paragraph numbers; references in *italics* are to page numbers.

Adams v Marylebone BC [1907] 2 KB 822; (1907) 97 LT 593; (1907) 23 TLR
702   6.6.1, 6.7, 6.8.1, 8.16, 17.2.2
Agromet Motoimport Ltd v Maulden Engineering Co (Beds) Ltd [1985] 2 All
ER 436; [1985] 1 WLR 762; (1985) 129 SJ 400   9.10
Allen v Gulf Oil Refining Ltd [1981] AC 1001; [1981] 1 All ER 353; [1981] 2
WLR 188, HL   15.8.1
Aly v Aly (1984) 128 SJ 65; (1984) 81 LS Gaz 283, CA   10.5
Amalgamated Investment and Property Co Ltd v Texas Commerce
International Bank Ltd [1982] QB 84; [1981] 3 All ER 577; [1981] 3 WLR
565   13.10
Amoco Australia Pty Ltd v Rocca Bros Motor Engineering Co Pty Ltd [1975]
AC 561; [1975] 1 All ER 968; [1975] 2 WLR 779, PC   10.8
Andreae v Selfridge & Co Ltd [1938] Ch 1; [1937] 3 All ER 255, CA   6.4, 15.8
Anisminic v Foreign Compensation Commission [1968] 2 QB 862; [1967] 2
All ER 986; [1967] 3 WLR 382, CA   10.7
Arenson v Casson Beckman Rutley & Co [1977] AC 405; [1975] 3 All ER 901;
[1975] 3 WLR 815, HL   8.20
Argyle Motors (Birkenhead) Ltd v Birkenhead Corpn [1975] AC 99; [1974] 2
WLR 71; [1974] 1 All ER 201   6.6.2
Arthur J Hall & Co v Simons [2000] 3 WLR 543, HL   8.20
Aubergine Enterprises Ltd v Lakewood International Ltd [2002] NPC 29   5.7.1
Austin Rover Group Ltd v Crouch Butler Savage Associates (A Firm) and
Others [1986] 3 All ER 50; [1986] 1 WLR 1102; (1986) 130 SJ 634, CA   13.4.3

Baggs v United Kingdom App No 9310/81 52 DR 29   15.13.3
Bater and Birkenhead Corp, Re [1893] 1 QB 679; [1893] 2 QBD 77, CA   6.6.2
Blue Circle Industries Plc v MoD [1998] 3 All ER 385; [1998] EGCS 93;
[1998] NPC 100, CA   6.6.2, 6.8
Brace v South East Regional Housing Association Ltd and Another [1984] 1
EGLR 144, CA   15.5
Burkett Sharp & Co v Eastcheap Dried Fruit Co [1962] 1 Lloyds Rep 267, CA,
affirming [1961] 1 Lloyd's Rep 80   8.9.1
Burlington Property Co Ltd v Odeon Theatres Ltd [1939] 1 KB 633; [1938] 3
All ER 469, CA   8.19

Camden London Borough Council v Marshall [1996] 1 WLR 1345; [1996]
EGCS 104   16.8
Cargill International SA v Sociedad Iberica de Molturacion SA [1998] 1
Lloyds Rep 489; [1998] CLC 231; (1998) 95(4) LSG 33   8.9.1
Carlish v Salt [1906] 1 Ch 335   11.8, 14.14
Caswell v Worcestershire Justices (1889) 53 JP 820   16.3
Cave v Horsell [1912] 3 KB 533; (1912) 81 LJKB 981; (1912) 107 LT 186, CA   2.5
Central London Property Trust Ltd v High Trees House Ltd [1947] KB 130;
[1956] 1 All ER 256; [1946] WN 175   13.10

Chartered Society of Physiotherapy v Simmonds Church Smiles [1995] 1
  EGLR 155; [1995] 14 EG 145; [1995] EGCS 25, QBD   8.3, 8.19, 10.2.1–10.3, 11.2.1
Christopher Brown Ltd v Genossenschaft Oesterreichischer Waldbesitzer
  [1954] 1 QB 8; [1953] 3 WLR 689; [1953] 2 All ER 1039   8.14
City of Westminster v London County Council [1902] 1 KB 326   4.5.1
Clark (Inspector of Taxes) v Perks and other applications [2002] 4 All ER 1   10.2.2
Clearbrook Properties Ltd v Verrier [1974] 1 WLR 243; [1973] 3 All ER 614;
  (1973) 27 P & CR 430   14.13.2
Cohen v Tannar [1900] 2 QB 609; (1900) 64 LJQB 904; (1900) 83 LT 64, CA   7.7
Colley v Council for Licensed Conveyancers [2001] 4 All ER 998   10.2.2
Collin v Duke of Westminster [1985] QB 581; [1985] 1 All ER 463; [1985] 2
  WLR 553, CA   9.10
Colls v Home and Colonial Stores Ltd [1904] AC 179; (1904) 73 LJ Ch 484;
  (1904) 53 WR 30, HL   15.4
Co-operative Insurance Society Ltd v Argyle Stores (Holdings) Ltd [1998] AC
  1   9.4
Cowper Essex v Acton Local Board (1880) 14 App Cas 153   6.6.4
Crofts v Haldane (1867) LR 2 QB 194; (1867) 36 LJQB 85; (1867) 16 LT 116   8.13, 15.4
Crosby v Alhambra Co Ltd [1907] 1 Ch 295; (1907) 76 LJ Ch 176   2.8, 13.8
Crown Estate Commissioners v Dorset County Council [1990] Ch 297; [1990]
  1 All ER 19; [1990] 2 WLR 89   8.14, 9.3
Cubitt v Porter (1828) 8 B & C 257; [1824–34] All ER Rep 267   6.4
Cullen v Chief Constable of the Royal Ulster Constabulary (Northern
  Ireland) [2003] 1 WLR 1763; [2003] UKHL 39; [2003] All ER (D) 174   15.10.2
Cutler v Wandsworth Stadium Ltd [1949] AC 398; [1949] 1 All ER 544;
  [1949] LJR 824, HL   9.4.2, 15.10

Dalton v Angus & Co (1881) 6 App Cas 740; (1881) 46 JP 132; (1881) 30 WR
  191   4.12, 15.5
Daniells v Mendonca (1999) 78 P & CR 401   3.2
Dean v Walker (1997) 73 P & CR 366; [1996] NPC 78, CA   15.11
Demolition & Construction Co Ltd v Kent River Board [1963] 2 Lloyd's Rep
  7   11.5
Director of Public Prosecutions v Kent and Sussex Contractors Ltd [1944] KB
  146; [1944] 1 All ER 119   16.2
Dodd Properties (Kent) Ltd v Canterbury City Council [1980] 1 All ER 928;
  [1980] 1 WLR 433; (1979) 124 SJ 84, CA   9.4.3
Drury v Army and Navy Auxiliary Co-operative Supply Ltd [1896] 2 QB 271;
  (1896) 60 JP 421   2.7
Dun and Bradstreet Software Services (England) Ltd and another v Provident
  Mutual Life Assurance Association and another [1998] 2 EGLR 175   13.10
Duncan v Dowding [1897] 1 QB 575; (1897) 61 JP 280; (1897) 66 LJQB 363   16.3
Dundee Corporation v Guthrie 1969 SLT 93   8.7

EWP Ltd v Moore Ltd [1992] QB 460; [1992] 1 All ER 880; [1992] 2 WLR
  184, CA   1.3
Ecclesiastical Commissioners for England's Conveyance, Re [1936] Ch 430;
  (1936) 105 LJ Ch 168   2.5
English v Emery Reimbold & Strick Ltd [2002] 3 All ER 385   10.2.2, 11.5

Eton College v Minister of Agriculture Fisheries and Food [1964] Ch 274;
  [1962] 3 All ER 290; [1962] 3 WLR 726   15.3.2

Fillingham v Wood [1891] 1 Ch 51; (1891) 64 LT 46; (1891) 7 TLR 66   2.8
Finchbourne v Rodrigues [1976] 3 All ER 581   8.3
Fitzgerald v Williams [1996] 2 All ER 171; [1996] 2 WLR 447, CA   12.3.2
Frances Holland School v Wassef [2001] 2 EGLR 88   2.5, 8.9.1, 8.9.2, 8.9.3, 10.2.3

Gyle-Thompson v Wall Street (Properties) Ltd [1974] 1 All ER 295; [1974] 1
  WLR 123; (1973) 117 SJ 526   3.1, 3.7, 8.3, 8.13, 10.7, 13.2, 13.9

Hammersmith and City Rly v Brand [1861–73] All ER Rep 60; (1869) LR 4
  HL 171; (1861) 21 LT 238   6.6.7
Hobbs Hart & Co v Grover [1899] 1 Ch 11; (1899) 68 LJCh 84; (1899) 79 LT
  454   3.8.1, 4.8, 13.2
Hobday v Nicholl [1944] 1 All ER 302; (1944) 113 LJKB 264; (1944) 42 LGR
  103   4.5.1
Hodgson v Armstrong [1967] 2 QB 299; [1967] 1 All ER 307; [1967] 2 WLR
  311, CA   10.5
Holbeck Hall Hotel v Scarborough Borough Council [2000] QB 836, CA   15.5, 15.7, 15.8
Holbeck Hall Hotel v Scarborough Borough Council (No 2) [2002] 2 WLR
  1396   4.12
Horner v Franklin [1905] 1 KB 479; (1905) 74 LJKB 291; (1905) 92 LT 178   10.3
Hughes v Percival (1883) 8 App Cas 443; (1883) 47 JP 772; (1883) 52 LJQB
  719   15.7

Imperial Gas Light and Coke Co v Broadbent (1859) 7 HL Cas 600; (1859)
  29 LJ Ch 377; (1859) 34 LTOS 1, HL   6.6.3
Ives (ER) Investment Ltd v High [1967] 2 QB 379; [1967] 1 All ER 504;
  [1967] 2 WLR 789, CA   14.13.3

James v United Kingdom (1986) 8 EHRR 123; (1986) 26 RVR 139   15.13.4
Jeune v Queen's Cross Properties Ltd [1974] Ch 97; [1973] 3 All ER 97;
  [1973] 3 WLR 378   9.4.4
John Henshall Quarries v Harvey [1965] 2 QB 233; [1965] 1 All ER 725;
  [1965] 2 WLR 758   16.2
Jolliffe v Woodhouse (1894) 10 TLR 553; (1894) 38 SJ 578   6.4, 15.7

Kammin's Ballrooms Co Ltd v Zenith Investments (Torquay) Ltd [1971] AC
  850; [1970] 2 All ER 871; [1970] 3 WLR 287, HL   10.5, 13.10
Kelly v Rogers [1892] 1 QB 910; (1892) 56 JP 789; (1892) 61 LJQB 604   7.7
Knight v Pursell (1879) 11 Ch D 412; (1879) 43 JP 622; (1879) 48 LJ Ch 395   2.7

Ladd v Marshall [1954] 1 WLR 1489; [1954] 3 All ER 745; (1954) 98 SJ 870   10.2.2
Langbrook Properties Ltd v Surrey County Council [1969] 3 All ER 1424;
  [1970] 1 WLR 161; (1969) 113 SJ 983   15.5
Larchbank, The [1943] AC 299; (1943) 168 LT 161; (1943) 59 TLR 116   7.4

Leadbetter v Marylebone Corp [1904] 2 KB 893; (1904) 91 LT 639; (1904) 20
TLR 778, CA   8.13, 8.19, 15.6
Leadbetter v Marylebone Corp [1905] 1 KB 661; (1905) 92 LT 819; (1905) 21
TLR 377   3.8.2, 4.10
Leakey v National Trust [1980] QB 485; [1980] 1 All ER 17; [1980] 2 WLR
65, CA   6.4, 15.8
Lehmann v Herman [1993] 1 EGLR 172; [1993] 16 EG 124   13.7, 13.9
Lewis v Haverfordwest Rural District Council [1953] 2 All ER 1599; [1953] 1
WLR 1486; (1953) 97 SJ 877   11.5
Lingké v Christchurch Corp [1912] 3 KB 595; (1912) 107 LT 476; (1912) 28
TLR 536   6.6.2
Livingstone v Rawyards Coal Co (1880) 5 App Cas 25; (1880) 44 JP 392, HL   9.4.3
London Corporation v Cusack-Smith [1955] AC 337; [1955] 2 WLR 363;
[1955] 1 All ER 302   1.3
London Chatham & Dover Railway Co v South Eastern Railway Co [1893] AC
429; (1893) 58 JP 36; (1893) 63 LJ Ch 93, HL   9.7
London Glos & N Hants Dairy Co v Morley & Lanceley [1911] 2 KB 257;
(1911) 9 LGR 738; (1911) 75 JP 437   2.7
Loost v Kremer (1997) (unreported) 12 May   8.3, 8.14
Lopes-Ostra v Spain (1994) 20 EHRR 277   15.12.3
Louis v Sadiq [1997] 1 EGLR 136; (1996) *The Times*, 22 November, CA   3.1, 8.13,
                                                              8.16, 9.5.4, 15.10
Lovell Partnerships (Northern) Ltd v AW Construction plc 81 BLR 83   10.2.2
Lowsley v Forbes (t/a LE Design Services) [1998] 3 All ER 897; [1998] 3 WLR
501; [1998] 2 Lloyds Rep 577, HL   1.3
Lowson v Percy Main & District Social Club & Institute [1979] ICR 568;
[1979] IRLR 227, EAT   16.3
Lubenham Fidelities v South Pembrokeshire District Council (1886) 33 BLR
39   8.3
Lucas (T) & Co Ltd v Mitchell [1974] Ch 129; [1972] 3 All ER 689; [1972] 3
WLR 934, CA   10.8

Maltglade Ltd v St Albans Rural District Council [1972] 3 All ER 129; [1972]
1 WLR 1230; (1972) 116 SJ 468, DC   13.4.2
Mannou Investments Co Ltd v Eagle Star Life Assurance Co Ltd [1997] AC
749   13.2
Marchant v Capital & Counties Plc [1983] 2 EGLR 156; (1983) 267 EG 843,
CA   6.6.7, 8.13, 15.6
Marine & General Mutual Life Assurance Society v St James' Real Estate Co
Ltd [1991] 2 EGLR 178; [1991] 38 EG 230   15.4
Mason v Fulham Corp [1910] 1 KB 631; (1910) 8 LGR 415; (1910) 74 JP 170   11.8,
                                                         14.9.1, 14.10.1, 14.10.2
Matania v National Provincial Bank Ltd [1936] 2 All ER 633; (1936) 106 LJKB
113, CA   15.8
Matos e Silva v Portugal (1996) 24 EHRR 573, ECHR   15.13.4
Metro-Cammell Hong Kong Ltd v FKI Engineering Plc (1996) 77 BLR 84   11.5
Metropolitan Building Act, ex parte McBryde, Re (1876) 4 Ch D 200; (1876)
46 LJ Ch 153   8.19

Midland Bank Plc v Bardgrove Property Services Ltd and John Willmott (WB)
(1992) 65 P & CR 153; [1992] 2 EGLR 168; [1992] 37 EG 126, CA 15.5, 15.10.2
Miller Construction v James Moore Earthmoving [2001] BLR 322 10.2.2
Mills & Rockleys v Leicester City Council [1946] KB 315 4.5.1
Montgomery, Jones & Co v Liebenthal & Co [1898] 1 QB 487; (1898) 67
LJQB 313 13.4.1
Mount Charlotte Investments plc v Prudential Assurance Co [1995] 1 EGLR
15; [1995] 10 EG 129; [1994] NPC 110, Ch D 10.2.2
Mount Eden Land Ltd v Prudential Assurance Co Ltd (1997) 74 P & CR 377;
[1997] 1 EGLR 37; [1997] 14 EG 130 5.7.1

National Westminster Bank Ltd v Betchworth Investments Ltd [1975] 1 EGLR
57; (1975) 234 EG 675, CA 13.4.3
News of the World Ltd v Allen Fairhead & Sons Ltd [1931] 2 Ch 402; (1931)
100 LJ Ch 394 15.4
North Eastern Co-operative Society v Newcastle upon Tyne City Council
(1987) 282 EG 1409; [1987] 1 EGLR 142 8.20
Northern Ireland Commissioner of Valuation v Fermanagh Protestant Board
of Education [1968] NI 89; [1969] 3 All ER 352; [1969] 1 WLR 1708, HL 16.6
Nunes v Davies Laing & Dick Ltd (1985) 51 P & CR 310; [1986] 1 EGLR 106;
(1985) 277 EG 416 13.2

Observatory Hill Ltd v Camtel Investments SA [1997] 1 EGLR 140; [1997] 18
EG 126, Ch D 14.13.2

Palacath Ltd v Flanagan [1985] 2 All ER 161; [1985] 1 EGLR 86; (1985) 274
EG 143 8.20
Palmer v Durnford Ford [1992] 1 QB 483; [1992] 2 WLR 407; [1992] 2 All
ER 122 8.20
Palmer v Southend-on-Sea Borough Council [1984] 1 All ER 945; [1984] 1
WLR 1129; [1984] ICR 372, CA 7.4
Penny and South Eastern Rly Co, Re (1857) 7 E & B 660; (1857) 26 LJQB
225; (1857) 5 WR 612 6.6.4
Pepper (Inspector of Taxes) v Hart [1993] AC 593; [1993] 1 All ER 42;
[1992] 3 WLR 1032, HL 1.5.14
Phipps v Pears [1965] 1 QB 76; [1964] 2 All ER 35; [1964] 2 WLR 996, CA 15.6
Pickering v Liverpool Daily Post and Echo Newspapers Plc and others [1991]
2 AC 370; [1991] 1 All ER 622; [1991] 2 WLR 513 15.10.2
Poplar Housing Association v Donoghue [2001] 4 All ER 604 10.7
Porter v Magill [2002] 1 All ER 465, HL 8.3
Poster v Slough Estates Ltd [1969] 1 Ch 495; [1968] 3 All ER 257; [1968] 1
WLR 1515 14.13.3
Prentice v Hereward Housing Association (1999) (unreported) QBD, 29
April 10.2.2
President of India v La Pintada Compania Navigacion SA [1985] AC 104;
[1984] 2 All ER 773; [1984] 3 WLR 10, HL 9.7
Prudential Insurance Ltd v Waterloo Real Estate Inc [1999] 2 EGLR 85;
[1999] 17 EG 131; [1999] EGCS 10 2.2.2

R v Ahmad (Zafar) (1987) 84 Cr App R 64; (1986) 18 HLR 416; (1986) 83 LS
Gaz 2569, CA 16.7

R v Birmingham City Council ex parte Ferrero Ltd [1993] 1 All ER 530
  (1991) LGR 977; (1991) 10 Tr LR 129, CA 10.7
R v Bow Road Domestic Proceedings Court ex parte Adediga [1968] 2 QB
  572; [1968] 2 All ER 89; [1968] 2 WLR 1143, CA 1.3
R v British Steel Plc [1995] 1 WLR 1356; [1995] ICR 586; [1995] IRLR 310,
  CA 16.2
R v Cornwall County Council ex parte Huntington [1994] 1 All ER 694, CA;
  affirming [1992] 3 All ER 566; [1992] COD 223 10.7
R v ICR Haulage [1944] KB 551; [1944] 1 All ER 691; (1944) 171 LT 180 16.2
R v Leonard Cheshire Foundation [2002] 2 All ER 936 10.7
R v London County Quarter Sessions Appeals Committee ex parte Rossi
  [1956] 1 QB 682; [1956] 1 All ER 670; [1956] 2 WLR 800, CA 13.4.2
R v Secretary of State ex parte Spath Holme Ltd [2001] 1 All ER 195, HL 1.5.14
R v White [1867] LR 2 QB 557 8.7
R v Wilcock (1845) 7 QB 317 15.3.2
Rees v Bennett [2001] 3 EGLR 1 4.12
Rees v Skerrett [2001] 1 WLR 1541, CA 15.6, 15.8
Rozel, The [1994] 2 Lloyd's Rep 161 11.5
Ruiz v Spain (2001) 31 EHRR 589 10.2.2
Ruxley Electronics and Construction Ltd v Forsyth [1996] AC 344; [1995] 3
  All ER 268; [1995] 3 WLR 118, HL 9.4.3

S v France App No 13728/88 65 DR 250 15.12.3
Selby v Whitbread & Co [1917] 1 KB 736; (1917) 15 LGR 279; (1917) 81 JP
  165   8.2, 8.15, 8.18, 8.19, 9.4.3, 9.4.4, 10.8, 14.9.2, 14.13.3, 15.5, 15.8.1
Sevcon Ltd v Lucas CAV Ltd [1986] 2 All ER 104; [1986] 1 WLR 462; (1986)
  130 SJ 340, HL 9.10
Sharma v Knight [1986] 1 WLR 757; (1986) 130 SJ 111; (1986) 136 New LJ
  332, CA 10.5
Shiloh Spinners Ltd v Harding [1973] AC 691; [1973] 1 All ER 90; [1973] 2
  WLR 28, HL 14.13.3
Shirley v Caswell (2001) Costs LR 1 11.5
Simeon and Isle of Wight RDC, Re [1937] Ch 525; [1937] 3 All ER 149;
  (1937) 157 LT 473 6.6.7
Smith v East Elloe Rural District Council [1956] AC 736; [1956] 1 All ER 855;
  [1956] 2 WLR 888, HL 10.5, 10.7
Solomons v R Gertzenstein Ltd [1954] 2 QB 243; [1954] 2 All ER 625; [1954]
  3 WLR 317, CA 2.5, 7.6
South Bucks District Council v Porter [2003] 3 All ER 1, HL 15.13.3
Spiers and Son Ltd v Troup (1915) 84 LJ KB 1986; (1915) 13 LGR 633;
  (1915) 112 LT 1135 2.5, 3.8, 4.8, 8.13, 11.7.1
Stainer v Secretary of State for the Environment and Shepway District
  Council (1992) 65 P & CR 310; [1994] JPL 44; [1993] EGCS 730 10.5
Standard Bank of British South America v Stokes (1878) 9 Ch D 68; (1878)
  43 JP 91; (1878) 47 LJ Ch 554 8.16, 10.6
Stanton v Callaghan [1999] 1 WLR 116 8.20
Stickey v Hooke [1906] 2 KB 20 10.3
Stone and Hastie, Re [1903] 2 KB 463; (1903) 68 JP 44; (1903) 72 LJKB 846,
  CA   8.13, 8.19, 10.7, 14.9.1, 14.10–14.10.2

Strachan & Henshaw Ltd v Stein Industrie (UK) Ltd (No 7) (1996) 13 Const
    LJ 418, QBD   10.2.2
Stran Greek Refineries and Stratis Andreadis v Greece (1995) 19 EHRR 293,
    ECHR   15.13.4
Sutcliffe v Thackrah [1974] AC 727; [1974] 1 All ER 859; [1974] 2 WLR 295,
    HL   8.3, 8.20

TO Supplies (London) Ltd v Jerry Creighton Ltd [1952] 1 KB 42; [1951] 2
    All ER 992; [1951] 2 TLR 993   13.4.4
Tanfern Ltd v Cameron Macdonald [2000] 1 WLR 1311   10.2.2
Tapling v Jones (1865) 29 JP 611; (1865) 11 HLC 290; (1865) 12 LT 555   15.4
Tesco Supermarkets Ltd v Nattrass [1972] AC 153; [1971] 2 All ER 127;
    [1971] 2 WLR 1166, HL   16.2
Thornhill's Settlements, Re [1941] Ch 24; [1940] 4 All ER 249; (1941) 164
    LT 190   8.8.2
Thornton v Kirklees Metropolitan Borough Council [1979] QB 626; [1979] 2
    All ER 349; [1979] 3 WLR 1, CA   9.4.2, 9.4.3
Tower Hamlets London Borough Council v Sherwood [2002] NPC 24, CA   4.5.1
Trafalgar House Construction (Regions) Ltd v General Surety & Guarantee
    Co Ltd [1996] AC 199; [1995] 3 All ER 737; [1995] 3 WLR 204, HL   12.5
Trendtex Trading Corp v Credit Suisse [1982] AC 679; [1981] 3 All ER 520;
    [1981] 3 WLR 766, HL   14.3
Trustees of Methodist Schools v O'Leary (1992) 66 P & CR 364; (1993) 25
    HLR 364; [1993] 16 EG 119, CA   16.6
Tucker v Hutchinson (1987) 54 P & CR 106   14.13.2

Upjohn v Seymour Estates Ltd [1938] 1 All ER 614; (1938) 54 TLR 465   3.1, 8.16

Video London Sound Studios v Asticus (GMS) Ltd, 2001, unreported,
    Technology and Construction Court   8.13

Wadham and North Eastern Rly Co, Re (1884) 14 QBD 747; (1885) 16 QBD
    227, CA   6.6.2
Ward v Cannock Chase District Council [1986] Ch 546; [1985] 3 All ER 537;
    [1986] 2 WLR 660   9.4.3
Warder v Cooper [1970] Ch 495; [1970] 1 All ER 1112; [1970] 2 WLR 975   9.4.4
Watson v Gray (1880) 14 Ch D 192; (1880) 44 JP 537; (1880) 49 LJ Ch 243   15.2
West Faulkner Associates v London Borough of Newham (1994) 71 BLR 1;
    (1995) 11 Const LJ 157, CA   4.10
Weston v Arnold (1873) 8 Ch App 1084; (1873) 43 LJ Ch 123; (1873) 22 WR
    284   2.7
Wigg v Lefèvre (1892) 8 TLR 493   2.5
Wildtree Hotels Ltd v Harrow LBC [2001] 2 AC 1   6.6.6
Willoughby v Eckstein (No 2) [1939] Ch 167; [1937] 1 All ER 257; (1937)
    156 LT 187   3.8.3
Woodhouse AC Israel Cocoa SA and another v Nigerian Produce Marketing
    Co Ltd [1972] AC 741; [1972] 2 All ER 261; [1972] 2 WLR 1090   13.10
Wilson v First County Trust Limited [2003] UKHL 40   15.12.3
Woodhouse v Consolidated Property Corp (1992) 66 P & CR 234; [1993] 1
    EGLR 174; [1993] 19 EG 134, CA   3.1, 8.13, 8.16, 9.5.4, 10.7

X and others (Minors) v Bedfordshire County Council [1995] 2 AC 633,
　[1995] 3 All ER 353; [1995] 2 FLR 276　　　　　　　　　　　　　　　15.10.2

Yorkshire Bank Plc v Hall [1999] 1 WLR 1713; [1999] 1 All ER 879; (1999) 78
　P & CR 136, CA　　　　　　　　　　　　　　　　　　　　　　　　　10.3
Yorkshire Electricity Board v British Telecom [1986] 2 All ER 961; [1986] 1
　WLR 1029; (1986) 130 SJ 613, HL　　　　　　　　　　　　　　　　　9.10
Yorkshire Water Services Ltd v Sun Alliance & London Insurance plc &
　Others (No 2) [1998] Env LR 204, QBD　　　　　　　　　　　　　　　15.5

TABLE OF STATUTES

References in the right-hand column are to paragraph numbers; references in *italics* are to page numbers. Page references printed in **bold** type indicate where an Act is set out in part or in full.

The 1667 Act	
s 8	1.2
Access to Neighbouring Land Act	
1992	15.1, 15.9, 15.11, 17.4
s 1(2)	**15.11**
(4)	**15.11**
s 2	15.11
s 2	15.11
s 2	15.10
(5)	15.10
Agricultural Tenancies Act 1995	
s 28	8.19
Arbitration Act 1889	8.18, 8.19
Arbitration Act 1950	8.18, 8.19
s 31	8, 8.19
Arbitration Act 1996	8.1, 8.14, 8.18–8.20
s 24	8.7
(1)(c)	8.7
s 29(1)	8.20
s 30	8.14
s 49	9.7
s 66	9.4
ss 94–97	8.19
Banking Act 1987	
s 40(3)	16.7
Bristol Improvement Act 1847	1.7
ss 27, 32	1.1
Building Act 1984	6.3, 15.12
ss 76–83	3.8
Civil Procedure Act 1997	10.2.2
Companies Act 1985	
s 725	13.4.4
s 726(1)	12.4
Compulsory Purchase Act 1965	
s 10(1)	6.6
Control of Pollution Act 1974	6.3, 7.5, *206*
County Courts Act 1984	10.3
s 15(1)	9.8
s 16	9.4.1

s 21	10.3
s 41	10.3
s 42	10.2.1, 10.3
s 69	9.7, *220*, *221*
s 74	9.7
Criminal Justice Act 1982	
s 37	16.8
Criminal Justice Act 1991	
s 17	16.8
Environmental Protection Act	
1990	*206*
Health and Safety at Work etc	
Act 1974	6.3, *206*
Human Rights Act 1998	4.5.3, 7.8, 15.13, 15.13.1–15.13.4, 17.2.2, *213*
s 2	15.13.3
s 3	15.13.1
s 6	15.13.1, 15.13.3
(3)	15.13.1
ss 7–9	15.13.3
Sch 1	15.13.2
Pts 1, 2	15.13.2
Interpretation Act 1978	
s 7	13.4.2
Sch 1	15.11
Judgments Act 1838	
s 17	9.7
Land Charges Act 1972	14.14.4
s 2(2), (3)	14.13.4
ss 5(7), 17(1)	14.13.1
Land Clauses Act 1845	
s 68	6.6, 6.6.2
Land Compensation Act 1973	
Pt I	6.6.7
s 1(3), (6)	6.6.7

Land Registration Act 2002	14.14.5	s 46(1)(j), (k)	*175*, *182*
s 34(2)(b)	14.14.5	(2)	*175*
s 42(1)(c)	14.14.5	(3)	5.4, *175*
Law of Property Act 1925	15.2	s 47	*175*
s 1(2)(e)	14.13.3	(1)–(3)	*175*
s 38	15.2	(4)	3.8.3, *176*
s 62	15.5	s 48	*176*, *182*
s 136	14.3	(1)–(4)	*176*
s 196(3)	13.6	s 49	*176*
Sch 1, Pt V, para 1	15.2	s 50	4.1, *177*
Limitation Act 1980	9.10	(1)(a)	4.2.1, *177*
ss 2, 7	9.10	(b)	4.2.2, *177*
s 7(1)–(3)	9.10	(2)	*177*
ss 8, 9, 34, 36	9.10	(a)–(c)	*177*
London Building Act 1894	1.2, 4.10, 6.6.1, 15.8.1	(d)	6.6.1, *177*
		(3)	*177*
s 91	8.15, 13.2	(4)	4.12, 15.8.1, *178*
(1)	8.15	s 51	*178*
s 95(2)(b)	6.5.2	(1)–(3)	*178*
s 96	11.7.1	(3)(a)	*178*
s 99	11.8	(b)	6.3, *178*
s 101	15.3.2	s 52	*178*
London Building Act 1905	1.2	(a)–(c)	*178*
London Building Act 1930	1.2	s 53	*179*
s 127	15.3.2	(1)–(3)	*179*
London Building Acts		s 54	15.3.2, *179*
(Amendment) Act 1939	1.3, 1.7, 3.5, 3.7, 5.4, 5.7, 6.6.1, 6.6.10, 7.5, 10.3, 12.1, 12.5, 13.2, 15.5, 17.2.2, 17.4, *171–184*	s 55	3.5, 8.1, 8.9.3, *179*
		(a)–(d)	*179*
		(e)–(l)	*180*
		(m)	*181*
Pt VI	1.1, 1.2, 1.7, *172–184*	(n)	10.2, 10.2.1, 10.3, *181*
s 1	1.2	(i)	8.15, 10.1, 10.2.1, *181*
s 44	5.2, *172*	(ii)	10.1, *181*
(i), (ii)	*172*	(o)	10.1–10.2.1, 10.3, *181*
s 45	*172*, *183*	(i)–(iii)	*181*
(1)	*172*	(iv)	10.2.1, *181*
(a), (b)	*173*	(v)	*181*
(c)	3.4.3, 3.5, *173*	s 56	*181*
(2)	*173*	(1)	*181*
s 46	*173*, *182*, *183*	(a)–(e)	*182*
(1)	*173*, *183*	(e)(i)	*182*
(a)	*173*, *182*	(ii)	6.5.2, *182*
(b)–(d)	*174*, *182*	(2)–(4)	*182*
(e)	*174*, *182*	(5), (6)	*183*
(i)	3.7, *174*	s 57	12.1, *183*
(ii)	*174*	(1)–(3)	*183*
(f)	*174*, *182*	s 58	*184*
(i)	3.7, *174*	(1)–(3)	*184*
(ii)	*174*	s 59	*184*
(g)–(i)	3.7, *174*, *182*	(1), (2)	*184*
		s 148	17.2.1

Table of Statutes

London Government Act 1963
s 43   1.3

Magistrates' Court Act 1980
ss 8, 64, 76, 92   9.4.1
s 127   16.8
Metropolitan Building Act 1855   2.5, 8.19
s 85(3)   6.4
Nuclear Installations Act 1965
s 12   6.6.2
Party Wall etc Act 1996   1.1, 1.4, 1.5–1.5.5, 1.5.9–1.5.11, 1.5.13, 1.5.14, 1.6, 1.7, 2.5, 2.6, 2.6.4, 2.6.5, 3.1, 3.2.3, 3.3.2, 3.4.3, 3.4.4, 4.3.5, 4.10, 4.12, 5.1, 5.3, 5.6, 5.7.2, 5.8.2, 6.3–6.5.1, 6.6, 6.6.3–6.6.5, 6.6.9, 6.8.1, 7.2, 7.5, 7.7, 8.1–8.4, 8.6.2, 8.9.3, 8.12–8.16, 8.20, 9.2, 9.3, 9.4.1, 9.4.2, 9.6, 9.7, 10.1, 10.2.2, 10.3, 10.6, 11.1–11.3, 11.5, 12.1, 12.2, 12.4, 12.5, 12.6.2, 12.8.1, 13.1–13.4, 13.7, 13.10, 14.1–14.6, 14.7.2, 14.8, 14.10.2–14.12, 14.13.3, 14.13.4, 14.14, 14.14.1, 14.14.3, 14.15, 15.1–15.3, 15.3.2, 15.5–15.11, 15.12.3, 15.13.4, 16.1, 16.5, 16.6, 17.1, 17.2.1–17.4, *151–169*, *171*, *186*, *190*, *192*, *194*, *195*, *197–199*, *201*, *203–205*, *207*, *208*, *219*, *222*, *223*
s 1   1.5.2, 2.6.2, 3.1–3.2.2, 3.4, 3.4.4, 3.5, 3.7, 4.1, 4.8, 4.9, 5.4, 7.2, 8.12, 13.9, 15.8.1, 15.10, 17.3, *152*
(1)   3.2.1, 3.2.2, *152*
(a)   3.2, *152*
(b)   2.6.4, 3.2, 3.2.1, *152*
(2)   3.2.3–3.3.3, 3.4–3.4.2, 5.4, 8.16, 15.10, *152*, *153*, *185*, *186*, *189–191*, *202–205*
(3)   3.2.3, 3.3, 3.3.2, 3.3.4, 3.5, 5.4, 11.8, 13.9, 14.5, *152*, *186*, *189*, *190*, *197*
(a)   *152*
(b)   3.3.2, 3.5, 11.2.2, 11.4.1, 11.8, 14.10–14.10.2, 14.12.1, 14.12.2, *152*, *163*
(4)   3.2.1, 3.2.3, 3.3, 3.3.3, 3.3.4, 3.4.1, 3.5, 11.3, 15.10, *152*, *153*, *186*, *189*, *197*, *227*

s 1(4)(a)   11.2.2, *152*
(b)   2.6.2, 2.6.3, 3.2.1, 3.4.4, *152*
(5)   3.2.1, 3.2.3, 3.4–3.4.2, 3.4.4, 5.4, 8.16, 15.10, 17.3, *153*, *185*, *189–191*, *202–205*, *227*
(6)   3.2.1, 3.2.3, 3.4, 3.4.2, 3.4.3, 5.4, *153*, *190*
(a), (b)   *153*
(7)   3.2.3, 3.4.3, 3.5, 6.6.2, 6.6.4, 9.5.2, 9.6, 11.2.2, 11.3, 12.3.1, *153*, *227*
(a), (b)   *153*
(8)   3.3.3, 3.5, 8.2, *153*, *227*
(9)   17.3
s 2   1.5.2, 3.1, 3.2.2, 3.4, 3.5–3.7, 3.8, 3.8.2, 4.1, 4.8, 4.9, 5.4, 5.7, 6.1, 6.9, 7.2, 8.13, 9.5.2, 15.5, 15.8.1, 15.10, 15.13.3, *153*, *155*, *156*, *193*
(1)   2.6.3, 2.6.4, 3.2.2, 3.7, 3.8.3, 8.13, *153*
(h)   2.2.1
(l)   15.4
(2)   3.7, 6.5.2, 13.2, 17.4, *153*, *192*
(a)   3.7, 5.4, 6.9, 11.4.2, *153*, *154*, *163*, *192*
(b)   3.7, 11.4.3, 17.3, *153*, *163*, *192*
(c)   3.7, 6.5.2, 17.3, *153*, *192*
(d)   3.7, 6.5.2, 17.3, *154*, *192*
(e)   3.7, 6.5.2, 6.9, 17.4, *154*, *155*, *163*, *192*
(f)   3.7, 6.9, 17.3, *154*, *155*, *192*
(g)   2.6.3, 2.6.4, 3.7, 5.4, 6.9, *154*, *155*, *192*
(h)   3.7, 6.5.2, 6.9, *154*, *155*, *192*
(j)   3.7, 6.9, 17.3, *154*, *155*, *192*
(k)   3.7, *154*, *192*
(l)   3.7, *154*, *192*
(m)   3.7, 6.5.2, 6.9, 11.4.4, *154*, *155*, *163*, *192*
(i), (ii)   *154*
(n)   3.7, *154*, *192*
(3)   3.7, 6.9, *154*
(a)   15.5, 17.3, *154*, *227*
(b)   2.6.3, 8.2, *155*
(4)   3.7, 6.9, *155*
(a)   3.7, 15.5, 17.3, *155*, *227*
(b)   *155*
(5)   3.7, 6.9, 15.5, 17.3, *155*, *227*
(6)   3.7, 6.9, 15.5, *155*
(7)   3.7, 6.9, *155*

Party Wall etc Act 1996 *cont.*
  s 2(7)(a), (b) **155**
  (8) 3.7, **155**
  s 3 1.5.2, 3.6, 3.8, 8.12, 8.16, 13.2,
       13.9, **155**, 157, 185, 192–194
  (1) 3.8.1, 15.10, 17.3, **155**, 189, 193,
      202–205
    (a) **155**
    (b) 5.5, **156**
    (c) **156**
  (2) **156**
    (a) 3.8.1, **156**, 193
    (b) 3.8.2, **156**
      (i), (ii) **156**
  (3) 5.6, **156**
    (a) 3.8, 3.8.3, 17.3, 17.4, **156**
    (b) 3.8, **156**
  s 4 1.5.2, 3.6, 3.8.2, 3.9, 11.4.5, 13.9,
       156, 157, 163, 192, 194, 197
  (1) 3.9.1, 12.1, 12.6.1, **156**, 186,
      189, 194
    (a) 17.3, **156**, 194
    (b) 5.6, 5.8.1, **156**, 194
      (i) **156**
      (ii) 5.8.2, **156**
  (2) 3.9.2, **156**
    (a) **156**, 194
    (b) **157**
  (3) 3.9.3, **157**, 197
    (a)–(c) **157**
  s 5 1.5.2, 3.8.2, 3.9.3, 3.10, 8.2, 14.5,
       157, 185, 186, 189, 194, 197
  s 6 1.5.3, 2.5, 3.2.3, 4.1, 4.3.4, 4.3.5,
       4.5, 4.5.1, 4.5.2, 4.8, 4.9, 4.11, 4.13,
       6.6.1, 7.2, 7.3, 8.12, 13.9, 15.8.1, 15.10,
       15.13.3, 17.3, 17.4, **157**, 168, 196
  (1) 4.1, 4.2.1, 4.3.2, **157**, 158, 185,
      195, 196
    (a) 4.3.1, 4.4, **157**
    (b) 4.3.2, **157**
  (2) 4.1, 4.2.2, 4.3.3, **157**, 158, 185,
      195, 196
    (a) 4.3.1, 4.4, **157**
    (b) 4.3.2, 4.3.3, **157**
  (3) 4.7, 5.8.1, 7.2, 11.3, 11.4.5, **158**,
      198
  (4) 2.5, 4.1, 4.8, **158**
  (5) 4.8, 4.9, 8.16, 15.10, **158**, 185,
      187, 189, 195, 196, 202–205
  (6) 4.8, **158**, 196

s 6(6)(a), (b) **158**
  (7) 4.8, 8.2, **158**, 187, 189,
      196, 197
  (8) 4.10, **158**
    (a) 4.10, **158**
    (b) **158**
  (9) 4.11, **158**
  (10) 4.12, 15.8.1, 15.10.2, **158**
s 7 1.5.4, 6.1, 6.2, 6.4, 6.5.1, 6.8.2,
     8.18, 11.6, 12.3.1, 15.8.1,
     15.8.2, **158**
  (1) 6.2, 6.4, 6.6.1, 6.6.6, 6.6.9, 6.7,
      6.8.1, 7.7, 9.2, 9.5.3, 9.6,
      15.8.1, **158**
  (2) 2.5, 3.4.3, 4.10, 6.2, 6.5.2, 6.6,
      6.6.6, 6.6.7, 6.6.10, 6.7, 6.8.1,
      7.7, 9.2, 9.5.2, 9.5.3, 9.6,
      12.2, 15.5, 15.6, 15.8.1,
      17.2.2, **159**, 227
  (3) 5.7.1, 6.2, 6.5, 6.5.2, 6.6.6, 6.7,
      7.7, 9.2, 9.5.3, 9.6, **159**
  (4) 3.9.1, 5.3, 5.4, 5.6, 5.7.1, 5.7.2,
      6.2, 17.4, **156**, **159**
  (5) 3.8.3, 4.10, 6.2, 6.3, 9.4.4, 17.4,
      159, 227
    (a) 15.12, **159**
s 7(5)(b) 8.2, **159**
s 8 1.5.4, 1.5.12, 2.5, 3.4.4, 5.7.2, 7.1,
     13.4, 14.3, 14.9, 14.9.2, 14.13.3, 15.9,
     15.13.3, 16.4, **159**
  (1) 3.3.3, 7.2, 7.3, 7.6, 9.2, 16.1,
      16.7, **159**, 166, 199
  (2) 17.3, **159**
  (3) 7.4, 9.6, 13.6, **159**, 186, 189,
      199, 200
    (a) 7.4, **159**, 200
    (b) **159**
  (4) **159**, 160
  (5) 7.3, 7.6, 16.1, 16.5, 16.7, **160**,
      166, 199
  (6) 7.4, 7.6, 9.6, **160**, 186, 189, 199,
      200
    (a) 7.4, **160**, 200
    (b) **160**
s 9 1.5.11, 8.13, 15.3, **160**
  (a) 6.6.3, 15.1, 15.3, 15.3.1, 15.4,
      15.5, 17.3, **160**
  (b) 15.3, 15.3.2, **160**, 227

Party Wall etc Act 1996 *cont.*
  s 10   1.5.4, 3.1, 3.3.3, 3.5, 3.7, 3.8.2,
          3.8.3, 3.9.3, 3.10, 4.1, 4.7, 4.9, 4.10,
          4.12, 5.3, 5.7.2, 5.8.2, 6.3, 6.4, 6.6.3,
          6.8, 6.10, 7.3, 8.1–8.4, 8.7, 8.7.1, 8.8.1,
          8.8.2, 8.9.2, 8.12, 8.14–8.17, 8.19, 9.4,
          9.4.2, 9.6, 10.2.2, 11.2.1, 11.5, 11.7.2,
          12.1, 12.2, 12.3.1, 12.6, 12.7, 15.5,
          15.13.3, 16.1, 16.5, 17.4, *153, 155, 159,*
          160, 163–165, 186, 190, 192, 196, 203,
          204, 208, 223, 227
  s 10(1)   3.5, 8.2, 8.5, 8.6, 8.10, 8.12,
                160, 161, 189
     (a)   8.5.1, *160, 189, 191, 193,*
                196, 203
     (b)   8.5.2, 8.5.3, 8.6.1, 8.7.2,
            8.9, *160, 161, 189, 201–204*
  (2)   8.4, *160*
  (3)   8.7.1, 8.8.1, *160*
     (a)   8.9.1, *160*
     (b)   *160*
     (c)   8.3, *160*
     (d)   *160*
  (4)   8.6.1, 8.7.2, 8.9, *161, 189, 203*
     (a)   *161*
     (b)   *161, 189, 201*
  (5)   8.3, 8.4, 8.6.1, 8.7.2, 8.9, *161,*
                                189, 203
  (6)   8.9–8.9.3, *161*
     (a), (b)   *161*
  (7)   8.7, 8.9–8.9.3, *161, 189, 201*
     (a), (b)   *161*
  (8)   8.4, 8.6.2, 8.7.3, *161, 168, 189,*
                            201, 204
     (a)   *161*
     (b)   8.3, *161*
  (9)   8.6.2, 8.7.3, 8.8.2, *161, 189,*
                        201, 202, 204
     (a)   8.9.1, *161*
     (b), (c)   *162*
  (10)   8.12, 8.13, 8.15, 9.5.1, 10.1,
                            162, 227
     (a)   6.8.1, *162*
     (b)   *162*
  (11)   8.10, 8.17, 9.5.1, 10.1, *162,*
                                202
  (12)   8.12, 8.16, 8.18, 9.5.1, 11.2.1,
                                162
     (a), (b)   *162*
     (c)   6.8.1, 8.12, 9.5.1, *162*

  s 10(13)   8.12, 8.18, 11.2.1, 11.5, 15.4,
                                162
     (a)   8.11, *162*
     (b)   *162*
     (c)   11.5, *162*
  (14)   8.11, *162*
  (15)   8.11, 11.2.1, *162*
     (a)   *162*, 227
     (b)   *162*
  (16)   8.19, 9.2, 10.1, 10.6, *162*
  (17)   10.1, 10.2, 10.3, 10.5, 11.2.1,
                        163, 189, 220
     (a), (b)   *163*
  s 11   1.5.7, 5.8, 11.2.2, 11.3, 11.7, *163,*
                                165
  (1)   11.3, 12.6.2, *163*
  (2)   8.2, *163*
  (3)   11.4.1, 11.4.6, *163*
  (4)   3.7, 11.4.2, 11.4.3, *163*
     (a), (b)   *163*
  (5)   3.7, 11.4.3, 17.3, *163*
     (a), (b)   *163*
  (6)   6.2, 6.5, 6.5.2, 6.9, 9.4, 9.5.2,
            9.6, 11.6, 12.2, 12.3.1, 17.4, *163*
  (7)   3.7, 3.9.1, 6.9, 11.4.4, 12.6.1,
                        154, 163, 186
     (a), (b)   *164*
  (8)   6.10, 8.2, 11.6, *164*
  (9)   3.9.1, 3.9.3, 4.7, 5.8.1, 11.4.5,
                        12.8.1, 17.3, *164*
     (a)   *164*
     (b)   5.8.1, 12.6.1, *164*
  (10)   5.7.2, 5.8.2, 12.3.1, 14.2, 14.3,
            14.10–14.10.2, 14.12.1, 14.14.1, *164,*
                                187
     (a), (b)   5.8.2, *164*
  (11)   11.4.6, 11.8, 14.10–14.10.2,
                    14.12.2, 14.14.1, *164*
  s 12   1.5.8, 5.7.2, 8.15, 11.2.2, 12.1,
                                12.2, *164*
  (1)   8.2, 12.1, 12.2, 12.8.2, *164,*
                        165, 187, 189, 208
  (2)   8.2, 12.1, 12.6, 13.9, *165, 185,*
                                189, 208
     (a)   12.6.1, 12.6.2, *165*
     (b)   12.6.2, *165*, 209
  (3)   12.1, 12.8.1, *165*
     (a), (b)   *165*
  (20)   17.4
  s 13 1.5.7, 5.8.2, 9.2, 11.2.2, 11.7, 11.8,
                                165

Party Wall etc Act 1996 *cont.*
  s 13(1)   11.7.1, *165*, *185*, *189*, 222
      (a), (b)   *165*
    (2)   5.8.2, 8.2, 8.13, 8.15, 11.7.2,
      13.9, 17.4, *165*, *187*, *189*, *222*, *223*
    (3)   11.7.2, *165*, 222
  s 14   1.5.7, 11.2.2, 11.7, 11.8, *166*
    (1)   11.8, *166*
    (2)   11.8, 14.3, 14.9.2, 14.10.2,
      14.12.2, 14.13.4, *166*, 222
  s 15   1.5.9, 5.8.2, 7.4, 10.5, 12.2, 13.4,
      166
    (1)   7.4, 13.4, *166*, 200
      (a)   *166*
      (b)   13.5, *166*
      (c)   13.4.4, *166*
    (2)   13.4, 13.6, *166*, 200
      (a), (b)   *166*
  s 16   1.5.12, 7.6, 9.2, 16.1, 16.8, *166*,
      199, *200*
    (1)   16.1, 16.2, *166*, 167
      (a)   *166*
      (b)   16.2, *166*
    (2)   16.7, 17.3, *166*, 167
      (a)   *166*
      (b)   *167*
    (3)   *167*
  s 17   9.4.1, 9.8, *167*
  s 18   1.6, *167*
    (1)–(2)   *167*
  s 19   1.6, *167*
    (1)–(2)   *167*
  s 20   1.5.1, 2.1, 2.5, 2.9, 3.8.1, 4.8, 5.2,
      5.8.2, 8.3, 8.6.2, 14.2, 16.6, 17.3, *167*,
      168, *204*, *227*
  s 21   *168*
    (1)   1.1, 1.7, *168*
    (2)   *168*
      (a), (b)   *169*
    (3)   *169*
  s 22   1.7, *169*
    (1)–(4)   *169*
Planning (Listed Buildings and
  Conservation Areas) Act 1990   15.12
Public Health Act 1936
  s 278(1)   6.6.2

Recorded Delivery Service Act
  1962
  s 1   13.4.4
Rent Act 1977   2.5

Supreme Court Act 1981
  s 35A   9.7

Town and Country Planning Act
  1990   15.12

TABLE OF STATUTORY INSTRUMENTS

References in the right-hand column are to paragraph numbers; references in *italics* are to page numbers.

Civil Proceedure Rules 1998, SI 1998/3132	9.4.1, 9.8, 10.2.2
Pt 2	10.2.2
Pt 7	10.2.2, *210*
r 7	9.9
Pt 8	8.7, 10.2.2, *210, 219–221*
r 8	9.9
PD 8, para 1.1	9.9
r 16.3	9.8
(6)	9.8
r 19	14.7.2
PD 29, para 2.2	9.8
r 30.3(1)	9.8
(2)	9.8
r 44.3(2)	11.5
Pt 52	10.2.2, 10.2.3, 10.4, *210–218*
r 52.3(b)	10.4
11(1)	10.2.2
(b)	10.2.2
(2)	10.2.2
13	10.2.2, 10.4
PD 52	10.2.2
para 9.1	10.2.2
section II	10.2.2
r 62.6(1)	8.7
Construction (Design and Management) Regulations 1994, SI 1994/3140	6.3
Control of Noise (Codes of Practice for Construction and Open Sites) Order 1984, SI 1984/1992	7.5
Control of Noise (Codes of Practice for Construction and Open Sites) Order 1987, SI 1987/1730	7.5
County Court Rules 1981, SI 1981/1687	10.2.2
High Court and County Courts Jurisdiction Order 1991, SI 1991/724	9.8
art 2(1)(1)	9.8
art 4A	9.8
Party Wall etc Act 1996 (Commencement) Order 1997, SI 1997/670	1.1, 1.7
art 4	1.7
Party Wall etc Act 1996 (Repeal of Local Enactments) Order 1997, SI 1997/671	1.1, 1.7
art 3	1.7
Rules of the Supreme Court 1965, SI 1965/1776	10.2.2

TABLE OF EUROPEAN LEGISLATION

References in the right-hand column are to paragraph numbers.

European Convention on the Protection of Human Rights and Fundamental
    Freedoms 1950   10.2.2, 15.12.1–15.12.3
    Art 6(1)   10.2.2
    Art 8   15.12.2, 15.12.3
European Convention on the Protection of Human Rights and Fundamental
    Freedoms Protocol 1   15.13.2
    Art 1   15.13.2, 15.13.4

Chapter 1
INTRODUCTION

1.1 SOURCE OF CURRENT LAW

The law relating to party walls is to be found in the Party Wall etc Act 1996[1] ('the Act'), which received Royal Assent on 18 July 1996. The Act was introduced as a Private Members Bill into the House of Lords by Lord Lytton, a practising chartered surveyor. Although a Private Members Bill, it received Government support. It completed its passage through the Lords on 22 May 1996, and passed all its stages in the Commons on 12 July 1996. The Act was brought into force on 1 July 1997, subject to transitional provisions.[2] Section 21(1) gives the Secretary of State power to amend or repeal earlier local Acts. Under this power, Part VI of the London Building Acts (Amendment) Act 1939 (as to which see below) and ss 27 and 32 of the Bristol Improvement Act 1847[3] have been repealed.[4]

1.2 Antecedents

After the fire of London in 1666, 'Commissioners for rebuilding' were appointed, on the basis of whose recommendations an Act for the rebuilding of London[5] was enacted. One of the primary purposes of that Act was to lay down requirements for new buildings to ensure that a general conflagration could not once again occur. Section 8 of the Act required:

> 'That there be party-walls and party-piers, set out equally on each building ground, to be built up by the first beginner of such building and that convenient toothing be left in the front wall by the said first builder, for the better joining of the next house that shall be built to the same: (2) and that no man may be permitted by the said surveyors, to build on the said party wall, or on his own contiguous ground, until he hath fully reimbursed the said first builder before full moiety of the charges of the said party-wall and pier ...'

The 1667 Act, which was limited in application to the City of London, made no provision for the demolition or alteration of party walls. Subsequent legislation in the eighteenth and nineteenth centuries elaborated the position. The culmination of two centuries of legislation, and the origin of the present law, is the London Building Act 1894, which was amended in 1905[6] and replaced in 1930 by the London Building Act 1930,[7] a consolidating statute. The relevant

---

1 1996 C40.
2 See the Party Wall etc Act 1996 (Commencement) Order 1997, SI 1997/670 and **1.7**.
3 10 & 11 Vict. C.XXIX.
4 The Party Wall etc Act 1996 (Repeal of Local Enactments) Order 1997, SI 1997/671.
5 19 Car II c.3.
6 57 & 58 Vict. C.CCXIII & 5 EDW.VII C.CCIX respectively.
7 20 & 21 Geo 5 C.CIVIII.

law was subsequently re-embodied with amendments in Part VI of the London Building Acts (Amendment) Act 1939.[8] By s 1 of that Act, it was to be read and construed as one with the 1930 Act. These Acts are hereafter referred to by date alone.

1.3 THE 1939 ACT

In all its essentials, the Act repeats provisions already contained in the 1939 Act, the material text of which is set out in Appendix 2. The 1939 Act was a local Act, applying only to the Inner London Boroughs.[9] Although the 1939 Act was repealed when the Act came into force, judicial decisions on its provisions and their predecessors will be of relevance in construing the corresponding provisions of the Act. In Parliament, it was stated that the purpose of the Act was to extend the 'tried and tested' provisions of the 1939 Act to the whole country,[10] and it is thought, therefore, that existing case-law on the previous legislation will continue to apply, except where a change in language compels a different conclusion: 'Where Parliament has continued to use words of which the meaning has been settled by decisions of the Court, it is to be presumed that Parliament intends the words to continue to have that meaning.'[11]

1.4 OPERATION OF THE ACT

Party walls separating the lands of adjoining owners are sensitive areas at common law. Since each owner has some interest in the wall, often neither can do any work to it without the consent of the other, which may lead to paralysis. The broad object of the Act is to set up machinery enabling the building owner to carry out works within the scope of the Act. The machinery starts with a notice under the Act, and, unless the adjoining owner consents, this sets in train an elaborate procedure for referring the matter to surveyors for determination. The surveyors embody their decision in an award which, subject to the possibility of appeal to the county court, is binding on both parties.

---

8   2 & 3 Geo 6 C.XCVII.
9   London Government Act 1963, s 43.
10 See Hansard HL Debates Vol 568 31 Jan 1996, col 1536.
11 *London Corporation v Cusack-Smith* [1955] AC 337, *per* Lord Reid at 361. See also *EWP Ltd v Moore* [1992] QB 460, CA; *Lowsley v Forbes (t/a LE Design Services)* [1998] 3 All ER 897, HL at 905 *per* Lord Lloyd. The presumption may not be followed where the previous interpretation is considered obsolete due, for example, to changed technical or social conditions – see eg *R v Bow Road Domestic Proceedings Court ex parte Adedigb* [1968] 2 All ER 89, CA.

1.5 STRUCTURE OF THE BOOK

This book attempts to explain the detailed workings of the Act. Its structure is as follows.

1.5.1 Definitions

Chapter 2 introduces the basic concepts of the Act, defined in s 20 (party wall, building owner, adjoining owner etc).

1.5.2 Substantive rights

Chapter 3 describes the principal substantive rights conferred by the Act, namely:

(a) rights to build where the boundary is not already built on (s 1);
(b) rights to build where the boundary is already built on (s 2).

This requires an explanation of the notices which the building owner has to serve (under ss 1 and 3), and the adjoining owner's right to serve a counter-notice (s 4), and the way disputes are deemed to arise (s 5).

1.5.3 Adjacent excavation

The Act also applies where the building owner's operations on his own land involve excavating to defined depths within 3 or 6 metres of a building of the adjoining owner (s 6). This is dealt with in Chapter 4.

1.5.4 Special foundations

The Act makes some miscellaneous provisions about 'special foundations'. These are brought together in Chapter 5.

1.5.5 Ancillary rights and obligations

The Act creates a number of ancillary rights (eg to compensation for damage) and obligations (eg not to cause unnecessary inconvenience). These are found mainly in s 7, but also elsewhere. They are dealt with in Chapter 6, except for the important rights of entry for the purposes of the Act (s 8), which are dealt with separately in Chapter 7.

1.5.6 Award

Section 10 enacts the complex machinery for the appointment of the surveyors, and the determination of disputes by their award. This is separated into three chapters: Chapter 8 on Procedure and Scope; Chapter 9 on Effect and Enforcement; and Chapter 10 on Rights of Appeal.

1.5.7 Financial matters

In general, the building owner has to pay the expenses of the works, but there are a number of circumstances in which the adjoining owner has to contribute. The complex financial provisions of s 11 are dealt with in Chapter 11, which also covers the machinery for recovering costs from an adjoining owner (ss 13 and 14).

1.5.8 Security

Chapter 12 is concerned with s 12, which enables each party to claim security for expenses against the other.

1.5.9 Notices

There are many forms of notice which the Act requires to be served. These are referred to throughout the text. Precedents are provided in Appendix 4, and checklists in Appendix 3. Chapter 13 deals only with the methods of service prescribed by the Act (s 15).

1.5.10 Successors in title

Although the Act affects land, and creates contingent liabilities for owners of land, it makes no reference to successors in title. Chapter 14 tackles this difficulty, and includes a brief look at the conveyancing problems.

1.5.11 Other areas of law

Chapter 15 covers s 9, which preserves certain common law rights, and deals with the Act's relationship to other areas of law, including statute law.

1.5.12 Criminal offences

Chapter 16 deals with s 16, which creates criminal offences in connection with the rights of entry under s 8.

1.5.13 Proposals for reform

Chapter 17 discusses criticisms of the workings of the Act and current proposals for reform.

1.5.14 Appendices

Appendix 1 contains the text of the Act, with cross-references to the commentary, and Appendix 5 lists the *Hansard* references to the Bill in both Houses of Parliament, since these are now admissible as an aid to construction.[12] Appendix 6 lists some glaring errors and inconsistencies in the Act, which ought to be removed. The other three appendices have already been introduced.

1.6 APPLICATION

The Act binds land belonging to the Crown,[13] but land in Inner London belonging to the Inns of Court is excepted.[14]

1.7 COMMENCEMENT AND TRANSITIONAL PROVISIONS

Section 21(1) gave the Secretary of State power to amend or repeal earlier local Acts. Section 22 provided for the Act to be brought into force by statutory instrument. The Party Wall etc Act 1996 (Commencement) Order 1997[15] provided that the Act should come into force on 1 July 1997. Where, outside Inner London work was commenced before 1 September pursuant to any agreement easement or right, other than a right arising under or by virtue of the Act, the Act does not apply.[16] In Inner London, where the 1939 Act applied prior to 1 July 1997 the general commencement date applied. The rationale of this was that the regime under the 1939 Act was essentially the same as that applied by the Act.

By the Party Wall etc Act 1996 (Repeal of Local Enactments) Order 1997 Part VI of the 1939 Act was repealed on 1 July 1997, as was the Bristol Improvement Act 1847.[17] Article 3 of the repeal order contained transitional provisions under which anywhere any work had been commenced, notice given or other action taken in accordance with either enactment, that enactment would continue to apply to the work, notice or other action.

The transitional provisions are now effectively spent. Local Acts containing provisions dealing with party wall matters other than those specifically repealed are unaffected by the Act and the commencement or repeal orders.

---

12 See *Pepper (Inspector of Taxes) v Hart* [1993] AC 593; *R v Secretary of State ex parte Spath Holme Ltd* [2001] 1 All ER 195, HL.
13 See s 19.
14 See s 18.
15 See the Party Wall etc Act 1996 (Commencement) Order 1997, SI 1997/670.
16 Ibid, Article 4.
17 10 & 11 Vict C. CXXIX.

Chapter 2

APPLICATION OF THE ACT

2.1 DEFINITIONS

The terms of art defined by the Act are set out in s 20. It is necessary to start with an explanation of the basic concepts.

2.2 PARTY WALL

This is defined as follows:

'(a) a wall which forms part of a building and stands on lands of different owners to a greater extent than the projection of any artificially formed support on which the wall rests; and
(b) so much of a wall not being a wall referred to in paragraph (a) above as separates buildings belonging to different owners.'

It will be seen that all party walls are, in a broad sense, boundary walls, which belong to one or more buildings. Paragraph (a) is concerned with external walls of single buildings. The wall must stand astride the boundary, partly (not necessarily equally) in one property and partly in the other; if the whole of the wall is on one side of the boundary, and only its foundations or footings project into the other side, it is not a party wall. Paragraph (b) is concerned with walls attached to buildings on both sides (eg between terraced houses). These do not have to stand astride the boundary, and may be wholly on one side of it; what matters is that they separate buildings belonging to different owners. The effect of these two definitions is illustrated in Figure 1 below. Both paragraphs carry difficulties.

2.2.1 Overhangs

Paragraph (a) does not define the status of overhangs. A wall may be entirely on one side of the boundary at ground level, but be corbelled out at a higher level, so as to overhang the adjoining land. Can such a wall, or its thickened upper part, be said to 'stand on' lands of different owners? Can 'on' include 'over' in this context? Upon the ordinary use of language, it is thought the answer to both questions is no. And this conclusion seems to be supported by s 2(2)(h), which expressly contemplates overhangs. It may, nevertheless, be arguable that a wall of this kind is a party wall to the extent that it overhangs the adjoining land.

2.2.2 Trespassing Buildings

Paragraph (b) gives rise to the question of the trespassing building. If a boundary wall is sited entirely on A's land, and B proceeds, without permission,

Party Wall

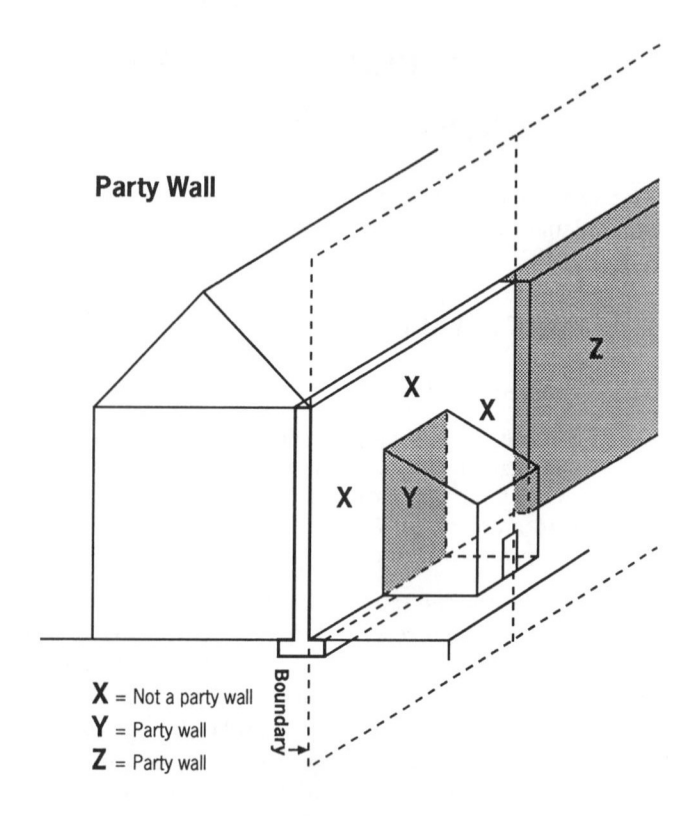

X = Not a party wall
Y = Party wall
Z = Party wall

Figure 1

to construct a building against it, the wall becomes a paragraph (b) party wall so far as the building extends. Does this mean that B becomes immediately entitled to claim the rights conferred by the Act? And if not immediately, how soon? It is considered that the answers lie in the law of adverse possession. By enclosing on A's wall, B is not merely trespassing, he is taking possession of its surface which is part of A's land.[1] If B serves some notice claiming rights which the Act appears to give him, A can negate the notice by suing for removal of the trespassing building, and will be entitled to succeed unless B has acquired title by 12 years' adverse possession. If B wants immediate rights which will not be vulnerable to this response, he must negotiate with A for them: and if A wants to keep full control of his wall, he should grant no more than a revocable licence to attach the building, which will prevent B's possession being adverse.[2]

---

1   This analysis appears to be supported by *Prudential Insurance Ltd v Waterloo Real Estate Inc* [1999] 2 EGLR 85.
2   See *Hesolp v Burns* [1974] 1 WLR 1241.

2.3 PARTY FENCE WALL

This is defined as:

> 'a wall (not being part of a building) which stands on land of different owners and is used or constructed to be used for separating such adjoining lands, but does not include a wall constructed on the land of one owner the artificially formed support of which projects into the land of another.'

Like a paragraph (a) party wall, a party fence wall is a wall which stands astride the boundary between two properties and, if only its foundations or footings project beyond the boundary, it is disqualified in the same way. The distinction is that the party wall fence does not form part of a building; it is essentially free-standing (eg a garden wall). See Figure 2 below.

2.4 PARTY STRUCTURE

This is defined as:

> 'a party wall and also a floor partition or other structure separating buildings or parts of buildings approached solely by separate staircases or separate entrances.'

This translates the concept of party wall from the vertical dimension to the horizontal, and also to the microcosm of parts of buildings approached by separate staircases or entrances (eg flats). The confusing qualifying words 'from without' have been pruned from the 1939 definition, thus removing

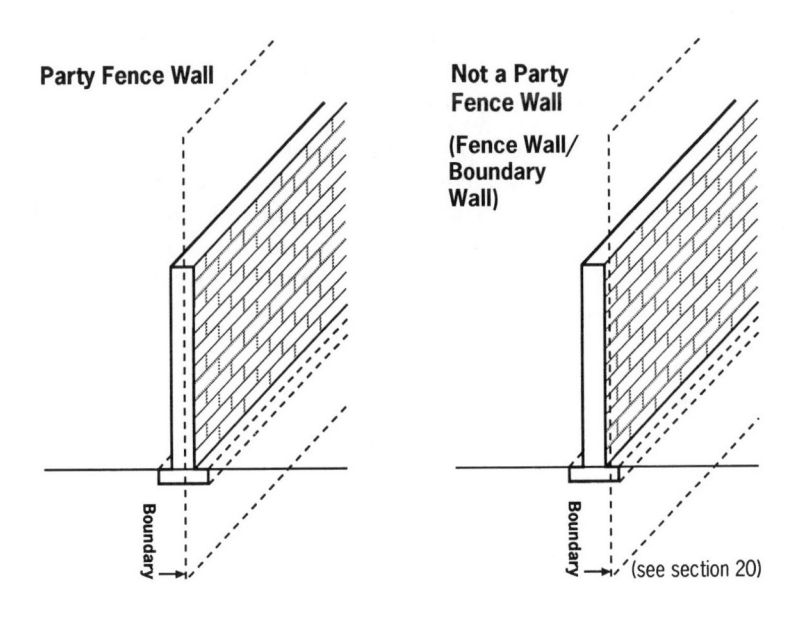

Figure 2 Fence Wall/Boundary Wall

doubts about the application to flats. All floors, ceilings and walls separating adjoining flats are party structures.

2.5 OWNER

There is a threefold definition of 'owner' which can be summarised as including:

(a) anyone receiving, or entitled to receive, the rents and profits;
(b) anyone in possession (except a mortgagee, a tenant at will, or a periodic tenant from year to year or a lesser period);
(c) a contractual purchaser of an interest in land, including a contract for a lease (other than a periodic tenancy of the kind excluded from (b)).

Authorities on predecessors of this definition should be approached with caution, since they turn on different wording, and sometimes apply provisions which no longer appear in the Act.[3] Limb (a), it seems, does not include a person, such as a receiver, who is in receipt of rent as agent for another.[4] Limb (b) does not include a statutory tenant under Rent Act 1977.[5] Limb (c) is new. It gives the standing of owner to a purchaser of the freehold or who has a contract for the grant of a qualifying lease.[6] It does not appear to deprive a vendor of his standing under (a) or (b).

This definition controls the subsidiary definitions of 'building owner', which simply means an owner who wishes to exercise rights under the Act, and 'adjoining owner' which means the owner of land, buildings, storeys or rooms adjoining that of the building owner. In this context 'adjoining' appears to carry its strict meaning of 'contiguous', 'having physical contact', since it needs express extension to embrace owners within the distances defined by s 6 (see ss 6(4) and 20, but see **2.9(b)**).[7]

This concept of ownership is fundamental to the Act. It gives rights to building owners, which are not controlled by competing rights which it gives to adjoining owners. But to adjoining occupiers who do not qualify as owners – and they include a large class of periodic tenants – it gives rights of compensation[8] and the right to receive notice before their property is entered[9],

---

3 For example *Wigg v Lefevre* (1892) 8 TLR 493, holding that a lessee for 35 years, who had sub-let, was not an owner under the Metropolitan Building Act 1855, is no longer applicable.
4 See *Solomons v R Gertzenstein Ltd* [1954] 2 All ER 625.
5 See *Frances Holland School v xx* [2001] 2 EGLR 88.
6 It is still not wide enough to include the plaintiff in *Spiers and Son Ltd v Troup* (1915) 84 LJKB 1986, who had not even exchanged contracts.
7 See *Re Ecclesiastical Commissioners for England's Conveyance* [1936] Ch 430. But if there are flat-owners who will be affected by works at a lower level, it might embrace them through its extended meaning of 'neighbouring': see *Cave v Horsell* [1912] 3 KB 533.
8 Section 7(2).
9 Section 8.

but they have no right to be heard in the deliberations leading to the award which determines what works are to be carried out.

2.6 OTHER EXPRESSIONS

It is somewhat confusing to find that the Act employs a number of other expressions which, although they appear to be used in a technical way which does not command immediate comprehension, are nevertheless not supplied with definitions. Their meaning has to be deduced from their context.

2.6.1 Wall

This everyday term is not defined, no doubt because the concept is so familiar. Yet it is not always clear whether a boundary structure can properly be regarded as a wall. Can a fence be a wall? A dictionary definition speaks of a 'solid structure of stones, bricks, concrete, timber, etc' (see *Concise Oxford Dictionary*). It is considered that a fence is not a wall, and that the distinguishing attributes of a wall are solidity and permanence. A boarded fence, for example, lacks these qualities and, it is thought, could not be regarded as a wall (and a fortiori post and wire or chain-link fences). There may be stockade-type structures which would be substantial enough to qualify, but in general timber seems insufficiently permanent.

2.6.2 Fence wall

This expression, which does not appear to have any ordinary meaning, is found in s 1(4)(b). It appears to be used there to denote a wall which is built wholly on one side of the boundary (and for this reason is outside the definition of 'party fence wall') except for its footings, which project over the boundary – a very specialised concept arising from the confused drafting of s 1 (see para 3.2, where this expression is adopted for this type of wall).

2.6.3 External wall

The normal meaning of this expression would be an outside wall, whether free-standing or part of a building. But in s 1(4)(b) it is used, in contradistinction to 'fence wall', of a wall which would be a party wall if it was not built wholly on the land of one owner. This suggests that its meaning is restricted to the outside wall of a building. On the other hand, in s 2(1) the use of the expression 'external wall of a building' suggests the normal meaning. There are other contexts which provide no guidance (eg ss 2(2)(g) and (3)(b)). Section 1(4)(b) probably does not provide sufficient reason to depart from the normal meaning.

2.6.4 Boundary wall

The normal meaning of this expression is a wall which marks a boundary, whether it stands on it or next to it, and whether it is the external wall of a building or free-standing. It is clear from the express qualifications attached to it in s 2(1) (where it means only a party fence wall or the external wall of a building) and s 1(1)(b) (where those meanings are excluded and it appears to be used in the specialised sense attached to 'fence wall' above) that the Act uses it in this broad, general sense. This is the sense it must bear when it is used without qualification (eg s 2(2)(g)).

2.6.5 Line of junction

The Act fights shy of the word 'boundary', except in the expression 'boundary wall' and uses this periphrasis instead. No doubt, this is in order to emphasise that what is meant is an incorporeal concept rather than any physical feature.

2.7 EXTENT

In general, it is clear that walls and structures are only party walls, party fence walls, and party structures to the extent that they satisfy the statutory definitions. In the case of paragraph (b) party walls, this appears expressly from the words 'so much of'. Thus, a wall which is a party wall not because it stands astride the boundary, but only because the neighbour's building is built against it, is a party wall only where it adjoins the neighbour's building: those parts of the wall which project above, or to either side of, the neighbour's building are not a party wall.[10] The same must apply to a party structure, so that the horizontal structure dividing two flats, the lower of which projects further sideways than the higher, will not be a party structure to the extent that it projects and forms the roof of the lower flat.

2.8 MULTIPLE OWNERS

The building owner, who wishes to exercise his statutory rights, may or may not own part of the party wall (in a paragraph (b) case it may belong entirely to the adjoining owner). In a simple case, the building owner will have only one adjoining owner to deal with, owning all the adjoining land. But if the party wall is the flank wall of a block of flats, there may be many persons who qualify as adjoining owners, including the landlord, the tenants of adjoining flats, and purchasers from either. The building owner will have to serve the requisite

---

10 See *Weston v Arnold* (1873) 8 Ch App 1084; *Drury v Army and Navy Auxilliary Co-operative Supply Ltd* [1896] 2 QB 271; *Knight v Pursell* (1879) 11 Ch D 412; *London Glos & N Hants Dairy Co v Morley & Lanceley* [1911] 2 KB 257. See also Figure 1.

notices on all of them,[11] and they will all be entitled to participate in the procedure leading to an award.

2.9 FLATS

There are other more specialised difficulties which arise in relation to flats. As an illustration, let us imagine two terraced buildings of different heights divided by an internal party wall, one (belonging to the building owner) of two storeys, the other (belonging to the adjoining owner) of three storeys, each separately tenanted under a 5-year lease. The top of the building owner's building is half way up the second storey of the adjoining building. Clearly the adjoining freeholder must be served with all requisite notices, but how many of his tenants have to be served? Two questions frequently arise.

(a) Suppose the tenancies all include the adjoining freeholder's interest in the party wall. It is clear that the tenants of the first two floors must be served, because they are owners of property which adjoins that of the building owner wherever the boundary is in relation to the wall. What of the third floor tenant? In his case the answer depends strictly on where the boundary between the two properties lies. If the party wall lies entirely on the adjoining owner's land, the third floor does not touch any property of the building owner. On the other hand, if the boundary lies in the middle of the party wall, the building owner will own the exterior half of the third floor wall. It would be a bold building owner who would neglect to serve this tenant. Not only would he have to prove that the boundary was on his side of the wall, he would also have to be prepared to meet the argument that contact with his airspace is enough to qualify the tenant as an adjoining owner.

(b) Let us now suppose that the adjoining owner has leased on terms which reserve to him the structure of his building, so that only the internal surface of the party wall is vested in his tenants. Strictly, in such a case, the tenants own nothing adjoining the building owner's property (unless the whole of the party wall is vested in him). Again, however, it is a strong step for the building owner to ignore their claim to be served. They will be more immediately affected than the freeholder by interference with the party wall. As a matter of construction the question comes down to the degree of contiguity required by the word 'adjoining' (see **2.5**). It may be significant that the definition (in s 20) speaks of 'storeys or rooms' as well as land and buildings. It is difficult to imagine a court denying such a tenant the right to a notice.

---

11 See *Fillingham v Wood* [1891] 1 Ch 5; *Crosby v Alhambra Co Ltd* [1907] Ch 295. For joint owners see **13.8**.

Chapter 3

RIGHTS OF BUILDING OWNER

3.1 INTRODUCTION

The substantive provisions of the Act, giving rights to building owners, are ss 1 and 2. It should be emphasised that these rights are conditional on the operation of the statutory machinery. Until an initiating notice has been served,[1] and, if a dispute ensues, until an award has been made under s 10, the building owner has only his rights at common law.[2] These procedures required by the Act must be strictly complied with, and in default the building owner will be liable for any tort (eg trespass or nuisance) against which the Act would have protected him. This is so whether he proceeds without serving any notice,[3] or serves a notice but proceeds before an award is made,[4] or proceeds under an award which turns out to be invalid.[5] In such circumstances all the usual remedies for tort will be available to the adjoining owner, including general and special damages,[6] and injunctions upon the usual equitable principles.[7]

A building owner must start by deciding whether to proceed under s 1 or s 2. These sections are mutually exclusive. Their common factor is that they apply 'where lands of different owners adjoin'. This is natural, since there could be no party wall if they did not. The distinction between them is, broadly, that s 1 applies where the boundary has not yet been built on, and s 2 applies where it has.

3.2 BOUNDARY NOT BUILT ON: SECTION 1

If the boundary is not built on at all (s 1(1)(a)), or is built on only to the extent of a boundary wall which is not a party fence wall nor the external wall of a building (s 1(1)(b)), and if either owner is about to build on the boundary, s 1 will apply. It provides two separate procedures for the building owner, according to whether he intends to build: (a) on the boundary (a party wall or party fence wall); or (b) wholly on his own land (a fence wall). There are a number of preliminary points to be made about the section.

---

1 For methods of service see Chapter 13.
2 See *Louis v Sadiq* [1997] 1 EGLR 136; *Upjohn v Seymour Estates Ltd* (1938) 54 TLR 465).
3 See *Louis v Sadiq* above.
4 See *Woodhouse v Consolidated Property Corporation Ltd* [1993] 1 EGLR 174.
5 See *Gyle-Thompson v Wall Street (Properties) Ltd* [1974] 1 All ER 295.
6 In *Louis v Sadiq* (above) the special damages included loan interest and additional building costs, both incurred because of the delay caused by the dispute, and general damages were awarded as well.
7 See *Daniells v Mendonca* (1999) 78 P&CR 401, where a mandatory injunction ordering the removal of unauthorised work was granted, as well as an injunction prohibiting work except in accordance with the 1939 Act.

3.2.1 Inherent contradictions

The application of s 1 has given rise to some difficulty. This is not surprising, since it contains the self-contradictory concept of a wall which is built on the boundary, and yet at the same time is placed wholly on the land of one owner. This is explicit in sub-ss (5) and (6), and implicit in sub-s (1)(b). This contradiction cannot be solved by attaching some artificial meaning to the word 'on' (such as 'hard up against', rather than 'astride'), since this will not work in sub-ss (4), (5) and (6). There is only one way of making sense of the concept. It must denote the type of wall illustrated in the right-hand half of Figure 2, which is outside the definition of 'party fence wall'. The whole width of the wall is on one side of the boundary (which is why it is outside that definition), so that the wall might be described as 'placed wholly on' one person's land. But the footings project over the boundary into the neighbouring land, and to this extent (irrelevant for the definition) the wall may also be described as 'built on the boundary'. It is convenient to refer to this specialised concept by the expression used in s 1(4)(b), namely 'fence wall' (see **2.6.2**).

Section 1(1) defines the scope of s 1. It applies where: (a) the boundary is not built on at all; or (b) is built on only to the extent of a boundary wall which is not a party fence wall or the external wall of a building. The description of the second category (s 1(1)(b)) can be answered only by a fence wall, and implicitly indicates that such a wall is regarded as 'built on' the boundary.

3.2.2 Extent of application

The final condition for application of the section is that one owner must be about to build on any part of the boundary. The reference to 'any part' highlights another imprecision in the drafting of the section. A comparison of ss 1(1) and 2(1) makes it quite clear that they are intended to be mutually exclusive. Circumstances may fall within one of them, but not both. But take a simple case where there is a party wall extending along half the common boundary, but nothing at all built along the other half. Two questions arise. First, does s 1 apply, and if so, to what extent? The answer must surely be yes, it applies to the length which has not been built on; the fact that the boundary has been partly built on does not prevent the section applying to the rest. The use of the compendious word 'where' to include a topographical sense assists this obvious conclusion. But secondly, what of the final explicit reference to an intention to build on 'any part' of the boundary? Does this mean that the section can give a right to build on the part already built on, or alternatively that it can apply only if the whole boundary is unbuilt-on? Neither position is acceptable. The first destroys the exclusivity of ss 1 and 2, by making s 1 trespass on the territory of s 2; the second renders s 1 useless in the simple case assumed. It is necessary to understand the reference to 'any part' as if it was to 'any **such** part', so that the effect of the section is restricted to the unbuilt-on part.

3.2.3 Works authorised

The building owner can use the section to obtain the right to build either: (a) a party wall or party fence wall on the boundary (sub-ss (2)–(4)), or (b) a wall placed wholly on his own land (sub-ss (5)–(7)). It should be remembered at this stage that category (b) is limited to the fence wall (ie with footings alone extending over the boundary). The section does not control the operations of an owner which are carried out entirely on his own land. Subject always to s 6 (see Chapter 4), such operations are part of the owner's rights of ownership, and the Act does not interfere with them.

3.3 BUILDING ON THE BOUNDARY (PARTY WALL OR PARTY FENCE WALL)

If the building owner wishes to build a boundary wall astride the boundary (ie a party wall or a party fence wall), he must follow the procedure prescribed by s 1(2), (3) and (4).

3.3.1 Originating notice

First, the building owner must serve a notice under s 1(2). There are four requirements:

(a) it must be served at least one month before the building owner intends the building work to start;
(b) it must be served on 'any' adjoining owner, ie all those whose land adjoins the intended work;
(c) it must indicate the building owner's desire to build;
(d) it must describe the intended wall.

Once the notice has been served under s 1(2), the building owner's rights depend on whether the adjoining owner serves on him a notice indicating his consent to the building of the proposed wall.

3.3.2 Consent notice

If the adjoining owner, having been duly served with notice under s 1(2), serves a notice indicating his consent to the building of the proposed wall, two consequences follow under s 1(3).

(a) The wall can be built. The two owners can agree its precise position, but unless they agree otherwise the building owner has a right to build it half on the land of each owner, ie centrally over the boundary.
(b) The second consequence is in respect of the cost of building the wall. Since the initiative comes from the building owner, it might be expected that he would normally have to pay all the costs. But the adjoining owner does not

have to consent, and if he does it will presumably be because he considers the proposal advantageous to himself. A wall which is built partly on the adjoining owner's land will belong partly to him, and it will be of some use to the adjoining owner, even if only for supporting climbing plants. This is the philosophy behind s 1(3)(b), under which the costs are shared by the two owners in proportions which have regard to the use 'made or to be made' of the wall by each of them. Nor is the initial sharing a once-for-all arrangement. The costs are to be shared 'from time to time', so that if one owner later makes greater use of the wall than was originally contemplated, he becomes liable to pay a further contribution. All contributions are assessed according to the cost of labour and materials prevailing at the time of assessment. This is one of the contingent liabilities imposed by the Act, which are considered in more detail later[8]. What may be noted here is that it can fall on either party, and can occur an unlimited number of times.

These consequences may or may not be regarded as equitable. The adjoining owner needs to appreciate that they are the terms to which he is agreeing, if he serves a consent notice.

3.3.3 No consent

If the adjoining owner does not serve a notice of consent within 14 days of the service on him of the building owner's notice under s 1(2), s 1(4) will apply. This gives the building owner limited rights which he can proceed to exercise without the need to serve any new notice. The building owner can build the wall, but entirely at his own expense, and wholly on his own land. For further consequences see **3.4.2** to **3.4.4**. The wall will be a 'work in pursuance of this Act' within s 8(1), so that the building owner will be entitled to exercise the statutory rights of entry for the purpose of executing the work (and see further **3.4.3**). These are the only works permitted by the section where there is no consent. If the building owner is not content with them, he must initiate a dispute, and go through the s 10 procedure (s 1(8)).

3.3.4 Time limit

Some confusion has arisen from the 14-day time limit for consent under s 1(4), which is new. It needs to be understood that its effect is not restricting, but enabling. For consent under s 1(3) no time limit is prescribed, so that a building owner who wishes to proceed under that section can wait, and, if so minded, cajole for as long as he likes, in the hope of a consent to those consequences. But if he is content to proceed under s 1(4), he does not have to put up with being strung along indefinitely: as soon as 14 days have gone by without a consent, he can go ahead with the works permitted by s 1(4).

---

8   See **14.10**.

3.4 BUILDING WHOLLY ON BUILDING OWNER'S LAND (FENCE WALL)

If the building owner wishes from the outset to build a boundary wall wholly on his own land, he must serve a notice on the adjoining owner under s 1(5), not 1(2). But why should he have to serve a notice if he intends to build wholly on his own land? And how can s 1 apply at all if he does not intend to build on the boundary? These questions highlight the contradiction already discussed (see **3.2.1**). The suggested answer lies in the chameleon nature of the fence wall, which is to be regarded for the purposes of the section as 'on' the boundary (by reason of its projecting footings) and at the same time as 'placed wholly on' the building owner's land (by reason of the above-ground position of the wall). This appears clearly enough from s 1(6), which deals with a wall 'wholly on' the building owner's land, and proceeds to give him the right to place projecting footings in the adjoining owner's land. This demonstrates that the fact that the footings are on the boundary does not prevent the wall being wholly on the building owner's land; such a wall will be a fence wall.[9]

Section 1(5) is available only where the new wall is to be built wholly on the building owner's land (apart from the footings). Thus, if there is already a boundary wall in position built wholly on the adjoining owner's land, the section enables the building owner to build close up to that wall. But the section does not appear to enable him to key his new wall into the old one, because the new wall will then not be wholly on his land. He must proceed under s 1(2), not s 1(5). (Of course if the above-ground part of the existing wall is astride the boundary, s 1 does not apply at all; s 2 must be used.)

3.4.1 Originating notice

The requirements for a notice under s 1(5) are exactly the same as those for a notice under s 1(2) (see **3.3.1**). The section does not interfere with the building owner's right to build on his own land, and there is no provision for consent or non-consent by the adjoining owner (but see **3.5**). But there are two prescribed consequences, which apply whether the wall is built wholly on the building owner's land under s 1(4) (see **3.3.3**) or s 1(5).

3.4.2 Footings and foundations

The first consequence is that under s 1(6) the building owner has the right, within a defined period, to place underground in the adjoining owner's land such projecting footings and foundations as are necessary for the construction of the walls. The defined period begins one month after the service of the

---

9 It does not resolve the contradiction to treat 'on' as having a special meaning such as 'hard up against': this will work for the references to 'on the line of the junction', but not for the references to 'wholly on' the building owner's land.

building owner's notice under s 1(2) or (5), as the case may be, and continues for one year.

3.4.3 Cost and compensation

The second consequence is financial (under s 1(7)). The building owner must build at his own expense, and must compensate any adjoining owner or occupier for any damage to his property occasioned by the building of the wall, and the placing of projecting footings or foundations in the adjoining owner's land under s 1(6). The express provision for compensation sits uneasily with the new s 7(2), which imposes on the building owner a general obligation to pay compensation for any loss or damage caused by work done in pursuance of the Act. If anything this provision is narrower in scope, since it is limited to compensating damage 'to property', which s 7(2) is not. And since this limitation did not feature in the parent provision (the 1939 Act, s 45(1)(c)), its insertion here appears to be deliberate and significant.

3.4.4 Rights of entry

Under s 8, the building owner is given special rights of entry on the adjoining owner's land (see Chapter 7) in aid of works 'in pursuance of this Act'. Works in conformity with notices served under s 1 will be works in pursuance of the Act, but where the work is a wall placed wholly on the building owner's land, the scope of the right of entry has been questioned. Is it limited to entry for the purpose of putting in the projecting footings, or does it also extend to the purpose of building the wall against the boundary? It is considered that the right applies to the building of the wall as well. Building wholly on the building owner's side of the boundary is expressly authorised by s 1(4)(b) and (5), so that it is scarcely arguable that such building is not in pursuance of the Act. Indeed it is a possible view that the only reason for this apparently unnecessary authority is to enable the rights of entry to be invoked in support of it.

It has been pointed out that a building owner who is content to put up a wall and its footings wholly on his own land does not need to use the Act at all (see **3.2.3**). If he chooses to do this, he must realise that he will be sacrificing the benefit of the statutory right of entry, since his work will not be in pursuance of the Act. He will also, presumably, be sacrificing a strip of his land on the far side of his wall, and the strip will be all the wider if it has to accommodate the work of building the wall.

3.5 DISPUTES

Any dispute arising from the procedures under s 1 is to be determined in accordance with s 10 (s 1(8)). But, in contrast to s 2 (see **3.10**), there is no provision for deemed disputes to arise. It follows that, if either party is not content with the result produced by the Act (eg if they cannot agree over the apportionment of costs under s 1(3)(b), or if the building owner is dissatisfied with his rights under s 1(3) or (4)), he must initiate the dispute procedure under s 10 by taking the first step of appointing a surveyor (see s 10(1)).

The reference to disputes with an adjoining 'occupier' is the first of several places where the Act's provisions are mutually inconsistent. Section 10 is restricted to disputes between a building owner and an adjoining owner, and makes no provision for third parties such as occupiers to participate in the procedure. The same inconsistency occurred in the 1939 Act (see ss 45(1)(c) and 55). The only scope for dispute under s 1 by an occupier is over compensation under s 1(7). It is tentatively suggested that an aggrieved occupier should in the first instance attempt to proceed under s 10, and resort to a civil claim if rebuffed.

3.6 BOUNDARY ALREADY BUILT ON: SECTION 2

Where the boundary has already been built on (and this includes the case of all party walls), or there is at the line of the boundary a boundary wall which is a party fence wall or the external wall of a building,[10] s 2 will apply. The building owner can use s 2 to acquire rights to do works to the party (fence) wall or structure, which he would not have at common law. These rights are enumerated, and closely defined, in 13 subsections, and some of them are subjected to special conditions. In order to acquire these rights, the building owner must first serve a 'party structure notice' (s 3), to which the adjoining owner may respond with a counter-notice (under s 4).

3.7 RIGHTS UNDER SECTION 2

The rights which the building owner can acquire under s 2 are as follows (s 2(2)).

(a) The right to underpin, thicken or raise: (i) a party structure; (ii) a party fence wall; or (iii) an external wall which belongs to the building owner and is built against (i) or (ii).

If work pursuant to this right is necessitated by a defect or want of repair of the structure or wall concerned, no special conditions are attached to the exercise of the right. If not, however, the following conditions are imposed (by s 2(3)).[11]

---

10 This includes the case of an external wall of a building which stands wholly on one owner's land, but with footings projecting into the neighbour's land.
11 For further reference to the conditions imposed by s 2, see Chapter 6.

(i) all damage occasioned by the work to the adjoining premises or to their internal furnishings and decorations must be made good;[12]

(ii) there is special protection for flues and chimney stacks which belong to the adjoining owner and either form part of, or rest on or against, the structure or wall affected. They must be carried up to a height agreed by the adjoining owner, or determined under s 10, and the materials used for doing so must be similarly agreed or determined.

Section 11(4) makes special provision for expenses incurred in exercising this right (see **11.4.2**).

(b) The right to make good, repair, or demolish and rebuild, a party structure or party fence wall, where such work is necessitated by a defect or want of repair of the structure or wall.

Section 11(5) makes special provision for expenses incurred in exercising this right (see **11.4.3**).

(c) The right to demolish a partition which separates buildings belonging to different owners but does not conform with statutory requirements, and to build instead a party wall which does so conform.

Throughout s 2, references to 'statutory requirements' import a special meaning. Buildings and structures which were erected before the passing of the Act (18 July 1996) are deemed to conform with statutory requirements if they conformed with the statutes regulating buildings or structures at the time when they were erected (s 2(8)). This right, therefore, is not applicable to such buildings and structures. But it will be applicable to buildings and structures erected after 18 July 1996, even though they conformed with statutory requirements when they were first built, if the statutory requirements are subsequently tightened.

(d) The right in the case of buildings connected by arches or structures over public ways, or over passages belonging to other persons, to demolish the whole or part of such buildings, arches or structures which do not conform with statutory requirements and to rebuild them so that they do so conform.

(e) The right to demolish a party structure which is of insufficient strength or height for the purposes of any intended building of the building owner, and to rebuild it of sufficient strength or height for those purposes (including rebuilding to a lesser height or thickness where the rebuilt structure is of sufficient strength and height for the purposes of any adjoining owner). This right is subject to the same conditions as affect right (a) above (s 2(4), (including the inappropriate reference to

---

12 The word 'furnishings' recurs in sub-ss (4)(a) and (5). It is thought to be an inept copying of 'finishings' from the 1939 Act (see s 46(1)(e)(i), (f)(i), (g), (h) and (i). The making good of chattels is probably outside the intention of the section.

'furnishings': see fn 6). The express right to rebuild to a lesser height reverses the decision of law in *Gyle-Thompson v Wall Street (Properties) Ltd* [1974] 1 All ER 295, but in view of the proviso safeguarding the purposes of the adjoining owner, a decision on similar facts might well be the same (since the lowering of the party wall diminished the adjoining owner's privacy).

This right applies only to a party structure which is of insufficient strength or height for the purposes specified, but there is an overlap with the right under sub-s (1), which may also apply in such circumstances (but only to a party wall) without being limited to them. This is the more unfortunate since the two rights are subject to different conditions, and therefore give different consequential rights to the adjoining owner. An award under s 10 will not usually specify which right is being exercised, so that in the case of overlap it is presumably open to the adjoining owner to enforce the conditions more favourable to him (but not both sets). If the building owner wishes to restrict the adjoining owner to conditions more favourable to *him*, he should take care not to rely on both sub-ss (e) and (l) in his notice, but only on the one with the less onerous conditions in the circumstances.

(f) The right to cut into a party structure for any purpose (which may be, or include, the purpose of inserting a damp proof course). The express reference to a damp proof course (which is new) is thought to be wide enough to include modern methods of damp prevention, such as chemical injection. This right is subject to the condition that all damage occasioned by the work to the adjoining premises or to their internal furnishings and decorations must be made good (s 2(5)).[13]

(g) The right to cut away from a party wall, party fence wall, external wall or boundary wall any footing or any projecting chimney breast, jamb or flue, or other projection on or over the land of the building owner in order to erect, raise, underpin any such wall for any other purpose. This right is subject to the same condition as (f).

(h) The right to cut away or demolish parts of any wall or building of an adjoining owner overhanging a party wall, to the extent that it is necessary to cut away or demolish the parts to enable a vertical wall to be erected or raised against the wall or building of the adjoining owner. This right is subject to the same condition as (f).

(j) The right to cut into the wall of an adjoining owner's building in order to insert a flashing or other weather-proofing of a wall erected against that wall. This right is subject to the condition that all damage occasioned by the work to the wall of the adjoining owner's building must be made good (s 2(6)).

---

13 See fn 6.

(k) The right to execute any other necessary works incidental to the connection of a party structure with the premises adjoining it.

(l) The right to raise a party fence wall, or to raise such a wall for use as a party wall, and to demolish a party fence wall and rebuild it as a party fence wall or as a party wall.

(m) The right to reduce, or to demolish and rebuild, a party wall or party fence wall to: (i) a height of not less than 2 metres where the wall is not used by an adjoining owner to any greater extent than a boundary wall; (ii) a height currently enclosed upon by the building of an adjoining owner. This right is subject to the condition that: (i) if there is an existing parapet, it must be reconstructed or replaced; or (ii) if not, a parapet must be constructed where one is needed (s 2(7)). If the adjoining owner by counter-notice requires the existing height of the wall to be maintained, he must pay a due proportion of the cost, so far as it exceeds the specified heights (s 11(7): see **11.4.4**). For the overlap with sub-s (e) and its consequences see under (e) above.

(n) The right to expose a party wall or party structure hitherto enclosed, subject to providing adequate weathering.

3.8 PARTY STRUCTURE NOTICE: SECTION 3

If the building owner can obtain the written consent of all adjoining owners and adjoining occupiers, he can exercise any of the rights conferred by s 2 without further formality (s 3(3)(a); see further at **3.8.3**). If he is served with a notice under the legislation relating to dangerous or neglected structures,[14] he can proceed without serving a party structure notice (s 3(3)(b)), if he has power to do the work under that legislation or otherwise.[15] Subject to those exceptions, however, he cannot exercise any of the rights granted by s 2 without first serving on any adjoining owner a party structure notice under s 3.

3.8.1 Requirements

The requirements of a party structure notice are as follows (s 3(1)):

(a) it must state the name and address of the building owner;
(b) it must state the nature and particulars of the proposed work. In *Hobbs, Hart & Co v Grover*[16] it was said that a notice should be sufficiently clear and intelligible to enable the adjoining owner to see what counter-notice he should give. For counter-notices see **3.9**. If the building owner is proposing

---

14 For example, the Building Act 1984, ss 76–83.
15 This dispensation applies only to work required by the statutory notice served on the building owner: see *Spiers and Son Ltd v Troup* (1915) 84 LJKB 1986.
16 [1899] 1 Ch 11, compare with **4.8**.

to construct special foundations,[17] it must include plans, sections and details of construction of the special foundations, together with reasonable particulars of the loads to be carried by them;
(c) it must state the date on which the proposed work will begin;
(d) it must be served at least 2 months before the date on which the proposed work is to begin (s 3(2)(a)).

3.8.2 Effect

A party structure notice is the first step towards enabling the building owner to exercise a right under s 2. The next step will depend on the response of the adjoining owner, who may react in one of three ways.

(a) If within 14 days of the service on him of the party structure notice the adjoining owner serves on the building owner a counter-notice indicating his consent (under s 5), there is no dispute and the building owner can proceed without further formality to carry out the works described in the party structure notice.
(b) The adjoining owner may within one month of service of the party structure notice serve on the building owner a counter-notice, in which case s 4 will apply.
(c) The adjoining owner may take neither of these steps, in which case there is a deemed dispute (under s 5), which has to be resolved under s 10.

In any event, a party structure notice ceases to have effect if the work to which it relates: (i) is not begun within the calendar year beginning on the date of its service;[18] and (ii) is not prosecuted with due diligence (s 3(2)(b)). If it ceases to have effect, the building owner must start again by serving a new party structure notice.[19]

3.8.3 Consents

The provision for written consent in s 3(3)(a) gives rise to two points. First, it is commonplace for clauses to be inserted in conveyances which enable the vendor to build on his retained land notwithstanding that the building may interfere with the access of light or air to the land being conveyed. The question arises whether a clause expressed to grant consent to the future exercise of any right conferred by s 2(1) of the Act, without the need for any party structure notice to be served (or some such provision), could operate according to its terms by force of s 3(3)(a). It is considered that it could not. For one thing, works pursuant to the Act have to follow without deviation plans which have been agreed or settled under s 10 (see s 7(5)), so that consent must be to

---

17 Ie foundations in which an assemblage of beams or rods is employed for the purpose of distributing any load: s 20. See further Chapter 5.
18 But this time-limit does not apply where there is a reference to surveyors within the year: see *Leadbetter v Marylebone Corp* [1905] 1 KB 661 and **4.10**.
19 For a discussion of the 'due diligence' requirement, see **4.10**.

defined works, not to undefined works at any time in the future. Further, it is hard to see how anyone other than the consenting party could be bound by his consent; it would not be binding on the land. The traditional 'light and air' clause works in quite a different way; it is a consent by the vendor to the enjoyment of light and air by the purchaser and his successors, which renders their enjoyment precarious and prevents them acquiring rights by prescription[20].

Secondly, it has been suggested (see para **17.3(f)**) that the requirement of consent by adjoining occupiers as well as owners is anomalous, and ought to be removed. It is not considered that there is any good case for such an amendment. The requirement is not new (see the 1939 Act, s 47(4)), and to do away with it would amount to an unwarrantable erosion of the flimsy protection which the Act offers to occupiers. Occupiers who do not qualify as owners (eg statutory tenants) are more closely affected than owners, who might bargain away their interests without proper regard to them. The anomaly is, if anything, that occupiers are not better protected.

3.9 COUNTER-NOTICE: SECTION 4

An adjoining owner who has been duly served with a party structure notice may serve a counter-notice on the building owner under s 4.

3.9.1 Objects

There are two legitimate objects of a counter-notice, which appear from the matters which have to be set out in it (s 4(1)).

(a) The adjoining owner can require modification for his own reasonable convenience in the building owner's proposals in respect of a party fence wall or party structure. He may require the building owner to build in or on the wall or structure such chimney copings, breasts, jambs, or flues, or such piers or recesses or other like works, as may reasonably be required for his convenience. For example, when the building owner is proposing to reduce the height of a wall, the adjoining owner can require him to maintain its existing height (s 11(7)).

(b) The second object concerns special foundations.[21] The building owner will have no right to install special foundations without the adjoining owner's consent in writing (s 7(4)). If he is prepared to consent subject to modifications, he can in the counter-notice require that they: (i) be placed at a specified greater depth than that proposed by the building owner; or (ii) be constructed of sufficient strength to bear the load to be carried by columns of any building which he may intend to build. If he makes such a

---

20 See *Willoughby v Eckstein* [1939] Ch 167.
21 See Chapter 5.

requirement he must be prepared to pay for the works which he requires (see s 11(9) and **11.4.5**).

3.9.2 Requirements

There are two requirements for a counter-notice (s 4(2)).

(a) It must specify the works (in the categories mentioned in **3.9.1**) which the adjoining owner requires to be executed, and must be accompanied by plans, sections and particulars of such works.
(b) It must be served within the month beginning on the date of service of the party structure notice.

3.9.3 Effect

Prima facie the building owner is bound to comply with the requirements set out in a duly served counter-notice, but he is not bound to comply if the works required would: (a) be injurious to him; (b) cause unnecessary inconvenience to him; or (c) cause unnecessary delay in the execution of the works pursuant to the party structure notice (s 4(3)). There are two courses open to the building owner.

(a) If he is content with the requirements set out in the counter-notice, he can within 14 days serve a notice indicating his consent (under s 5), in which case he can proceed with the works in the party structure notice, as modified by the counter-notice, without further formality.
(b) He can abstain from serving a notice of consent, in which case there is a deemed dispute, which must be resolved under s 10 (s 5).

The adjoining owner has to pay the expenses of carrying out the works required by his counter-notice (see s 11(9) and **11.4.5**).

3.10 DISPUTES: SECTION 5

An owner who is served with a party structure notice or a counter-notice can serve a notice indicating his consent within 14 days. In default of any such consent notice, a dispute is deemed to arise under s 5, which must be resolved under s 10.

# Chapter 4

ADJACENT EXCAVATION AND CONSTRUCTION

4.1 INTRODUCTION

Unlike ss 1 and 2, which enlarge the building owner's rights, the principal effect of s 6 of the Act is to restrict his right to conduct operations wholly on his own land. It applies where a building owner proposes to carry out excavations or to excavate for and erect a building or structure within certain distances of any building belonging to an adjoining owner. All owners of buildings within the specified distances are adjoining owners (s 6(4)). The object is to protect their buildings from subsidence caused by the proposed operations. The building owner must serve an initiating notice, and unless a notice of consent is served, a dispute is deemed to have arisen between the building owner and the adjoining owner, which is referred for an award under s 10.

Section 6 contains two separate provisions, according to the distance within which the adjacent excavation is to be carried out from the building of the adjoining owner. Section 6(1) deals with excavation within 3 metres of the building, and s 6(2) applies where the work is to be carried out within 6 metres of the building. These provisions reproduce (in metric form) the provisions of s 50 of the 1939 Act, where the relevant distances were 10 feet and 20 feet respectively.

4.2 DISTANCES

There are two critical distances

4.2.1 3-metre notice

Section 6(1) of the Act is derived from s 50(1)(a) of the 1939 Act. It applies where any excavation building or structure is within 3 metres measured horizontally from any part of a building or structure of the adjoining owner if the excavation proposed will, within the 3-metre limit, extend to a lower level than the bottom of the foundations of the building or structure of the adjoining owner.

4.2.2 6-metre notice

This is governed by s 6(2), which again reproduces a provision of the 1939 Act, namely s 50(1)(b), with the substitution of 6 metres for the 20 feet of the earlier provision. The section applies in the case of excavation works within 6 metres of the adjoining owner's building, where any part of the proposed excavation building or structure will, within the 6 metres, meet a plane drawn downwards in the direction of the excavation building or structure of the building owner at an angle of 45° to the horizontal from the line formed by the intersection of the plane of the level of the bottom of the foundations of the building or structure of the adjoining owner with the plane of the external face of the external wall of the building or structure of the adjoining owner.

These descriptions can be more easily understood from a diagram, see Figure 3 below.

4.3 MEASUREMENTS

It is important to understand exactly what measurements these sections require.

4.3.1 Horizontal

First there is the horizontal measurement of 3 or 6 metres (s 6(1)(a) and (2)(a)). This is taken from a fixed point on the adjoining owner's land, namely 'any part of a building or structure' on his land. 'Any part' must mean the nearest part. If the nearest part is at ground level, the measurement is simple. If

6-Metre Notice

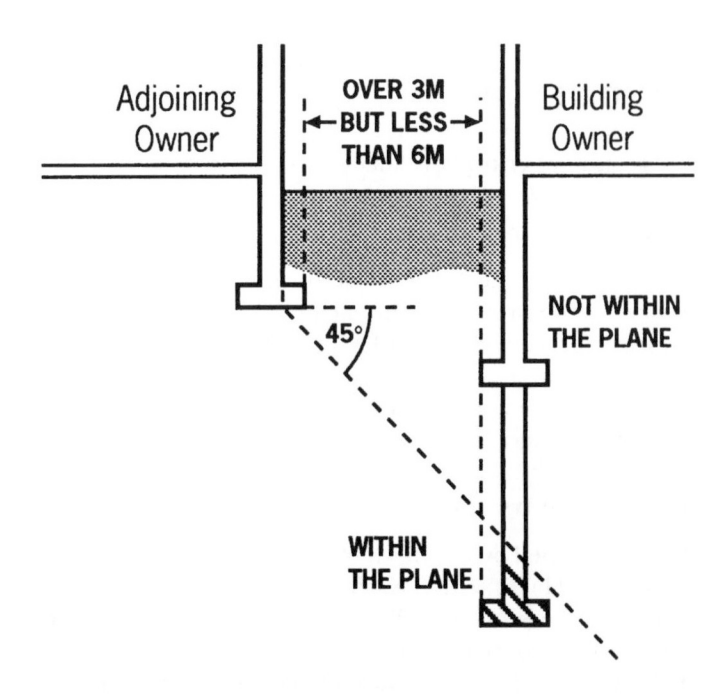

Figure 3

it is some projection above ground level, the measurement must still be made horizontally. That is to say, a vertical plane must be imagined, dropped (as if by a plumb-line) from the nearest edge of the projection, and the measurement must be taken from the place where the plane (plumb-line) touches the ground. For the difficulties posed by invisible underground projections see **4.3.5**. The distances so measured will define the sensitive areas.

4.3.2 Depth: 3-metre area

Having ascertained the sensitive areas it is necessary to determine whether the building owner's operations will, within a sensitive area, be intruding below a sensitive depth (ss 6(1)(b) and (2)(b)). The first step is to determine how far the operations will involve any excavation building or structure below ground within the sensitive area. Intrusions within the sensitive areas above ground are for this purpose irrelevant; so are excavations etc which are not within the sensitive area. The second step is to ascertain the sensitive depth. This is related to 'the level of the bottom on the foundations' of the adjoining owner's building or structure. In the 3-metre area the relation is simple: the sensitive depth is any depth below that level. Any excavation etc within the sensitive area and below the sensitive depth brings s 6(1) into play.

4.3.3 Depth: 6-metre area

Under s 6(2) it is only the last step (ascertaining the sensitive depth) which is different. The sensitive depth is still related to the bottom of the foundations of the adjoining owner's building or structure, but in the more complex way described in s 6(2)(b) and illustrated by Figure 3. The vertical plane of the external face of the external wall of the adjoining owner's building or structure (in this context projections are ignored) must be produced downwards until it intersects the horizontal plane of the foundations, and from the point of intersection a plane must be drawn downwards at 45° from the horizontal towards the building owner's works. The sensitive depth is below this 45° plane. Again it is only excavations etc within the sensitive area and the sensitive depth which bring s 6(2) into play.

4.3.4 Points to note

The following points may be emphasised.

(a) Works which attract s 6 include not only the finished building or structure, but any excavation within the sensitive area and depth. There is no exception for excavations which are designed to be filled in before completion.

(b) The new works can go below the sensitive depth provided they are not witin the sensitive area. Piles, for example, will not attract s 6, whatever their depth, if they are more than 6 metres horizontally from the adjoining owner's building or structure.

(c) No linear measurement is taken to or from the bottom of the adjoining owner's foundations. What is relevant is 'the level' of that bottom, ie the depth of a horizontal plane drawn from the lowest point, wherever it may be. The fact that the lowest point is outside the sensitive area does not affect the determination of the sensitive depth.

4.3.5 Non-apparent structures

Ascertainment of the sensitive depth will be impossible without knowledge of the position and depth of the adjoining owner's foundations, and the sensitive area may depend on underground projections (eg a cellar). This puts the building owner in an impossible position. The Act gives him no right to enter and explore these underground features (see **7.2(c)**), but if he proceeds without a s 6 notice, he runs the risk of being stopped by injunction. This intractable difficulty is as old as the legislation, yet has given rise to no reported authority. No doubt it has been solved by the commonsense guesswork and risk-taking of building owners down the years. The following advice seems prudent.

(a) Insure.
(b) If in doubt, write to the adjoining owner requesting information and permission to enter and explore. If these are refused, this may inhibit the grant of equitable relief.
(c) If still in doubt, serve a s 6 notice, adding a paragraph repeating the requests and stating that it is served without prejudice and will be of no effect if it is found that s 6 does not apply (for a precedent see Appendix 4).

4.4 MEANING OF 'EXCAVATION'

'Excavation' involves hollowing out the ground, and does not include the demolition of a building which has a pre-existing cellar, even though the effect of such demolition is to leave the void created by the cellar exposed to the elements. On the other hand, if the retaining wall of the existing cellar is removed, to form the foundations and cellar walls of a new building, this will involve excavation. Presumably, the simple drilling of a small diameter hole into the ground, for example to take core samples, will not be excavation, but the construction of a large shaft will be. Further, it would seem excavation remains excavation even if it is later backfilled or occupied by elements of the construction during the works. Sections 6(1)(a) and (2)(a) refer to proposing to 'excavate' on the one hand, and to 'excavate for and erect a building or structure' on the other, as alternatives. The distinction is between activities which involve simple excavation and activities which are the prelude to the erection of a building or structure. Thus it is clear that the section applies even where the void formed by the excavation is designed to be occupied by a building or structure. It is considered that the digging of trenches in connection with repairs to, or installation of, services is an example of excavation within the first part of the provision. An example of the second part would be the digging ot deep excavations in which several levels of basement are intended to be installed as part of a new building.

4.5 MEANING OF 'BUILDING OR STRUCTURE'

These are not terms of art, and the Act does not define them. Their exact scope will be a question of fact and degree varying in each individual case. This gives rise to practical difficulties over the application of s 6.

4.5.1 General

The concept of a 'building' is relatively well understood: it denotes a structure of some permanence, usually capable of being entered, and often built of brick. It would not include, for example, a wooden fence. But 'structure' is much wider. It has been said to mean anything constructed and put together[1] and has been held to include a wall, ie something constructed,[2] and a kiosk used for trading in the highway.[3] It is a term capable of embracing the wooden fence, or, by way of further example, a prefaricated wooden shed. In the context of s 6 the width of the expression gives rise to two particular areas of difficulty.

4.5.2 Structures with no foundations

Section 6 requires measurements to be related to 'the bottom of the foundations' of the building or structure. A natural inference is that structures which have no true foundations are not within the expression, and are therefore not protected by s 6. But is this inference sound? It is considered that it is not. The section must be construed in the light of the mischief which it aims to cure, ie damage by subsidence arising from the building owner's operations. Lightweight structures with no proper foundations are not immune to subsidence. Indeed they are, if anything, more vulnerable to it than more substantial structures which are properly supported. For this reason it is thought unlikely that, if the matter was tested, the absence of foundations would be held to be decisive (notwithstanding the contrary arguments suggested below). This reasoning applies primarily to buildings and structures of the adjoining owner, but it would be difficult to support a different meaning for the same words (in the same subsection) in relation to the building owner.

4.5.3 Underground services

More doubtful is the question whether underground pipes, drains and other services are to be regarded as structures. Mere cables, it is thought, could not,

---

1   See *Hobday v Nicholl* [1944] 1 All ER 302.
2   See *Mills & Rockleys v Leicester City Council* [1946] KB 315.
3   See *Tower Hamlets London Borough Council v Sherwood* [2002] NPC 24, CA.

since they are not in the ordinary sense constructed, and are commonly not even rigid. But pipes and conduits which are jointed and rigid are probably within the widest concept of a structure. Are there any grounds for supposing that they are not within the true construction of that word in s 6? It is tentatively suggested that there are grounds, as follows.

(a) They are less vulnerable to the mischief of subsidence.
(b) Being by definition underground they pose intractable practical difficulties for the building owner (see **4.3.5**). The Act should not be so strictly construed as to interfere unreasonably with the building owner's operations, especially as s 6 is concerned with operations conducted on his own land.
(c) The last point may be reinforced by the impact of the Human Rights Act 1998.

4.6 BOTTOM OF THE FOUNDATIONS

This expression is not defined, and is not thought to need much elaboration. It is considered to denote the lowest point of the building or structure in question. If it has no proper foundations, it will be the foot of any supporting columns, if any, or the floor or other base. If there are raft foundations, it will be the underside of the raft; if there are piles, the foot of the piles.

4.7 SECTION 6(3)

Where excavation work is contemplated within the distance limits, the building owner is given the right to underpin or otherwise strengthen or safeguard the foundations of the building and structure of the adjoining owner so far as may be necessary (s 6(3)). He is also bound to do this, if required to by the adjoining owner. In either case, these operations must be at the expense of the building owner.[4] Note that the obligation is not limited to those parts of the adjoining owner's building which fall within the defined distances. The extent of work required must in the case of dispute be decided in accordance with s 10.

4.8 NOTICES

At least one month before beginning to excavate, the building owner must serve on the adjoining owner a notice indicating his proposals and stating whether he proposes to underpin or otherwise strengthen or safeguard the foundations of the building or structure of the adjoining owner (s 6(5)). The notice must be accompanied by plans and sections showing the site and depth

---

4 Notwithstanding s 11(9).

of any excavation the building owner proposes to make, and, if he proposes to erect a building or structure, its site (s 6(6)). If a consent by the adjoining owner is not served within 14 days, a dispute is deemed to have arisen (s 6(7)).

The notice must be served on all adjoining owners, as defined by s 6(4), ie all owners of buildings or structures within the 3 or 6 metre distances. It will be recalled that these distances are measured horizontally. That is to say, a vertical plane must be imagined rising from the side of the excavation, and any building or structure within the horizontal distance of 3 or 6 metres from that plane qualifies. If there is a block of flats, all flats with any part within those distances will qualify, and all their owners (as defined in s 20: see para **2.5**) must be served.

The notice must indicate the proposals in reasonable detail, and must be sufficiently clear and intelligible to enable the adjoining owner to decide what action to take[5].

Where the adjoining owner owns the ground floor, it is prudent for the notice to include requests for information about underground structures and foundations, and for a right to enter and explore (see **4.3.5**).

If a building owner wishes to invoke s 1 or s 2 as well as s 6, it will be advisable to serve two separate notices. In theory a single notice, observing the time limits and other requirements of both sections, could suffice, but confusion is almost certain to result.

4.9 SCOPE OF DISPUTE

Where there is only a s 6 notice, and no notice under s 1 or 2, any dispute must relate only to matters arising under s 6. The jurisdiction of the surveyors under s 10 cannot extend to any other matter. It is considered that a s 6 notice and award can confer no right on the building owner to enter the adjoining owner's land except for the purposes of excavation and underpinning etc under s 6(5). In particular, such an award cannot allow the building owner access to the adjoining owner's land for the purpose of constructing his building above ground level, for example by using the adjoining owner's land for the execution of scaffolding.

4.10 LAPSE OF NOTICE

A notice ceases to have effect if the work to which it relates has not begun within the period of 12 months beginning with the day on which the notice was served

---

5   *Hobbs Hart & Co v Grover* [1899] 1 Ch 11. *Spiers & Son Ltd v Troup* (1915) 84 LJKB 1986. (1915) 13 LGR 633. Cf **3.81**.

and is not prosecuted with due diligence (s 6(8)). The 12-month time-limit does not apply, if it expires while a dispute is still being resolved pursuant to s 10.[6] It is considered that 'due diligence' involves the application of men, materials and plant industriously and efficiently towards the completion of the works.[7]

If the work is not prosecuted with due diligence the notice by the building owner ceases to have effect. The notice is not rendered invalid *ab initio*, so that work already carried out under it does not cease to be authorised by the Act. But it appears that the right to carry out further work lapses. No machinery is provided for reviving the right to proceed under the notice. It seems that the building owner can only serve a fresh notice.

Nor is any provision made about work already carried out. In practical terms, this raises a considerable difficulty if the work has been left in an unsafe or unsatisfactory state from the adjoining owner's point of view. The adjoining owner is given no right to sue for the expense of reinstatement, or for damages for failure to prosecute with due diligence. He would have to sue for damages under s 7(2) and (5) of the Act claiming the cost of reinstatement.

4.11 PLANS

On completion of any work under s 6, the building owner must, on request, supply the adjoining owner with particulars including plans and sections of the work (s 6(9)). The purpose of this is presumably to enable the adjoining owner to plan any future work of his own, or to take appropriate remedial steps if structural distress subsequently occurs in his building. This provision creates a statutory duty, which would be enforceable by damages and (where appropriate) a mandatory injunction.

4.12 COMMON LAW LIABILITY

Section 6(10) repeats s 50(4) of the 1939 Act, and provides that the section does not relieve the building owner of any liability to an adjoining owner or occupier to which he may be exposed by reason of any works which he executes. Thus even though the building owner has operated entirely on his own land, and even though he goes through the machinery of the Act and builds entirely in accordance with an award under s 10, he will still be liable at common law for

---

6   See *Leadbetter v Marylebone Corp* [1905] KB 661. Although the wording of s 6(8)(a) is different from s 90(4) of the 1894 Act, it is not thought that the differences will affect this commonsense decision, which has stood for so long.
7   See *West Faulkner Associates v London Borough of Newham* (1995) 11 Const LJ 157, CA.

any injury suffered by adjoining owners and occupiers by reason of his work. At common law, a prescriptive right of support may arise, to have one's building supported by the ground.[8] Liability for withdrawal of support may also arise in negligence, though the duty may be limited.[9]

4.13 FURTHER REFERENCES

The fact that s 6 is concerned with operations exclusively upon the building owner's land raises special considerations in other contexts: for rights of entry see **7.2(d)-(f)**, and for the nature of the statutory duty see **15.10**.

---

8   *Dalton v Angus & Co* (1881) 6 App Cas 740, *Rees v Bennett* [2001] 3 EGLR 1.
9   See, eg *Holbeck Hall Hotel Ltd v Scarborough Borough Council* (No 2) [2002] 2 WLR 1396.

Chapter 5

SPECIAL FOUNDATIONS

5.1 INTRODUCTION

Special foundations are a side issue in the Act. They are not dealt with comprehensively, but they crop up in three separate contexts, which can conveniently be brought together.

5.2 DEFINITION

In s 20, special foundations are defined as:

> 'foundations in which an assemblage of beams or rods is employed for the purpose of distributing any load.'

In deference to modern methods of construction, the word 'steel' before 'beams' has been dropped. As it stands, the definition (which derives from s 44 of the 1939 Act) refers primarily to reinforced concrete and grillage foundations. The expression is not restricted to the foundation of a wall. It seems clear therefore that the definition encompasses pad and raft foundations and, probably, ground beams supported on piles. It is thought, however, that jet slurry grouting, is not included. This involves stabilising the ground by injecting cement slung through tubes at high pressure. The cement mixes with the soil and forms 'columns' or 'tubes' of hard material.

5.3 GENERAL PRINCIPLE

The general principle is that the Act does not authorise the building owner to place special foundations in the adjoining owner's land without his previous consent in writing (s 7(4)). The building owner may propose them, but the adjoining owner has an absolute right to veto them. Even an award under s 10 cannot authorise them without the required consent

5.4 SECTIONS 1 AND 2

In accordance with the general principle, ss 1 and 2, although they contemplate projecting footings and foundations (s 1(6)) and underpinning (s 2(2)(a), (g)), do not give any right to construct special foundations in the adjoining owner's land.

Under s 1 there is nothing to prevent a building owner proposing special foundations in his notice under s 1(2) or (5). A notice of consent from the adjoining owner under s 1(3) will then satisfy s 7(4), provided that the nature of the foundations and the fact that they are to be placed in the adjoining owner's land have been clearly specified. But the foundations authorised by s 1(6) cannot, in the absence of a written consent satisfying s 7(4), be special foundations, even if the building owner considers them 'necessary for the construction of the wall'. This is a new restriction, since the equivalent in the 1939 Act (s 46(3)) applied only to what is now s 2.

5.5 PARTY STRUCTURE NOTICE

It is one of the requirements of a party structure notice that, if the building owner proposes to construct special foundations, the notice must give full particulars of their construction and the loads they are to be designed to carry (s 3(1)(b)). Consistently with the general principle, it might be expected that such a proposal would be limited to special foundations to be constructed in the building owner's land. The next section, however, shows otherwise.

5.6 COUNTER-NOTICE

Section 4(1)(b) enables the adjoining owner to use his counter-notice for the purpose of consenting to a proposal for special foundations under s 7(4) while imposing requirements for his own advantage. The reference to s 7(4) shows that special foundations in the adjoining owner's land are meant here, because that section does not apply to special foundations in the building owner's land. Thus, the Act contemplates that the special foundations proposed in a party structure notice may legitimately include special foundations in the adjoining owner's land. The requirements which the adjoining owner can impose in his counter-notice under s 4(1)(b) are:

(a) that the foundations be placed at a specified greater depth than that proposed by the building owner; and
(b) that they be constructed of sufficient strength to bear the load to be carried by columns of any building which the adjoining owner may intend to build on his land.

Thus, the adjoining owner can impose conditions requiring the special foundations to be strong enough for his own future purposes. The building owner must comply unless one of the exceptions in s 3(3) is applicable.[1]

---

1 See **3.9.3**.

5.7 CONSENT IN WRITING

It has already been pointed out (see **5.4**) that the requirement of consent in writing, although not new, is now much more sweeping than formerly, since in the 1939 Act it affected only the rights given by what is now s 2.

5.7.1 Requirements

Section 7(4) requires the 'previous consent in writing' of the adjoining owner. 'Previous' means that it must be given before work is started on the special foundations in his land. The consent must, consistently with s 7(3), be to particular works described in plans and sections. It is considered that the building owner could rely on a conditional consent, provided he can show that the condition has been properly observed.[2] The requirement of writing is unambiguous; it should be signed by the adjoining owner or an authorised agent.

5.7.2 Oral Consent

An oral consent cannot satisfy s 7(4) because it is not in writing. However, the form of the section opens the door to the technical possibility of oral consent. It states:

> 'Nothing in this Act shall authorise the building owner to place special foundations on land of an adjoining owner without his previous consent in writing.'

This is not the same as saying 'a building owner shall not etc'. It is simply saying that the Act does not authorise it. Without the authority of the Act, the building owner cannot place foundations in another's land, but only because it would normally involve trespass. However, consent can authorise what would otherwise be a trespass, and there is no general rule that such a consent must be in writing. It is therefore arguable that an oral consent can be relied on independently of the Act but the resulting position would not be satisfactory for either party. The building owner would have difficulty in proving the consent, if it was disputed. Further, the work being outside the Act, could not be included in any award under s 10, nor would it carry rights of entry under s 8. The adjoining owner would not have the benefit of the right of compensation under s 11(10) (see **5.8.2**), which requires consent to have been given in writing, nor of the right to security for the expense of work (under s 12).

5.8 EXPENSES

In general, the building owner must bear the expenses of special foundations which he proposes. However, there are two special provisions in s 11.

---

2   Compare *Aubergine Enterprises Ltd v Lakewood International Ltd* [2002] NPC 29; *Mount Eden Land Ltd v Prudential Assurance Co Ltd* (1997) 74 P & CR 377.

5.8.1 Section 11(9)

Under s 11(9)(b), the adjoining owner is liable for the expenses of carrying out works 'requested or required' by him. Expenses he has 'required' will include additional expenses caused by any requirement which he has imposed in respect of special foundations under s 4(1)(b), but not the expense of underpinning which he has required (see s 6(3)).

5.8.2 Section 11(10)

Section 11(10) deals specifically with special foundations. It applies where an adjoining owner has consented to the construction of special foundations on his land, and when he later constructs a building on his land its cost is increased by their existence. In such a case, the adjoining owner can, after completion of the work, claim so much of the cost as was due to the existence of the special foundations from the owner of the building to which they belong. In order to make this claim he must (as under s 13), within 2 months of the completion of the work, ensure that the responsible owner receives an account, together with any necessary invoices and other supporting documents. This provision gives rise to a number of difficulties.

This is one of the contingent liabilities imposed by the Act. Like the others,[3] it gives rise to questions relating to benefit and burden.

(a) Burden
The burden is carefully imposed not on the building owner, but on 'the owner of the building to which the foundations belong'. This shows that the burden falls on the owner at the material time, and is not personal to the original building owner who installed the special foundations. Thus, like the other contingent liabilities, it may fall on a purchaser without notice who had no reliable means of discovering it.

(b) Benefit
The benefit is even more problematical. If the burden falls on future owners, one would expect the benefit to run with the adjoining owner's land. The language, however, is ill-suited to this result. The person entitled is 'the adjoining owner', and this must mean the adjoining owner who fulfils the condition in s 11(10)(b) by erecting the building on his land. Clearly, the original adjoining owner who fulfilled the condition in s 11(10)(a), by consenting to the foundations, will qualify. But what if it is a successor who erects the building? Can he be 'the adjoining owner' within s 11(10)(b)? It is hard to wrest this meaning from the words. 'Adjoining owner' is defined (s 20) by reference to his relation to the building owner, who is in turn defined by his desire to exercise rights under the Act. Thus, in the context of s 11(10)(b), there is no current building owner or adjoining owner: 'the adjoining owner' can only be a description of the original adjoining owner by his former status. If his successor had been

---

3   See Chapter 14, **14.10**.

intended to be included, the expression should have been 'the owner of that land' (ie the land mentioned in s 11(10)(a)). This, however, is the sense in which the words must be construed if they are to produce a rational result.[4]

There are other ways in which the wording of this section is unsatisfactory.

(a) The concept of foundations 'belonging' to a building is imprecise. The Act itself contemplates that the adjoining owner may make use of special foundations constructed in his land by the building owner.[5] If he does so, but later finds that those foundations hinder building operations on his land (eg demolition and redevelopment), it is unclear whether they 'belong' to the neighbouring building sufficiently to support total, or even partial, liability for the increased expenses.

(b) It is not provided that the account must be served on the owner responsible (ie under s 15), but liability arises only if he *receives* it within the time-limit. Service and receipt are not the same thing. Part of the object of machinery for service is to enable service to be proved whether a document has actually been received or not. It seems the expense and embarrassment of personal service may be needed.

(c) In contrast to s 13(2), no provision is made for objections to the account nor for determination under s 10. No doubt this will be a matter within the jurisdiction of the surveyors, if any notice has been served under the Act. But the operations are, ex hypothesi, on the adjoining owner's land, and he may not have needed to serve any notice. In that case, it is not clear whether there is jurisdiction under s 10 (the deeming in s 13(2) suggests otherwise), or only in the court.

---

4 See further **14.2**.
5 See s 4(1)(b)(ii).

Chapter 6

ANCILLARY RIGHTS AND OBLIGATIONS

6.1 INTRODUCTION

Section 7 of the Act imposes duties on the building owner, regulating the exercise of his rights under the Act, and gives valuable rights to the adjoining owner. This chapter also deals with the building owner's obligations to make good any damage (under s 2) and to pay compensation.

6.2 SECTION 7

Section 7 groups together five subsections, whose unifying thread is that they are designed to protect adjoining owners. But they do not develop logically, and some are general, some specific.

(a) Subsections (1) and (2) are general, and protect adjoining occupiers as well as owners. But subsection (1) (unnecessary inconvenience) is concerned with the way rights are exercised (ie the carrying out of works), while (2) (compensation) is also concerned with the effect of works once executed.
(b) Subsection (3) (hoardings etc) gives specific protection, again to occupiers as well as owners, while work is proceeding, when it has the effect of 'laying open' the adjoining land or building. A counterpart of this protection is s 11(6), which provides an allowance for disturbance (again for occupiers as well as owners) where premises are laid open.
(c) Subsection (4) is concerned with special foundations, and is dealt with in Chapter 5.
(d) Subsection (5) (plans) controls the works which can be carried out, as between building owner and adjoining owner.

It is convenient to start with the subsections which are concerned with the carrying out of work, namely (5), (1) and (3) with 11(6).

6.3 SECTION 7(5): WHAT WORK MAY BE CARRIED OUT

This subsection is an essential part of the machinery of the Act, operating between building owner and adjoining owner. It strictly defines what work the building owner can carry out.

(a) The works must comply with statutory requirements. The obvious requirements are those of the Building Regulations, and the Building Act 1984. But all other relevant statutory provisions, are included. For

example, the provisions of the Control of Pollution Act 1974 regarding noise on construction sites, and of the Health and Safety at Work etc Act 1974 and Regulations regarding site safety (eg the Construction (Design and Management) Regulations 1994).
(b) There must be plans, sections and particulars, which may be agreed between the owners or determined by an award (under s 10), and the works must be executed in accordance with them.
(c) There can be no deviation from the plans, except such as may be agreed between the owners (or between surveyors acting on their behalf), or determined by a further award. The words in parenthesis are new (see the 1939 Act s 51(3)(b)) and seem to be at the same time unnecessary and inappropriate; unnecessary because without them the agreement can be reached through agents anyway, and inappropriate because it is not the function of surveyors appointed under s 10 to act as agents for the parties.

6.4 SECTION 7(1): UNNECESSARY INCONVENIENCE

This subsection provides that a building owner shall not exercise any right conferred on him by the Act in such manner or at such time as to cause unnecessary inconvenience to any adjoining owner or occupier.

This is a general obligation restricting the way the defined works are to be carried out. It may be expressly embodied in the award, but it will apply even if it is not.

The inclusion of adjoining occupiers extends the benefit to tenants and other residents who do not satisfy the definition of owners.[1] They will not have had any right to participate in the determination under s 10, but their interests are to some extent protected by s 7.

The concept of unnecessary inconvenience appears to impose a stricter duty than the tort of nuisance, where the criterion is unreasonable interference with the enjoyment of land. An interference may be reasonable, but not necessary, and a method of working may cause inconvenience without amounting to an interference.[2] No doubt there must, as in the law of nuisance, be a balancing of the interests of the parties.[3]

The case of *Jolliffe v Woodhouse*[4] is Court of Appeal authority for the following useful propositions: (a) the duty imposed by this section[5] is broken when there is unreasonable delay in carrying out the work; (b) the duty is personal to the

---

1 See para **2.5**.
2 See *Clerk and Lindsell on Torts* (17th edn) para 18.12, *Andreae v Selfridge & Co Ltd* [1938] Ch 1.
3 See eg *Leakey v National Trust* [1980] QB 485.
4 (1894) 10 TLR 553.
5 The section under consideration was s 85(3) of the Metropolitan Building Act 1855, which does not appear to differ significantly.

building owner, and it is no defence that the breach was that of his contractor; (c) breach of the duty gives rise to a claim in damages, and (d) this is so even though the work could have been done without recourse to the statutory power.[6]

6.5 SECTIONS 7(3) AND 11(6): PREMISES LAID OPEN

These provisions are necessitated by the very radical works which may be authorised under the Act, involving, for example, the removal of a wall which exposes the interior of the adjoining building.

6.5.1 Section 7: Duty to Provide Protection

This subsection imposes a specific obligation on the building owner, whenever his operations under the Act involve laying open any part of the adjoining land or building. He must provide, for as long as may be necessary, a proper hoarding, shoring, fans or temporary construction for the protection of the adjoining land or building, and the security of any adjoining occupier. What is proper, and the time for which it is necessary, will depend on the facts of each case. Normally the award will make suitable provisions for protection and security, but they will not detract from the duty; if the measures provided by the award are not adequate, the building owner is still under an obligation to do what is proper for protection and security, and breach of this duty can give rise to a claim in damages.

The need where a building is exposed is obvious. But it is less obvious where it is just part of the land which is laid open. Even a modest trench for the purpose of installing footings involves, in ordinary language, a laying open of the land. It is considered that the use of the word 'proper' indicates that there is no need to provide hoardings etc unless they are appropriate. A deep trench may need support to prevent subsidence; a shallow one may not require any special measures.

6.5.2 Section 11(6): Allowance for disturbance

This subsection should also be noticed under this heading. It provides that where adjoining premises are laid open pursuant to s 2(2)(e) (ie by demolition of a party structure) a 'fair allowance in respect of disturbance and inconvenience' shall be paid by the building owner to the adjoining owner or occupier. This is a partial counterpart to s 7(3). It is not thought there is any significance in the reference to 'premises' rather than 'land or building'; these expressions are not defined, and clearly cover the same ground. What is surprising and illogical about the provision is the narrowness of its scope

---

6   The work was demolition of a wall for the purpose of rebuilding it, which could be done at common law: *Cubitt v Porter* (1828) 8 B & C 257.

(which has been carried forward from s 56(1)(e)(ii) of the 1939 Act). There are plenty of other subsections of s 2(2) which grant rights which may lead to the laying open of adjoining premises (eg (c), (d), (h), (m)), but only sub-s (e) attracts this specific privilege.[7]

The use of the expression 'fair allowance' rather than 'compensation' is strange. It goes back to s 95(2)(b) of the 1984 Act, where it is not restricted to laying open. It is more appropriate to a sum designed to reimburse outgoings rather than to represent damages, and may reflect a reluctance to regard disturbance and inconvenience as proper subjects for damages.

This right does not appear to have been much exploited in the past (no reported authority on it has been found). In view of the wider right to compensation under s 7(2) it is thought unlikely that it will prove any more fruitful in the future.

6.6 SECTION 7(2): COMPENSATION

This important subsection imposes on the building owner an obligation to compensate adjoining owners and occupiers for 'any loss or damage which may result to any of them by reason of any work executed in pursuance of this Act'. In considering its effect it is instructive to keep in mind the extensive law affecting the comparable case of compensation for injurious affection.[8]

6.6.1 History

The wording is drawn from s 50(2)(d) of the 1939 Act, where, however, it applied only to work done in pursuance of what is now s 6.[9] This extension in the scope of statutory compensation is an innovation, since it had been decided under the 1894 Act in *Adams v Marylebone BC*[10] that no compensation was payable for work authorised by the statutory procedure.

6.6.2 Scope

The words 'any loss or damage' are comprehensive, and appear to cover any form of loss suffered by the adjoining owner or occupier. Prima facie the measure of general damage will be the tortious measure, namely the difference in the market value of the adjoining owner's land before and after the execution of the work.[11] But there is no reason to limit the compensation to

---

7 But of course the duty under s 7(3) applies to all cases of laying open.
8 Under Land Clauses Act 1845, s 68 (as amended) and Compulsory Purchase Act 1965, s 10(1).
9 The 1939 Act section embraced 'inconvenience' as well as loss and damage, but the omission is not thought to be significant in the light of s 7(1).
10 [1907] 2 KB 822.
11 As with compensation for injurious affection: see *Re Wadham and North Eastern Rly Co* (1884) 14 QBD 747, (1885) 16 QBD 227, CA.

damage to land,[12] especially in the light of the limitation of compensation under s 1(7) to damage 'to property'.[13] It is considered that the words are amply wide enough to cover other categories of loss, such as interference with a business carried on on the land, or loss of a chance to sell property advantageously.[14]

6.6.3 Authorised work

It is clear that the work must have been 'executed in pursuance of the Act'. That is to say it must have been authorised by a valid award under s 10. If it was not so authorised, either because there was no award, or because the award was for some reason invalid, the claim must be for damages at common law and not for statutory compensation.[15] This would apply, for example, if the work interfered with an easement, such as an established right of light, since this would be contrary to s 9(a).

6.6.4 Work otherwise actionable

More doubtful is the question whether the work must be such that it would have been actionable if not carried out under the authority of the Act. Suppose that an award authorises the raising of a wall so as to deprive the adjoining owner of a beautiful view, or the lowering of a wall so as to expose him to being overlooked; is the resulting diminution in the value of the adjoining land a loss within the section? It is a well established principle that such loss is not covered by compensation for injurious affection.[16] On the other hand there is no such restriction where the injuriously affected land was held with other land compulsorily acquired.[17] Such fine distinctions, however, are out of place in the simpler context of party walls. It is tentatively suggested that, although the word 'damage' may be restricted to damage recognised by the law, the word 'loss' may be designed to go further. Again there is a telling contrast with s 1(7), where 'loss' is not mentioned.

6.6.5 Effect of completed work

The loss must result from 'any work executed' pursuant to the Act. This is an ambiguous expression. It seems undoubtedly to mean loss resulting from the

---

12 Unlike compensation for injurious affection, where this limitation is derived from the different statutory context of s 68: see *Argyle Motors (Birkenhead) Ltd v Birkenhead Corpn* [1975] AC 99.
13 See **3.4.3**.
14 Compare cases on the predecessor of Public Health Act 1936, s 278(1); *Re Bater and Birkenhead Corp* [1893] 1 QB 679, 2 QB 77 CA; *Lingké v Christchurch Corp* [1912] 3 KB 595; see also *Blue Circle Industries Plc v MoD* [1998] 3 All ER 385, CA (Nuclear Installations Act 1965, s 12).
15 See the authorities on injurious affection, eg *Imperial Gas Light and Coke Co v Broadbent* (1859) 7 HL Cas 600.
16 See eg *Re Penny and South Eastern Rly Co* (1857) 7 E & B 660.
17 See eg *Cowper Essex v Acton Local Board* (1880) 14 App Cas 153.

existence of the work, once executed, but it is also capable of bearing a portmanteau meaning, so as to embrace in addition loss resulting from the process of carrying out the work. The wider meaning is examined in **6.6.6**. The narrower meaning is considered to be the primary field of operation of the section. Loss resulting from works executed must include loss resulting from the execution of the works. This is the same primary criterion as applies in the case of injurious affection,[18] and leads to the before-and-after comparison for the general measure of loss (see **6.6.2**).

6.6.6 Loss during execution of work

Temporary loss suffered during the execution of the statutory work is recognised as a compensatable head of injurious affection.[19] But here the interrelationship of s 7(2) with sections 7(1) and (3) becomes significant. Those sections impose specific duties in respect of the carrying out of the works, breach of which sounds in damages (see **6.4** and **6.5.1**). There appears to be little, if any, room for s 7(1) to provide additional compensation during the period which they cover.[20]

6.6.7 Loss from use of completed works

Loss arising from the use of statutory works, once completed, (eg from noise, smell, fumes, vibration) is not normally a compensatable head of injurious affection.[21] Exceptionally, however, it may be where statute authorises continuing works, and the compensation provision is wide enough.[22] The words of s 7(2) are probably wide enough, but the Act is not concerned with, and awards do not normally authorise, continuing works.[23] In addition there is, in limited circumstances, an independent right under Part I of the Land Compensation Act 1973 to compensation for certain loss arising from the use of public works, but this is unlikely to be applicable.[24] Apart from those exceptional cases, the adjoining owner's only claim will be under the law of nuisance.

6.6.8 Interest

This is dealt with later (see **9.7**).

---

18 The statutes refer to injurious affection from 'the execution of the works'.
19 See *Wildtree Hotels Ltd v Harrow LBC* [2001] 2 AC 1.
20 Unless, for example, the adjoining owner was to sell during the construction period, thereby suffering a permanent capital loss in addition to temporary inconvenience.
21 See *Hammersmith and City Rly v Brand* (1869) LR 4 HL 171.
22 See *Re Simeon and Isle of Wight RDC* [1937] Ch 525.
23 But it is not ultra vires for an award to impose an obligation to repair (see *Marchant v Capital & Counties Plc* [1983] 2 EGLR 156 and **8.13(g)**), and in such a case the question of compensation for use could arise.
24 See *Halsbury's Laws* vol 8(1) (4th edn), para 359 *et seq*. 'Public works' includes works provided in the exercise of statutory powers (s 1(3)), but compensation is available only if the statute confers immunity from actions for nuisance (s 1(6) as amended).

6.6.9 No-fault compensation

It should be noted that the obligation to pay compensation, where it applies, in no way depends on any fault on the part of the building owner. On the contrary, work executed in pursuance of the Act is necessarily authorised and lawful, and the compensation is payable even if the award has been followed to the letter. It is the price which the building owner has to pay for the right to carry out the works. If he acts unlawfully (eg by travelling outside the award, by building negligently, or by causing unnecessary inconvenience), he will not be acting in pursuance of the Act, and the adjoining owner's cause of action for any resulting loss will not be under this section, but elsewhere.[25]

6.6.10 Proposal for reform

In the first edition of this book the advent of s 7(2) was welcomed (see para 6.6 fn 6). The Government has now suggested that it should be repealed, with a return to the piecemeal provisions of the 1939 Act. For the authors' comments on this suggestion see para **17.2.2**.

6.7 RELATION OF SECTION 7(2) TO OTHER COMPENSATORY PROVISIONS

This is a topic which has caused some disagreement among commentators[26] and deserves examination. Two views may be mentioned.

(a) One theory is that ss 7(1) and (2) should be read together, so that the scope of s 7(2) is limited to compensation for inconvenience. This view is respectfully considered to be untenable. The words 'any loss or damage' in s 7(2) are not expressly limited to damage arising from, or consisting of, inconvenience, nor does the section's proximity to s 7(1) lead to any such implication.

(b) Another view is that s 7(1) defines the limit of the statutory rights, while s 7(2) imposes a condition on their exercise.[27] This is more convincing in that it recognises the independence of s 7(2) from s 7(1). But the distinction between defining the limit and imposing a condition is of doubtful substance and utility. It is based on obiter remarks in the Court of Appeal in *Adams v Marylebone BC*[28] and it leads to a questionable limitation on the jurisdiction of the surveyors (see **6.8.1**).

---

25 Ie in tort for trespass, negligence or breach of s 7(1) respectively.
26 See P Chynoweth 'Unnecessary inconvenience and compensation within the party wall legislation' (2000) 18 *Structural Survey* 99. This summarises the opposing views with references.
27 See Chynoweth op cit.
28 [1907] 2 KB 822.

52   Party Walls – Law and Practice

The view has already been expressed that the presence of s 7(1) and (3), imposing specific duties in respect of the carrying out of works (for breach of which damages can be awarded), leaves virtually no room for the additional application of s 7(2) during that period (see **6.6.6**). Beyond that it is doubted whether it is profitable to seek theoretical consistency in a statute with such an essentially empirical history as this one. Its provisions must, of course, be construed so as to be consistent with each other and so as to produce a rational result. This may involve the rejection of unhelpful distinctions as well as untenable implications.

6.8 ENFORCEMENT

All the sections mentioned above impose obligations on the building owner for the benefit of the adjoining owner, and in most cases for the benefit of adjoining occupiers as well. These are statutory duties, breach of which is capable of giving rise to an action in tort.[29] This is the only form of enforcement available to adjoining occupiers, since they have no access to the award procedure under s 10. But adjoining owners are in a position to have recourse to the s 10 procedure, which will have been invoked by the building owner in the first place. How do these competing jurisdictions interact?

6.8.1 Extent of surveyors' jurisdiction

The surveyors have jurisdiction to settle by award 'any matter which is connected with any work to which [the] Act relates' (s 10(10)(a)), and the award may determine 'any matter arising out of or incidental to the dispute' (s 10(12)(c)). Prima facie these words are wide enough to embrace matters such as the inconvenience or loss caused by works executed in pursuance of the Act, and indeed there appears to be no doubt that the surveyors' jurisdiction includes the determination of loss or damage under s 7(2).[30] But the analysis outlined in **6.7(b)** has led to the view that under s 7(1), while the surveyors' award must give effect to the duty to avoid unnecessary inconvenience, only the court can adjudicate on any question of breach of the duty.[31] The reasoning is logically tidy, but it is considered, with all respect, that the consequence is not supported by the *dictum* of Fletcher Moulton LJ relied on.[32] Vaughan Williams

---

29 Compare *Blue Circle Industries Plc v MoD* [1998] 3 All ER 385, CA.
30 In the *Adams* case (above) Vaughan Williams LJ thought so ([1907] 2 KB 822); Fletcher Moulton LJ is not in point (see fn 33); Buckley LJ did not comment.
31 See Chynoweth, op cit at p 103.
32 See the *Adams* case where he said (at p 841):
    '... I personally am disposed to think that with regard to any act of the building owner outside the provisions of [the Act] the [surveyors] would have no jurisdiction; but at the same time I think that [they] would have the widest powers of determining the

LJ in the same case expressed the opposite view. He, having acknowledged[33] that the surveyors' power to prescribe convenient works did not necessarily include power to decide on compensation for inconvenience, said:[34]

> '... I am disposed to think that in all the cases in which the Act provides for compensation[35] the intention is that the amount of compensation is to be determined by the [surveyors] ... it would be extremely inconvenient if two inquiries were necessary, one by the [surveyors] to ascertain whether the conditions precedent to the right to compensation existed and another before some other tribunal to determine the amount of the compensation.'

It is considered that there is great force in this reasoning, and that it would be decisive in the new context. Thus, it would seem that the surveyors' jurisdiction extends also to issues arising under sections, such as s 7(1), which can be regarded as defining the limits of the statutory rights.

6.8.2 Surveyors or court?

If the analysis in the last two paragraphs is correct, the surveyors jurisdiction extends to awarding compensation for breach of the statutory duties in s 7. Thus an adjoining owner (but not an adjoining occupier) who wishes to pursue a claim for compensation will need to know whether he is bound to apply to the surveyors, or whether he has the alternative of bringing an action in court. This is considered later (see **9.5.1**).

6.9 DUTY TO MAKE GOOD

It has already been noticed that certain rights under s 2 are conditional.[36] The conditions imposed on the building owner consist of obligations: (a) to make good any damage; and (b) to carry out specified works. The rights and their respective conditions can be summarised in tabular form.

---

manner and time of doing the work so as not to cause unnecessary inconvenience to the adjoining owner or occupier. But it appears to me to be unnecessary to decide these questions, because I hold that *the adjoining owner has no right to compensation for any inconvenience caused by operations which the Act has given the building owner a right to carry out ... for ... his action is lawful*'.

This *dictum* is restricted to 'acts outside the Act', ie which not merely cause inconvenience but go beyond the authorised works. Further these are explicitly not words of decision, and the italicised passage suggests that this tentative view is not compatible with the presence of s 7(2).

33 See ibid at p 833.
34 See ibid at p 834–835.
35 His earlier reference to compensation for inconvenience shows that he is not here confining himself to *express* provision for compensation.
36 See **3.6** and **3.7**.

Right	Conditions
Section 2(2)(a): underpinning etc	Section 2(3). Unless work is necessitated by defect or want of repair: (a) make good; (b) specified works, if work to party structure or external wall.
Section 2(2)(e): demolition etc	Section 2(4): (a) make good; (b) specified works. (NB Also liability under s 11(6)).
Section 2(2)(f): cutting into (g): away from, etc (h): overhangs	Section 2(5). Make good.
Section 2(2)(j): Weather-proofing	Section 2(6). Make good.
Section 2(2)(m): Reducing height	Section 2(7). Specified works. (NB Liability for adjoining owner under s 11(7)).

6.10 SECTION 11(8): PAYMENT IN LIEU

Where the building owner has to make good specified damage by reason of the conditions mentioned above, the adjoining owner can require that the expenses of making good be determined under s 10 and paid to him in lieu of carrying out the work (s 11(8)). The following points should be noted.

(a) The adjoining owner has an absolute right to make the requirement. The surveyors have no jurisdiction to enquire into its reasonableness.
(b) The section does not say that the requirement must be in writing, but it clearly should be. It does not have to be served in any particular way.
(c) The requirement cannot be made until it has been determined that works are to be carried out which are conditional on making good. It must clearly be made promptly after that, and certainly before the building owner embarks on making good.
(d) The right applies where the building owner has to 'make damage good', and applies only to the expenses of 'making good'. It does not appear to apply to the further expenses of the specified works mentioned above, even if the adjoining owner does not wish them to be carried out.

Chapter 7

RIGHTS OF ENTRY

7.1 INTRODUCTION

Section 8 confers rights of entry on land in favour of the building owner and the surveyors, subject to the prior service of notice. These rights are exercisable against occupiers as well as adjoining owners.

7.2 RIGHT OF BUILDING OWNER

Section 8(1) entitles the building owner to enter any land or premises for the purpose of executing work pursuant to the Act, and to remove any furniture or fittings or take any other action necessary for that purpose. The right may be exercised during usual working hours.

(a) The section expressly authorises the building owner to bring servants, agents, employees and workmen (who will include contractors and sub-contractors and their employees) onto the land. But they must be there for the purpose of executing work pursuant to the Act.
(b) The right is limited to executing work in pursuance of the Act. Therefore, there is no right to enter in respect of unrelated work even if it is part of the same project. Normally, the right will not be exercisable until the works pursuant to the Act have been defined by an award. To the extent that any award is ultra vires or otherwise invalid, no entry will be authorised.
(c) The words at the end of the subsection 'take any other action necessary for that purpose' relate back to 'for the purpose of executing any work in pursuance of this Act' and not to the removal of any furniture or fittings. The only 'purpose' expressly referred to earlier in the subsection is the purpose of executing any work in pursuance of the Act.
(d) Works in pursuance of the Act are defined in ss 1, 2 and 6. They do not include preparatory works of exploration for the purpose of ascertaining whether works on the building owner's own land fall within the distances prescribed in s 6, which requires intimate knowledge of the adjoining owner's foundations. The rights of entry are therefore not available for this purpose. It has already been pointed out that this may put the building owner in an impossible position (see **4.3.5**).
(e) Section 6 is concerned with the depth of foundations, and works pursuant to the section are normally sited entirely on the building owner's land. It is considered that the rights of entry do not extend to entry for the purpose of carrying out such works, even if it would be convenient for the building owner to have access to the adjoining land for that purpose. Still less would they extend to the siting on the adjoining land of temporary structures

such as scaffolding to assist the erection of the buildings supported by the new foundations.

(f) But there is a necessary exception to the limitation mentioned in (e) above. Section 6(3) allows the building owner to underpin or otherwise strengthen the adjoining owner's building (and obliges him to do so if the adjoining owner so requires). Work of this character necessarily has to be carried out on the adjoining land. If such work is authorised by the award, it must be work in pursuance of the Act, and the rights of entry must extend to it.

7.3 RIGHT OF SURVEYORS

Under s 8(5), a surveyor is entitled to enter any land or premises during usual working hours for the purpose of carrying out the object for which he is appointed or selected.

(a) The purposes for which a surveyor is appointed or selected are the purposes of s 10, ie determination of a dispute. Again there is no right of entry for exploratory purposes, for example to determine whether a notice is necessary under s 6.
(b) In contrast to s 8(1), there is no express right for anyone other than the surveyor to enter. It is thought, however, that it may be legitimate for him to take an assistant for ministerial duties, such as measuring and note-taking.

7.4 NOTICE BEFORE ENTRY

It is an essential pre-condition to the exercise of these rights of entry that notice is served on all owners and occupiers of the land (s 8(3) and (6)). The methods of serving notices are dealt with in Chapter 13, and a precedent is provided in Appendix 4. At least 14 days' notice must be given, except in a case of emergency, when 'such notice of the intention to enter as may be reasonably practicable' is all that is required (s 8(3)(a), (6)(a)).

(a) 'Emergency' has been held to mean the sudden occurrence of facts causing an apprehension of danger or difficulty.[1] Examples might include unexpected movement in the party wall, collapse of excavations, etc.
(b) Subsections (3) and (6) are concerned with the length of notice required, and not its form. But it is considered that they cannot be satisfied by oral notice, since their references to 'serving' imply a document to be served under s 15. It follows that, even in an extreme emergency, a written notice must be handed over at the time of entry. This view is supported by s. 15(1) which refers to 'notice *or other document*'.

---

1 See *The Larchbank* [1943] AC 299.

(c) 'Reasonably practicable' is not the equivalent of reasonable, nor does it mean simply what is reasonably capable physically of being done. It has been held to mean 'feasible in all the circumstances'.[2]

7.5 USUAL WORKING HOURS

Both rights are exercisable during 'usual working hours', which are not specified by the Act and give rise to some uncertainties. Whatever the meaning of this expression when the 1939 Act was passed, there has in recent years been a major change in the hours during which business activities are carried on. Retail stores are frequently open until late in the evening and, at least in major centres, trade 7 days a week. What limits are implied by the use of the expression today? The following suggestions are made.

(a) Since the hours must be 'usual', the hours worked by supermarkets or late night grocers etc, are irrelevant.
(b) The primary purpose of the limitation on hours is to protect adjoining owners and occupiers against unreasonable disturbance of their rest and privacy. The concept is of the hours between which a reasonable householder would regard it as usual for someone to be at work. Typically, it is thought, this would be under modern conditions between approximately 8.30 am and 5.30 am 5 days per week. Saturday mornings might also be included, but not Sundays.[3]
(c) The concept may vary with the neighbourhood. What is usual in an industrial estate may differ from what is usual in a residential road.

7.6 CIVIL REMEDY

These rights of entry are enforceable by criminal sanctions under s 16.[4] Can they also be enforced by civil proceedings (ie for a declaration or injunction)?

(a) It is considered that s 8(1) is apt to create a private right in favour of the building owner, breach of which entitles him to seek relief from the civil courts.[5]
(b) On the other hand, it is considered that under s 8(5) the surveyors have no right. It is the building owner who has to serve the notice under s 8(6), so it appears to be his right which a surveyor exercises. Here too, therefore, it is

---

2 Compare *Palmer v Southend-on-Sea Borough Council* [1984] 1 All ER 945, CA.
3 Under the Control of Pollution Act 1974, notices relating to noise caused by work on construction sites generally specify hours within these periods: see Control of Noise (Codes of Practice for Construction and Open Sites) Orders 1984 and 1987, SI 1984/1992, SI 1987/1730.
4 See Chapter 16.
5 Compare *Solomons v R Gertzenstein Ltd* [1954] 2 All ER 625, CA.

the building owner who has a right of action if a surveyor is obstructed or denied entry.

7.7 OCCUPIERS

The adjoining owner whose land is entered will at least have had the opportunity to participate in the procedure leading to the award, and to make representations to the surveyor. Mere occupiers of the adjoining land are not so privileged. It may be that a 14-day notice, carrying a warning of potential criminal liability for obstruction, will be the first and only intimation that they are about to be seriously disturbed. The consolation provided by the Act is principally the right to compensation under s 7(2), and less importantly the further rights under s 7(1) and (3). In addition, an occupier who is a tenant with a qualified covenant for quiet enjoyment in the traditional form may, in some circumstances, have a claim against his landlord (the adjoining owner) for any interference with his possession. If the adjoining owner has opposed the award, or taken no part in the procedure, the building owner's entry will be by title paramount, and there will be no claim.[6] But if the adjoining owner has actively consented or agreed to operations which could not otherwise have been authorised, he may be liable for the interference.[7]

7.8 HUMAN RIGHTS ASPECTS

The impact of rights of entry on owners and occupiers may raise issues under the Human Rights Act 1998.[8] These are discussed at **15.13**.

---

6 See *Kelly v Rogers* [1892] 1 QB 910.
7 Compare *Cohen v Tannar* [1900] 2 QB 609.
8 1998 C42.

Chapter 8

THE AWARD – PROCEDURE AND SCOPE

8.1 INTRODUCTION

One of the principal features of the Act is the establishment of a special disputes resolution procedure. This is contained in s 10, derived from s 55 of the 1939 Act. When a dispute arises or is deemed to have arisen between building owner and adjoining owner, they must either agree jointly on the appointment of a single surveyor (called in the Act the 'agreed surveyor') or each must appoint a surveyor, and the two surveyors so appointed ('the parties' surveyors') must forthwith select a third surveyor (called in the Act the 'third surveyor') who is to resolve any disagreement between the parties' surveyors. The parties' surveyors and the third surveyor are together known as the 'three surveyors'. In this book the expression 'the surveyors' is used to refer to the surveyor or surveyors acting under s 10, whichever procedure has been used. In practice, most disputes involve the three-surveyor procedure, but the third surveyor is rarely called in.

The status of surveyors is considered below. Although appointed (except in the case of a third surveyor) by the parties, they must act independently at all times. They should not regard the party who appointed them as their client, but simply as their 'appointing party'. The better view is that they are not arbitrators[1] and thus are, for example, under no duty to act judicially, to give reasons for their decisions, or comply with the Arbitration Act 1996. The mechanism by which the surveyors produce their decision is an award (or if necessary more than one award), which once issued and unless challenged on appeal (see Chapter 10) is final and binding on the parties.

8.2 DISPUTE

Section 10 is headed 'Resolution of disputes', and it is the occurrence of a dispute which necessitates the appointment of surveyors. A dispute is a difference between a building owner and an adjoining owner in respect of any matter connected with any work to which the Act relates (s 10(1)). Disputes fall into three categories.

(a) There are many contexts in which the Act expressly contemplates the possibility of disputes arising and provides that they are to be resolved under s 10 (ss 1(8), 2(3)(b), 7(5)(b), 11(2), 12(1), 12(2)). Indeed, there is one context where the s 10 procedure is invoked without any reference to a dispute (s 11(8)).

---

1 See **8.19**.

(b) The Act deems a dispute to arise in certain circumstances. Mostly, this occurs when a notice under the Act is not consented to (ss 5, 6(7)), but it also applies, perhaps unnecessarily, where the adjoining owner serves a notice of objection to an account from the building owner (s 13(2)).
(c) Actual disputes may arise which fall into neither of the foregoing categories.[2]

8.3 QUALIFICATION AND INDEPENDENCE OF SURVEYORS

Remarkably the Act does not require surveyors to be qualified in any particular way, or indeed at all. 'Surveyor' is defined simply as any person 'not being a party to the matter' appointed or selected under s 10 to determine disputes (s 20).

So neither the building owner nor the adjoining owner can be appointed under s 10, but the section offers no other express guidance. Is this the only restriction, or are others to be implied? It is considered that there are two material implications carried by the section. First, the disqualification of the parties implies that a degree of genuine independence and impartiality is required. Secondly, s 10(8)(b), which disqualifies the appointing officer from appointing if he is employed by a party (see **8.6.2**) appears to equate employee with employer for the purposes of the section. This is the context from which the competence of candidates has to be collected.[3]

There is little authority on the degree of independence required. Surveyors are not judges,[4] who may be disqualified by any circumstances which would lead a fair-minded and informed observer to conclude that there is 'a real possibility' that the tribunal is biased.[5] But their position has been described as 'quasi-judicial',[6] and the definition in s 20 implies, as has been suggested, that they must be genuinely independent. It has been said that their function is 'in the nature of an expert determination', but that they are 'not obliged to act

---

2   See *Selby v Whitbread & Co* [1917] 1 KB 736 at 744–745.
3   For further discussion see P Chynoweth *Impartiality and the Party Wall Surveyor* 17 Const LJ 93.
4   The question whether they are arbitrators is considered in **8.19**.
5   See *Porter v Magill* [2002] 1 All ER 465, HL.
6   See *Gyle-Thompson v Wall Street (Properties) Ltd* [1974] 1 All ER 295 at 303a per Brightman J.

without regard to the interests of the party who appointed them'.[7] For the degree of impartiality required, the nearest analogy seems to be an architect under standard forms of building contract, who has obligations 'to act in a wholly disinterested and unbiased way in the interests of both the parties concerned'[8] and 'in a fair and unbiased manner, holding the balance between his client and the contractor'.[9]

It is obvious that a qualified professional is the most suitable person to discharge the duty of impartiality, and therefore the most suitable candidate for appointment or selection under s 10. However, the Act does not require any professional qualification, and it is therefore clear that a non-professional is not disqualified. It is considered, however, that there are limits to be derived from the implications suggested above. First, the appointee must genuinely be a separate person from the appointing party: a company wholly owned by the party would not be competent.[10] Indeed it has been held that no company can be appointed because of the references to death in s 10(3)(c) and (5).[11] Secondly, there is the question whether the employee of a party is competent. This is considered doubtful, by reason of the equation implied by s 10(8)(b): it is true that the equation affects the competence of the appointor, but the competence of the appointee is more sensitive, and it would be strange if it was not similarly affected.

8.4 MACHINERY OF APPOINTMENT

There is elaborate machinery for the appointment and selection of surveyors. The following preliminary points may be noted.

(a) The Act uses the word 'appoint' for surveyors appointed by the parties, and 'select' for the selection of the third surveyor.[12]
(b) All appointments and selections must be in writing (s 10(2)).
(c) All appointments and selections 'shall not be rescinded by either party' (s 10(2)). This clearly makes appointments, which are made by the parties, irrevocable. So if a surveyor is appointed, and he is at the time a member of a particular professional practice, he remains in post notwithstanding any change in his employment or other circumstances. Even being convicted of serious criminal offences would not result per se in termination of his

---

7 See *Chartered Society of Physiotherapy v Simmonds Church Smiles* [1995] 1 EGLR 155 at 159 per Lloyd CCJ.
8 See *Lubenham Fidelities v South Pembrokeshire District Council* (1886) 33 BLR 39 at 52.
9 See *Sutcliffe v Thackrah* [1974] AC 727 at 737D per Lord Reid.
10 See *Finchbourne v Rodrigues* [1976] 3 All ER 581. Quaere whether the incapacity would extend to a (non-professional) spouse or close family member.
11 See *Loost v Kremer* (unreported) 12 May 1997 (HH Judge Cowell CCJ), at p 25 of the transcript.
12 But not consistently: the choice of the term 'appointing officer' (s 10(8)) is anomalous, and the reference to 'appointments' in the definition of this term (s 10) is a solecism.

appointment, but an imprisoned surveyor would no doubt become incapable of acting.[13] The effect of s 10(2) on selections which are not made by the parties is unclear.

8.5 METHODS OF APPOINTMENT AND SELECTION

The primary methods of appointment and selection are prescribed by s 10(1).

8.5.1 Agreed surveyor

The parties can concur in the appointment of a single surveyor (s 10(1)(a)). This is unusual, and normally the next subsection is followed.

8.5.2 Parties' surveyors

If there is no agreed surveyor, each party must appoint a surveyor (s 10(1)(b)).

8.5.3 Third surveyor

The two surveyors appointed by the parties must forthwith select the third surveyor (s 10(1)(b)).

8.6 SECONDARY METHODS

There are fall-back methods of appointment and selection, if the directions prescribed by s 10(1) are not followed.

8.6.1 Parties' surveyors

If either party to the dispute refuses to make an appointment under s 10(1)(b), or neglects to do so for 10 days after being served with a request by the other party, the other party may make the appointment on behalf of the defaulting party (s 10(4)). There appears to be nothing to prevent the other party appointing the surveyor he has already appointed himself, so as to convert him into an agreed surveyor. This procedure applies only to failure to appoint under s 10(1)(b), and apparently not to failure to appoint under s 10(5).[14]

8.6.2 Third surveyor

If either of the parties' surveyors refuses to select a third surveyor, or neglects to do so for 10 days after being served with a request by the other surveyor, the other surveyor can apply for the selection to be made by: (a) the appointing

---

13 See s 10(5) and **8.7**.
14 See **8.7.2**.

officer[15] or, if the appointing officer or his employer is a party to the dispute, by (b) the Secretary of State (s 10(8)). This same procedure also applies if one of the parties' surveyors refuses or neglects to select a replacement third surveyor under s 10(9).[16]

8.7 DEATH AND INCAPACITY OF SURVEYORS

Once the surveyors have been duly appointed, the procedure under s 10 may nevertheless break down for a variety of reasons, which the section proceeds to cater for. The first group of reasons involve no question of fault. A surveyor may, before the dispute is settled: (a) die; (b) become incapable of acting; or (c) deem himself incapable of acting. This last category is new, and seems to be designed to enable a surveyor to withdraw for any reason which he personally considers sufficient (eg ill health, overwork). It is thought that the term 'incapable of acting' should not be restricted to mental or physical incapacity. The object of the procedure is to provide a speedy and efficient resolution of disputes in the context of on-going building works. This object would be frustrated by such a narrow construction.[17] Any supervening event which makes a surveyor's proper discharge of his functions practically or legally impossible should qualify.

If there is a dispute over incapacity, it should be noted that no power of removal is given to the court. Either party can, no doubt, bring an action[18] for a declaration that a surveyor is incapable of acting, and if the declaration is made the consequences under s 10 will follow. In practice it is more likely to be the surveyor's own appointing party who may wish to take this step, since the opposing surveyor will presumably be able to proceed under s 10(7) (see **8.9.2**). The consequences vary according to the category of surveyor concerned.

8.7.1 Agreed surveyor

If it is an agreed surveyor who dies etc, the procedure under s 10 has to begin all over again (s 10(3)).

8.7.2 Parties' surveyors

If it is a surveyor appointed by a party, that party can appoint another surveyor in his place (s 10(5)). Steps taken by his predecessor are not invalidated, and he

---

15 Ie the person appointed under the Act for the purpose by the local authority: s 20.
16 See **8.8.2**.
17 See *R v White* [1867] LR 2 QB 557. *Dundee Corporation v Guthrie* 1969 SLT 93. For 'incapacity' in arbitration see Arbitration Act 1996, s 24(1)(c), expressly limited to physical or mental incapacity, but applying to non-supervening incapacity as well.
18 By claim under CPR Part 8 against the surveyor and the other party (by analogy with applications under the Arbitration Act 1996, s 24: see CPR r 62.6(1)).

must presumably take up where the predecessor left off. If the party does not make the appointment, the other party does not appear to have power to make it on his behalf, since s 10(4) applies only to failure to appoint under s 10(1)(b).

8.7.3 Third surveyor

If it is the third surveyor, the other two surveyors must forthwith select another surveyor in his place (s 10(9)). If they fail to agree, either of them can invoke the secondary procedure under s 10(8).[19]

8.8 REFUSAL AND NEGLECT BY SURVEYORS – GENERAL

The procedure may also break down because a surveyor refuses or neglects to act. This too is provided for. In the cases of an agreed surveyor and a third surveyor, refusal and neglect are assimilated to death and incapacity.

8.8.1 Agreed surveyor

Thus if an agreed surveyor refuses to act, or neglects to do so for 10 days after being served with a request by either party, the procedure under s 10 has to begin all over again (s 10(3)).

8.8.2 Third surveyor

Similarly, if a third surveyor refuses to act, or neglects to do so for 10 days after being served with a request by either party or either party's surveyor, a new third surveyor must forthwith be selected (s 10(9)).

It should be noted that in these provisions there is a distinction between 'refuses to act' and 'neglects to act' after being served with a request. This repeated distinction throughout s 10 seems to imply that refusal involves an express refusal, whereas neglect merely involves inaction.[20] This is discussed below.

8.9 REFUSAL AND NEGLECT BY PARTIES' SURVEYORS

More elaborate provision is made in s 10(6) and (7) for refusal or neglect by the parties' surveyors. These sections apply to the parties' surveyors, whether appointed under s 10(1)(b), (4) or (5). They introduce the new and more rigorous concept of refusing or neglecting to act 'effectively'.

---

19 See **8.6.2**.
20 Compare *Re Thornhill's Settlements* [1941] Ch 24.

8.9.1 Section 10(6): refusal

Section 10(6) is very sweeping. If a surveyor refuses to act effectively, the other party's surveyor can proceed to act ex parte (ie on his own), and anything he does is as effectual as if he had been an agreed surveyor. In effect, therefore, the refusing surveyor is completely superseded by the other party's surveyor, who assumes the authority of an agreed surveyor, and is thus enabled to proceed to make an award on his own. There appears to be no opportunity for the refusing surveyor to retrieve his position: once the section applies he is completely ousted. It is considered that only very obstructive conduct could justify such a consequence. The contrast between refusing and neglecting suggests that there must be an express refusal to do something. In *Frances Holland School v Wassef*[21] it was held there had been no refusal where the surveyor had continued discussions on technical matters in correspondence and expressed the view that there was no need for an award at that time. In cases relating to arbitration, it has been held that there has been a refusal where an arbitrator unjustifiably refused to sign an award unless it included his reasons for dissenting;[22] but that a refusal to act must be 'definite and final', and a refusal to act in a particular manner is not sufficient.[23] The word 'effectively' dilutes the refusal to some extent. It does not have to be a refusal to take any step at all (which may be what is necessary under s 10(3)(a) and (9)(a)), but a refusal to take any effective step. For example, it does not have to be 'I refuse to consider this matter at all', but might be 'I refuse to consider any plans embodying this proposal'. What is more difficult is the question whether a refusal to take a specific effective step (eg attending a meeting), as opposed to a refusal to take *any* effective step, could satisfy the section. On the whole, it is considered that a refusal related only to a specific step is more suitable to be dealt with under s 10(7).

8.9.2 Section 10(7): neglect

Under s 10(7), either party or one party's surveyor, can serve on the other surveyor a request to take some action. If he does not act effectively within 10 days the requesting party's surveyor is entitled to act ex parte 'in respect of the subject matter of the request', and what he does will be as effectual as if he were an agreed surveyor. This is less draconian than s 10(6). It contemplates that the request will have a limited subject matter, and that the defaulting surveyor will be superseded only in respect of that subject matter. Again, the criterion is not total inaction but failure to take any effective step. This will include, for example, not only failure to answer correspondence at all, but also giving answers which amount to deliberate procrastination.[24] It should be

---

21 [2001] 2 EGLR 88.
22 *Cargill International SA v Sociedad Iberica de Molturacion SA* [1998] 1 Lloyds Rep 489.
23 *Burkett Sharp & Co v Eastcheap Dried Fruit Co* [1962] 1 Lloyds Rep 267 CA, affirming [1961] 1 Lloyds Rep 80.
24 *Frances Holland School v Wassef* [2001] 2 EGLR 88.

remembered, however, that if the request procedure is to be usefully exploited, the subject matter must be some concrete step which the requesting surveyor could effectually take on his own (eg appointing a third surveyor, or deciding a specific issue, such as security under s 12).

8.9.3 Requirements common to refusal and neglect

A surveyor wishing to avail himself of s 10(6) or (7) must comply strictly with the provisions of the Act. He can rely on a refusal or a neglect (with appropriate prior notice) or both. The relevant grounds must be expressly stated in the ex parte award. Thus, in *Frances Holland School v Wassef*[25] a surveyor served a 10-day notice (under s 55 of the 1939 Act). He then proceeded to issue an ex parte award, after the period had expired, on the basis of a refusal to act. In holding the award was invalid on its face His Honour Judge Crawford Lindsay QC said:[26]

> 'The relevant grounds must be expressed accurately in the ex parte award. In this case, there was no reference to a neglect to act by Mr Johnson after the written request in the ex parte award. The only reference was to a refusal to act. Accordingly, the ex parte award is inconsistent with the reference to the 10-day time limit in the letter of 21 January 2000. The award accordingly refers to a ground, namely refusal, upon which Mr Davies did not rely. It does not refer to the ground upon which he purported to rely. In those circumstances, I consider that the ex parte award is bad on its face and invalid.'

8.10 MAKING THE AWARD

The award is settled by:

(a) the agreed surveyor, if there is one (s 10(1)); and if not
(b) by the three surveyors (s 10(1)); or
(c) by any two of them (s 10(1)). In practice, the award is normally settled jointly by the two surveyors appointed by the parties, who have recourse to the third surveyor only if they cannot reach agreement between themselves. Normally, therefore, the third surveyor takes an active part only if the other two do not agree, and his vote can then decide the issue.

But there is a fourth possibility:

(d) either of the parties, or either of their surveyors can at any time call on the third surveyor to determine the disputed matters (s 10(11)). If this happens, the settling of the award is wholly in his hands.

---

25   [2001] 2 EGLR 88.
26   [2001] 2 EGLR 88 at 91 A–B.

8.11 SERVICE OF THE AWARD

Provision is made for the award, once it is made, to be served on the parties.

If the award is made by the parties' surveyors, they must serve it on the parties forthwith (s 10(14)).

If, however, the award is made by the third surveyor, he is under no obligation to serve it until after 'payment of the cost of the award': he must then serve it on either the parties or their surveyors, and if he chooses to serve on the surveyors, they in turn must forthwith serve it on the parties (s 10(15)). This is a new section, yet it is hard to accept that the phrase cited means what it says. In the context of s 10(13)(a), the natural meaning of 'the costs of the award' is the costs of making and obtaining the award, whose incidence will be determined by the award. These costs will be unquantified, and the paying party will not be known until the award is published. Yet, s 10(15) requires them to be paid before the third surveyor parts with his award. This is absurd. The reference to 'the costs of the award' must be understood as a reference to the third surveyor's fees. The object is to assimilate his right to payment to that of an arbitrator.

8.12 SCOPE OF AWARD: SURVEYORS' JURISDICTION

Section 10 is concerned with disputes between a building owner and an adjoining owner 'in respect of any matter connected with any work to which this Act relates' (s 10(1)), and the subject matter of the award is, in general, described in exactly the same terms (s 10(10)). But s 10 is also more specific in prescribing the contents of an award.

The award may determine (s 10(12)):

(a) the right to execute any work;
(b) the time and manner of executing any work (but unless the parties agree, the time is not to start running until after the expiry of the minimum notice period prescribed by the Act);[27]
(c) any other matter arising out of or incidental to the dispute, including the costs of making the award.

The award can also determine (s 10(13)) the incidence between the parties of the reasonable costs incurred in:

(a) making or obtaining the award;
(b) reasonable inspection of the work to which the award relates;
(c) any other matter arising out of the dispute.

---

27 Ie one month for notices under ss 1 and 6, 2 months for notices under s 3.

The words of s 10(12)(c) are deliberately wide. They are designed to give the surveyors jurisdiction not only over the subjects of dispute expressly mentioned in the Act[28] but over any incidental question which can arise in the course of a dispute resulting from the service of a notice under the Act. Thus they must determine not only the fundamental questions of what work is to be carried out, within what time, and with what precautions, but also ancillary questions such as what compensation is to be paid,[29] what contributions made to expenses, and who is to pay the costs.

8.13 LIMITS OF JURISDICTION

There are, however, limits to the surveyors' jurisdiction in making their award. Their powers derive wholly from the Act, and if they travel outside those powers, the award may be wholly or partly void.

A number of examples may be given.

(a) The Act can be invoked only by the service of a valid initiating notice. If the initiating notice is invalid (eg because it is served in circumstances where the Act does not in truth apply), or has not been properly served on the right party, any resulting award must be wholly void for want of jurisdiction.[30]

(b) Similarly, if a building owner carries out works and then serves a belated notice, but the premature works cause a disastrous collapse, the question of responsibility for the collapse arises purely at common law, and the surveyors have no jurisdiction to determine it by award under the Act.[31]

(c) An award cannot override the requirements of the Act, properly construed. Thus if an account is not served within the period allowed by s 13(2), no award can be based on it.[32]

(d) An award cannot authorise works which will permanently interfere with an easement of light,[33] or otherwise infringe s 9.

(e) An award cannot direct a payment to be made to a person who is not entitled to it under the Act.[34]

---

28 See **8.2(a)**.
29 See **6.8.1**.
30 See *Gyle-Thompson v Wall Street (Properties) Ltd* [1974] 1 All ER 295. The same applies if the surveyors are not properly appointed: ibid.
31 See *Woodhouse v Consolidated Property Corp* [1993] 1 EGLR 174, CA: it is not thought that the new wording of s 10(10) affects this decision. See also *Louis v Sadiq* [1997] 1 EGLR 136.
32 See *Spiers and Son Ltd v Troup* (1915) 84 LJKB 1986.
33 See *Crofts v Haldane* (1867) LR 2 QB 194, decided before there was any equivalent of s 9.
34 See *Re Stone and Hastie* [1903] 2 KB 463.

(f) An award cannot authorise work under s 2 unless it falls within one of the descriptions in s 2(1).[35]
(g) An award cannot grant dispensation from the need to serve notice before carrying out work in the future.[36] It was thought to follow that an award could not impose continuing obligations, but the Court of Appeal has held that an award can impose an obligation to maintain a wall.[37]
(h) An award cannot require the building owner to compensate the adjoining owner for damage to chattels not attached to the land, under s 2(3)(a) or 2(4)(a), since these are not internal furnishings and decorations.[38] This decision seems questionable. 'Furnishings' is not a word limited to fixtures, in ordinary speech, but includes general furniture (ie chattels).

8.14 PRELIMINARY DETERMINATION OF JURISDICTION

It is clear from **8.13** that the surveyors' first step must be to determine whether in the circumstances they have jurisdiction to proceed to resolve the dispute brought before them. For example, they must ask themselves: do the proposals fall within the Act? Will the completed work interfere with an easement of the adjoining owner? And so forth. If the answer to such questions is negative, any award they make may be void. Equally, if they wrongly answer them in the affirmative, that cannot prevent a court later holding their award void for want of jurisdiction.[39] This dilemma has long been familiar to arbitrators and it was well established before the Arbitration Act 1996 that they had power to consider such questions, and reach their own conclusions, although they could, if they saw fit, refer the matter to the court.[40] There can be no doubt that surveyors acting under s 10 have the same powers,[41] and normally they reach their own conclusion in the interests of the expedition which is a prime object of the proceedings.

---

35 See *Gyle-Thompson v Wall Street (Properties) Ltd* [1974] 1 All ER 295.
36 See *Leadbetter v Marylebone Corp* [1904] 2 KB 893, CA.
37 See *Marchant v Capital & Counties Plc* [1983] 2 EGLR 156.
38 *Video London Sound Studios Ltd v Asticus (GMS)*, 2001, unreported, Technology and Construction Court.
39 They cannot by their own decision validly enlarge or diminish their jurisdiction: see *Crown Estate Commissioners v Dorset County Council* [1990] Ch 297.
40 See *Christopher Brown Ltd v Genossenschaft Oesterreichischer Waldbesitzer* [1953] 2 All ER 1039, and see now the Arbitration Act 1996, s 30.
41 See *Loost v Kremer* (above).

8.15 SUCCESSIVE AWARDS

Section 10(10), which is new, has dropped the reference to settling matters in dispute 'from time to time during the continuance of the work.[42] It was partly this phrase which enabled McCardie J to describe the jurisdiction of the surveyors as follows:[43]

> 'Section 91 of the [1894] Act provides that the arbitrators ... shall settle from time to time all matters in dispute. Their jurisdiction is, I think, continuous and exclusive, subject to the rights of appeal ... It remains unimpaired until the final adjustment of all questions in difference between the building owners who gave the notice and the adjoining owner who received the notice, and until the operations involved in the notice are concluded.'

It is not thought, however, that the removal of the key reference to settling matters 'from time to time' has deprived the surveyors of their power to make successive awards as separate issues arise. This power is not only useful, it is an essential feature of the procedure under the Act. While the principal issue is always likely to be what work can be done, and how, the Act itself provides for quite separate matters to be determined under s 10[44] which can conveniently, and in some cases, only[45] be dealt with by separate awards. It is considered that this framework is enough to demonstrate that the surveyors can make a succession of awards, determining different issues, as necessary.

8.16 RETROSPECTIVE AWARDS

The Act requires notices to be served before the exercise of any of the rights which it grants.[46] If the notice leads to agreement or consent, no award is needed, but if, as is more usual, it leads to an actual or deemed dispute, only an award under s 10 can resolve the dispute, and authorise the works and the time and manner of their execution (s 10(12)). It has long been established, not only that works which are started without the service of any notice are unlawful and can be restrained, but that the same applies even after the service of a notice if the works have not yet been authorised by an award.[47] Thus the position is that the statutory rights are (in the absence of consent) conditional on the completion of an award as well as on the service of a proper notice. As Evans LJ put it in *Louis v Sadiq* [1997] 1 EGLR 136, at 139c:

---

[42] See 1939 Act, s 55(n)(i); 1894 Act, s 91(1).
[43] See *Selby v Whitbread & Co* [1917] 1 KB 736 at 742.
[44] For example security under s 12.
[45] For example objections to an account under s 13(2).
[46] See ss 1(2), (5), 3, 6(5).
[47] See *Standard Bank of British South America v Stokes* (1878) 9 Ch D 68; *Upjohn v Seymour Estates Ltd* (1938) 54 TLR 465, when an award had been drawn up but not signed; *Louis v Sadiq* [1997] 1 EGLR 136.

'... the statutory scheme is clear. The building owner has certain express rights, but these can only be exercised (1) with the adjoining owner's written consent, or (2) in accordance with a valid award by the surveyor or surveyors ...'

Thus works carried out before an award is made, and their consequences, are subject to the common law regime and are outside any jurisdiction of the surveyors.[48] It follows that the surveyors have no jurisdiction to make a subsequent award assessing compensation for any damage such works may have caused,[49] still less authorising them retrospectively.

The logic of this position is unquestioned, but its rigour can cause serious inconvenience to both parties, for example, by delaying the sale of properties while the position is regularised.[50] In such circumstances it may be advantageous for both parties to agree to authorise the surveyors to act as if a proper notice had been served, and to proceed to make whatever award is needed. There are cases in which such a course has been noted by the court without disapproval.[51]

8.17 MULTIPLE PARTIES

The complexities of the procedure under s 10 are compounded if there is more than one adjoining owner. There is no right to require all adjoining owners to appoint the same surveyor, and no procedure for consolidating disputes which are being adjudicated by different surveyors. Nor can an award against one adjoining owner create any estoppel against another. Thus the building owner is faced with the possibility of inconsistent awards leading to paralysis. If all adjoining owners do appoint the same surveyor, it should be possible to minimise this risk by arrangements equivalent to consolidation. Alternatively, if the same third surveyor is selected in each case, he can be called on (under s 10(11)) to make all the awards.

8.18 PROCEDURE AND FORM OF AWARD

The surveyors are not arbitrators[52] and do not have the benefit of the procedural powers conferred on arbitrators by the Arbitration Acts. They are not bound to hold a hearing at which the views of the parties can be put forward. Their award should deal with the matters mentioned in s 10(12) and (13).[53] It is also usual for it to make detailed provisions for matters required by s 7, for example measures designed to minimise inconvenience to adjoining

---

48 See *Woodhouse v Consolidated Property Corp* [1993] 1 EGLR 174.
49 Ibid.
50 The time-scale and the losses suffered in *Louis v Sadiq* (above) form a cautionary tale.
51 See *Adams v Marylebone BC* [1907] 2 KB 822; *Louis v Sadiq* (above) at 139M.
52 See **8.19**.
53 See **8.12**.

owners and occupiers. An award is to be given a reasonably benevolent construction 'without pedantic strictness or meticulous severity'.[54] A specimen form of award is included in Appendix 4.

8.19 SURVEYORS AS ARBITRATORS

It is considered that the Arbitration Acts do not apply to the surveyors, although the authorities are not altogether consistent.

There are a number of earlier authorities which speak of the surveyors as arbitrators,[55] but only one (decided at first instance upon the Metropolitan Building Act 1855) which has actually held that they are subject to the provisions of the Arbitration Acts.[56]

More recently, it has been held that the Arbitration Acts are 'plainly' excluded by what is now s 10(16), which provides that the award is conclusive.[57] In the light of ss 94–97 of the Arbitration Act 1996 (formerly Arbitration Act 1950, s 31), this conclusion is not quite so plain, since s 94 of that Act applies the arbitration legislation (with modifications) to 'statutory arbitrations' except so far as this produces inconsistency. It is nevertheless submitted that the conclusion remains correct. The procedure under s 10 is a self-contained code, designed to work informally and expeditiously. It is more akin to a determination by experts than to arbitration.[58] The expression 'statutory arbitration' should be reserved for procedures expressly described as arbitration in their parent statutes[59] which are intended to take advantage of the arbitration machinery.

8.20 IMMUNITY OF SURVEYORS

The question arises whether the surveyors are vulnerable to claims in negligence by the parties, or enjoy quasi-judicial immunity. It is difficult to provide a confident answer. The leading authorities are the decisions of the House of Lords in *Sutcliffe v Thackrah*[60] and *Arenson v Casson Beckman Rutley & Co*[61] ('*Sutcliffe*' and '*Arenson*').

---

54   See *Selby v Whitbread & Co* [1917] 1 KB 736 at 744.
55   Notably *Re Stone and Hastie* [1903] 2 KB 463, where a procedure under the Arbitration Act 1889 was followed, but its applicability was assumed, not decided; *Leadbetter v Marylebone Corp* [1904] 2 KB 893, CA; *Selby v Whitbread & Co* [1917] 1 KB 736; *Burlington Property Co Ltd v Odeon Theatres Ltd* [1939] 1 KB 633.
56   *Re Metropolitan Building Act ex parte McBryde* (1876) 4 Ch D 200.
57   See *Chartered Society of Physiotherapy v Simmonds Church Smiles* [1995] 1 EGLR 155.
58   Ibid.
59   For example Agricultural Tenancies Act 1995, s 28.
60   [1974] AC 727.
61   [1977] AC 405.

The general principle is not that people who decide differences or disputes between rival parties are immune because they have to act fairly, but that they owe a duty of care to the parties, and any immunity is exceptional (see *Arenson*). Thus the surveyor will owe a duty of care to both parties.

In *Sutcliffe* it was assumed that arbitrators enjoyed an immunity, which extended also to 'quasi-arbitrators'.[62] But in *Arenson* so much doubt was cast on the arbitrator's immunity[63] that arbitrators have now been expressly protected by statute.[64] If it is correct that the surveyors are not arbitrators[65] this will not assist them.

Thus, the question is whether the surveyors are immune as quasi-arbitrators. They satisfy the most important criterion identified in *Arenson*, ie they determine formulated disputes. On the other hand, their procedure has been characterised as in the nature of an expert determination,[66] and experts are not normally immune, particularly if they are entitled to act solely on their own opinion, rather than upon evidence presented to them.[67] The general trend is to restrict immunities from negligence claims.[68] On the other hand, the surveyors are charged with the statutory duty of deciding what are declared by the Act to be disputes, and hence are more than mutually agreed valuers.

In this state of the authorities, any prudent surveyor will wish to make sure that his insurance covers his activities under the Act. He may also wish to consider stipulating for immunity.

---

62 See [1974] AC 727, at pp 752–753 per Lord Morris.
63 See [1977] AC 405, at p 431 per Lord Kilbrandon (for example).
64 See Arbitration Act 1996, s 29(1).
65 See **8.19**.
66 See **8.19**.
67 See *Palacath Ltd v Flanagan* [1985] 2 All ER 161; *North Eastern Co-operative Society v Newcastle upon Tyne City Council* [1987] 1 EGLR 142.
68 *Arthur J Hall & Co v Simons* [2000] 3 WLR 543, HL (barristers); *Palmer v Durnford Ford* [1992] 1 QB 483. *Stanton v Callaghan* [1999] 1 WLR 116 (experts).

Chapter 9

THE AWARD – EFFECT AND ENFORCEMENT

9.1 INTRODUCTION

The procedure leading to an award, and the scope of the award and the surveyors' jurisdiction, are considered in Chapter 8. The procedures for upsetting an award by appeal or for excess of jurisdiction are considered in Chapter 10. This chapter is concerned with the effect of an award and its enforcement.

9.2 EFFECT

A valid award which is not appealed conclusively determines the dispute which had arisen, or had been deemed to arise, under the Act, and it cannot be questioned in any court (s 10(16)). This has the following consequences.

(a) The building owner can carry out the works authorised by the award, even though they infringe the owner's rights at common law.
(b) The authorised works become works 'in pursuance of this Act', so that the rights of entry for the purpose of executing them become exercisable (s 8(1)), and must be respected by the adjoining owner, on pain of criminal liability (under s 16).
(c) Both parties must observe the terms of the award, and each will be able to enforce them against the other. Whatever the terms of the award, the building owner must carry out the works without causing unnecessary inconvenience to the adjoining owner. If the adjoining owner is ordered to pay a contribution to expenses, then (subject to due service of an account under s 13) he must do so.
(d) Adjoining occupiers are also affected. They have no right of appeal, and can only resist an award if they can show that it was made without jurisdiction. Subject to that, they too must observe the rights of entry, and rely on ss 7(1), (2) and (3) for any redress.[1]

9.3 ESTOPPEL

A judgment of a competent court creates an estoppel by record, which prevents the parties and their successors from reopening the same cause of action. It also creates issue estoppel, which prevents them later raising issues which were raised, or could have been raised, in the earlier proceedings.[2] By extension,

---

1 See Chapter 6.
2 See *Halsbury's Laws* (4th edn, Vol 16) paras 974–982.

these doctrines also apply to arbitration awards and decisions of all kinds of domestic tribunals.[3] In principle, therefore, an award under the Act appears to be capable of creating both cause of action estoppel and issue estoppel between the parties.

The nature of the issues settled by an award, however, leaves relatively little scope for the operation of estoppel. For example, an award may, without addressing any issue of law, direct that certain work can be done within a certain time. If the time expires without a start being made, the building owner may serve a fresh notice proposing the same work. The fact that time has passed, and the circumstances may have changed, probably means that neither party is effectively estopped from advancing the same factual arguments as before.

Further, a tribunal of limited jurisdiction cannot by its own decision enlarge or diminish its jurisdiction, so that its decisions on its own jurisdiction create no estoppel.[4] Thus a decision by the surveyors that, for example, some structure is a party structure will create no estoppel if they would not otherwise have had jurisdiction.

Nevertheless, it may be that an award involves decisions capable of creating estoppel. For example, the surveyors may have to decide whether a right to light exists before deciding what work can be carried out.[5] This may go not to jurisdiction, but to the manner of its exercise, and so be capable of giving rise to an estoppel.

9.4 ENFORCEMENT: ACTION ON THE AWARD

It is assumed here that a valid award has been made, and that one party is in breach of one of its terms. The term may have required the payment of money,[6] or, more likely, the carrying out of work in a particular way, for example by using bricks of a particular description. How is the aggrieved party to go about enforcing the terms of the award?

Since the better view is that the procedure under s 10 is not an arbitration,[7] enforcement under s 66 of the Arbitration Act 1996 will not be possible. The appropriate course is an action in court on the award. The procedures available vary according to the nature of the term which has been broken, and the remedy which is desired.

---

3 See ibid, paras 1012-1016: estoppel quasi by record.
4 See *Crown Estate Commissioners v Dorset County Council* [1990] Ch 297.
5 See **15.4**.
6 Eg an allowance for disturbance under s 11(6).
7 See **8.19**.

9.4.1 Payment of money

There are two procedures for recovering sums of money which an award directs to be paid.

(a) Any sum payable in pursuance of the Act (other than a fine) is recoverable summarily as a civil debt.[8] This summary procedure is by way of complaint to the magistrates' court and is governed by the Magistrates' Court Act 1980, s 8.[9] The magistrates' court has power to award costs;[10] payment may be enforced by distress warrant;[11] there is no power to impose a sentence of imprisonment in default of payment.[12]
(b) Section 17 does not provide that the summary procedure is to be the only way of recovering money payable in pursuance of the Act. It therefore leaves unimpaired the county court's jurisdiction to try actions for sums recoverable by virtue of any enactment.[13] Since sums directed to be paid by an award are recoverable by virtue of the Act, a civil action in the county court for payment is available as an alternative. Equally, if the sum in question is more than £50,000, the action could be brought in the High Court.

Claims with estimate values of less than £50,000 must generally be brought in the County Court (see p 98). It is thought that in general the more straightforward course is to utilise the County Court (or High Court if appropriate) rather than the Magistrates' Court. The Magistrates' Court is likely to be wholly unfamiliar with the Act and this is likely to give rise to practical difficulties. Also, in the County Court and High Court the Civil Procedures Rules 1998 apply. These contain provisions appropriate to actions for recovery of monies due, for example by requiring the parties to formulate their cases in statement of case, by providing for disclosure of document, and by allowing summary judgment to bring a speedy end to hopeless claims and defences. These are not available in the Magistrates' Court.

9.4.2 Breach of non-monetary term

For breach of a non-monetary term the aggrieved party may wish to claim either damages or specific relief. It is not altogether clear what the nature of this cause of action is. It cannot be breach of contract, since an award is not, and is nowhere deemed to be, a contract. It is considered that it is implicit in s 10 that both parties are under a statutory duty to observe the terms of an award, so that the cause of action is breach of statutory duty. The duty is not a public duty, which might be enforceable only by the Attorney-General, but a private duty

---

8   See s 17.
9   Magistrates' Court Act 1980, ch 43.
10 Ibid, s 64.
11 Ibid, s 76.
12 Ibid, s 92.
13 Under the County Courts Act 1984, s 16.

owed by the parties to each other. And since the Act provides no remedy for its breach, there is no difficulty in concluding that the parties are entitled to enforce it against each other. As Lord Simonds said:[14]

> '... if a statutory duty is prescribed but no remedy by way of penalty or otherwise is imposed, it can be assumed that a right of civil action accrues to the person who is damnified by the breach. For, if it were not so, the statute would be but a pious aspiration.'

9.4.3 Damages

In principle, therefore, the aggrieved party can claim damages for breach of the terms of an award.[15] In this connection the following points can be mentioned.

(a) Since breach of statutory duty is a tort,[16] the measure of damages is the tortious measure. The classic formulation is that of Lord Blackburn:[17]

> '... the sum of money which will put the party who has been injured...in the same position as he would have been in if he had not sustained the wrong...'

(b) It is likely that the breach will consist of failure by the building owner to provide some work intended to benefit the adjoining owner, or failure to provide it to an adequate standard. This is a notoriously difficult area for the assessment of damages, since the cost of carrying out the necessary work often exceeds the diminution in value of the claimant's property. In such a case, the claimant will normally recover the cost of the work only if he genuinely intends to carry it out.[18]

(c) Such costs will normally be assessed at the date of the hearing, but might be assessed at an earlier date if the claimant ought reasonably to have done the work earlier.[19]

(d) If the diminution in value is nil, and the cost of reinstatement disproportionate, the court may award a modest sum for loss of amenity.[20]

9.4.4 Specific Relief

Specific relief is by way of the equitable remedies of specific performance and injunction. Specific performance is a remedy normally available only in contract.[21] But an injunction can be granted to restrain a breach of statutory

---

14 See *Cutler v Wandsworth Stadium Ltd* [1949] AC 398, at 407; *Thornton v Kirklees Metropolitan Borough Council* [1979] 2 All ER 349, CA.
15 As happened in *Selby v Whitbread & Co* [1917] 1 KB 736.
16 See *Thornton v Kirklees Metropolitan Borough Council* [1979] 2 All ER 349, CA.
17 See *Livingstone v Rawyards Coal Co* (1880) 5 App Cas 25, at 39.
18 See *Ward v Cannock Chase District Council* [1986] Ch 546.
19 See *Dodd Properties (Kent) Ltd v Canterbury City Council* [1980] 1 All ER 928.
20 See *Ruxley Electronics and Construction Ltd v Forsyth* [1995] 3 All ER 268, which, however, is a contract case.
21 But in *Selby v Whitbread & Co* [1917] 1 KB 736, 753 McCardie J would have been prepared to award it in an appropriate case to enforce a positive term of an award.

duty, and a suitably framed mandatory injunction will have the same effect as an order for specific performance.[22] Historically, the court has been reluctant to enforce specifically an obligation build[23], but the court is nowadays prepared to order specific performance where the works are sufficiently defined,[24] and this requirement ought to be supplied by the compulsory plans (under s 7(5)).

9.5 ENFORCEMENT: ACTION OUTSIDE THE AWARD

The assumption here is that there is no term in the award which deals with the matter in dispute, so that no action can be brought on the award. This may occur for a variety of reasons. It may be, for example, that unforeseen circumstances give rise to some collapse, or to greater delay, or other damage, to the adjoining owner than was expected; or it may be that the building owner goes beyond what the award authorised, or carries out the authorised works in such a manner as to cause unnecessary inconvenience, or negligently. Any such event may give the adjoining owner[25] a potential cause of action. What steps are open to him?

9.5.1 Further award

The first question must be whether the surveyors have jurisdiction to make a further award to deal with the unforeseen dispute. It has been pointed out that the surveyors' jurisdiction extends to all matters 'arising out of or incidental to' the original dispute (s 10(12)(c)), and that this includes the making of successive awards as separate issues arise (see **8.15**). Moreover, it is considered that the mandatory wording of s 10(10), (11) and (12) is sufficient to indicate that their jurisdiction, so far as it legitimately extends, is exclusive. That is to say, if the new dispute falls within the surveyors' jurisdiction, the proper course is to submit it to them for a further award, even if it gives rise to a claim for breach of statutory duty which could otherwise be pursued by court action. The possibilities outlined above need to be examined in this light.

9.5.2 Compensation

Insofar as authorised works result in loss or damage to the adjoining owner he has a claim to compensation under s 7(2). It is considered that this is a claim which is within the jurisdiction of the surveyors (see **6.8.1**), and that they can be asked to make an award to deal with such a claim. The same applies to any claim for compensation under s 1(7), or an allowance for disturbance under s 11(6).

---

22   See *Warder v Cooper* [1970] Ch 495, where a mandatory injunction (ordering possession) was granted as well as a negative injunction.
23   But see note 17 above.
24   See *Jeune v Queen's Cross Properties Ltd* [1974] Ch 97; *Co-operative Insurance Society Ltd v Argyle Stores (Holdings) Ltd* [1998] AC 1.
25   For the special position of the adjoining occupier see **9.6**.

There are many other possible sources of dispute which will clearly be within their jurisdiction (eg due performance of conditions imposed by s 2).

9.5.3 Inconvenience: inadequate protection

More controversial is the question whether the surveyors' jurisdiction includes examining, and perhaps awarding, compensation or damages for unnecessary inconvenience caused in breach of s 7(1) (see **6.8.1**, where it is argued that it does). Similar considerations could affect a claim for breach of duty to provide adequate protection and security where a building is laid open (s 7(3)). It may be that the comprehensive nature of the right to compensation under s 7(2) makes it unlikely that these questions will need to be resolved, but there is another possibility raised by the specific duties imposed by s 7(1) and (3). One of the functions of the original award will have been to consider, and make provisions catering for, the performance of these duties. If damage (eg a collapse) is suffered without breach of any such precautionary provisions, a question may arise whether the surveyors exercised sufficient care in framing their original award. That would create a position of conflict which would make it impossible for them to adjudicate impartially on the issue. Strictly an embarrassment of this kind does not appear to affect the question of jurisdiction, but it would mean that the surveyors had become incapable of acting.

9.5.4 Unauthorised work

If the complaint is that work has been done which was not authorised by the award, it is outside the jurisdiction of the surveyors, and a court action is appropriate. Unauthorised work will, if it could not have been carried out without authority, be trespass or nuisance, giving rise to a cause of action in tort.[26] The surveyors have no jurisdiction to make a subsequent award authorising it retrospectively, even if they could have authorised it in the first place (see **8.16**). It can make no difference whether the award was for some reason void, or merely silent.

9.5.5 Other tort

Whether there is any other scope for actions in tort (eg for negligence) is considered later (see Chapter 15).

9.6 ADJOINING OCCUPIERS

Adjoining occupiers have no access to the s 10 procedure, and the jurisdiction of the surveyors is of no use to them. Where the Act makes express provision for

---

26 See *Woodhouse v Consolidated Property Corp* (1992) 66 P & CR 234; *Louis v Sadiq* [1997] 1 EGLR 136.

their protection[27] the only method of enforcement open to them is a court action for breach of the statutory duty in question. For the characteristics of such an action see **9.4**. This is anomalous. It involves the possibility of parallel claims under, say, s 7(2) being separately but simultaneously pursued by an adjoining owner before the surveyors and by an adjoining occupier in court, with an attendant risk of differing approaches.

9.7 INTEREST

Courts have power to award interest on any debt or damages.[28] Interest accrues automatically on judgment debts at a prescribed rate, which is varied from time to time by statutory instrument.[29] Arbitrators can award interest.[30] These are all statutory powers: there is no power to award interest at common law.[31] Interest is not mentioned anywhere in the Act and thus it is clear that the surveyors cannot include any provision for interest in the award.

9.8 VENUE

For the summary procedure under s 17 for recovering money see **9.4.1(a)**. The other causes of action considered above, including those for breach of statutory duty, are founded in tort. The High Court and county court now have co-ordinate jurisdiction over all claims in tort, regulated by a single set of rules, the Civil Procedure Rules 1998. The county court has jurisdiction whatever the amount involved,[32] but there are relatively strict guidelines. Where money is being claimed, the claim form has to include a statement of the financial value of the claim[33] and in calculating what he expects to recover, the claimant must disregard certain specified matters, such as interest and costs.[34] A claim for money may be commenced in the High Court only if the financial value of the claim is £15,000 or more,[35] and it will normally be transferred to the county court if its estimated value is less than £50,000.[36] The sources of jurisdiction for transfer between courts are set out in CPR r 30.3(1), and the compulsory criteria for deciding the appropriate court are listed in CPR r 30.3(2).

---

27 See ss 1(7), 7(1), (2), (3), 8(3), (6), 11(6).
28 See Supreme Court Act 1981, s 35A; County Courts Act 1984, s 69.
29 Judgments Act 1838, s 17; County Courts Act 1984, s 74.
30 Arbitration Act 1996, s 49.
31 See *London Chatham & Dover Railway Co v South Eastern Railway Co* [1893] AC 429, HL; *President of India v La Pintada Compania Navigacion SA* [1985] AC 104.
32 See High Court and County Court Jurisdiction Order 1991, SI 1991/724 (as amended), art 2(1)(1) and County Courts Act 1984, s 15(1).
33 Under CPR r 16.3.
34 See CPR r 16.3(6).
35 See High Court and County Courts Jurisdiction Order 1991, art 4A.
36 See Practice Direction 29, para 2.2.

9.9 PROCEDURE

For actions on an award it will often be appropriate to start proceedings under CPR r 8, since the presence of an uncontested award as the basis of the action should mean that there is no substantial dispute of fact, so that formerly an originating summons would have been used.[37] For actions not based on an award it is more likely that there will be sufficient issues of fact to require proceeding under CPR r 7.

9.10 LIMITATION

The application of the Limitation Act 1980 to the causes of action which have been discussed raises difficult questions. Reference should be made to specialised works on limitation.[38] However, some general points may be made here. There are several competing sections of the 1980 Act which may be applicable.

(a) Section 2 provides a 6-year period for actions in tort. Whether an action for breach of statutory duty is an action founded on tort for limitation purposes is doubtful. A purely statutory cause of action has been assumed in the House of Lords to be governed by this section.[39]

(b) Section 7 provides a 6-year period for actions 'to enforce an award, where the submission is not by an instrument under seal'. In s 34, 'award' is defined in terms of arbitration, but that definition does not apply to s 7. It probably does not apply to the surveyors' award, which does not result from any submission.

(c) Section 9 provides a 6-year period for actions to recover 'any sum recoverable by virtue of any enactment'. Fine distinctions have been drawn under this section and its predecessor,[40] but it is thought that it probably applies to liquidated and unliquidated sums whether due under an award or outside an award (eg under s 7(2)). But it does not apply to claims for specific relief by injunction.

(d) Section 8 provides a 12-year period for actions 'upon a specialty', unless a shorter period is prescribed elsewhere. A statute is a specialty. This section does not extend the 6-year period where ss 2 or 9 apply, but may be applicable (by analogy) to claims for specific relief by injunction.[41]

(e) Section 36 provides that the time-limits under ss 2, 7, 8 and 9 do not apply to claims for an injunction or other equitable relief, except by analogy, but the equitable doctrines of laches and acquiescence do apply.

---

37 See PD8, para 1.1.
38 For example McGee *Limitation Periods* (Sweet & Maxwell, 4th edn, 2002).
39 See *Sevcon Ltd v Lucas CAV Ltd* [1986] 2 All ER 104.
40 See McGee, op cit, pp 52ff, 190ff.
41 See *Collin v Duke of Westminster* [1985] QB 581.

The date of accrual of a cause of action under a statute often gives rise to difficulty,[42] but it is not thought that causes of action under the Act will raise serious doubts. The cause of action on an award will accrue when there is a breach of any term of the award.[43] The direct causes of action under s 7 will accrue when the breach of duty occurs (under s 7(1) or (3)), or the work is done which causes the loss or damage (s 7(2)).

---

42 See eg *Yorkshire Electricity Board v British Telecom* [1986] 2 All ER 961.
43 Compare *Agromet Motoimport Ltd v Maulden Engineering Co (Beds) Ltd* [1985] 2 All ER 436.

Chapter 10
RIGHTS OF APPEAL

10.1 INTRODUCTION

Section 10(17) of the Act provides that:

> 'Either of the parties to the dispute may, within the period of fourteen days beginning with the day on which an award made under this section is served upon him, appeal to the county court against the award and the county court may –
> (a) rescind the award or modify it in such manner as the court thinks fit; and
> (b) make such order as to costs as the court thinks fit.'

This provision re-enacts s 55(n)(i) of the 1939 Act. Section 55(n)(ii) and (o) of the 1939 Act, concerned with appeals to the High Court, are not repeated in the Act.

The scheme of the Act is to provide a statutory right of appeal from any award by the surveyors. The right of appeal arises in the case of all awards, and therefore covers awards by an agreed surveyor, awards by any two of the three surveyors, and awards by the third surveyor alone.[1]

Section 10(16) provides that (subject to any appeal) 'The award shall be conclusive and shall not except as provided by this section be questioned in any court'.

10.2 EXTENT OF MATTERS WHICH CAN BE RAISED ON APPEAL, AND MODE OF APPEAL

The wording of s 10(17) is wide and general, and suggests that the court has complete discretion as to what order to make. It removes the dual procedures for appeal under s 55(n) and (o) of the 1939 Act.

10.2.1 *Chartered Society of Physiotherapy v Simmonds Church Smiles*

This view is supported by the only decided case directly in point, *Chartered Society of Physiotherapy v Simmonds Church Smiles*.[2] That case related to an appeal against a third surveyor's award, which was made to the county court, but was transferred to the High Court under s 42 of the County Courts Act 1984. The case was heard by an Official Referee (His Honour Judge Humphrey Lloyd

---

1 See s 10(10) and (11).
2 [1995] 1 EGLR 155.

QC).[3] The court rejected an argument that the court's powers on appeal were akin to those of the Court of Appeal hearing an appeal from the High Court after a trial of fact and law so that, for example, no new evidence could be admitted which was not before whoever made the award.

Judge Lloyd expressed the principle as follows:[4]

> 'Looking at the whole of s 55(n) and (o) it is, in my judgment, clear that the award is one which may be completely reopened if an appeal is duly made. S 55 (n) (1) provides that the county court may, "... modify it in such manner and make such order as to costs as it thinks fit". In my view, the words, "as it thinks fit" plainly qualify "modify in such manner" and are not limited to an "order as to costs" for otherwise "such manner" is left hanging in the air. Thus the Court has, in my judgment, wide powers to alter any award and to do so must have the power to substitute its own finding or conclusion for any finding or conclusion that the surveyor(s) made or may be presumed to have made.'

In rejecting the argument that fresh evidence would not be admissible before the court on an appeal, he stated:[5]

> 'Essentially the question which the Court has to resolve is what award ought now to be made, taking into account all the facts established by admissible evidence, rather than the narrow question contended for by the Respondent which is close to an investigation as to whether the award was made by a competent surveyor or surveyors. Depending on the point or points at issue on the appeal there may have to be a re-hearing. As I have stated that indeed is, in my judgment, exactly what is envisaged by s 55 (o)(iv).'

10.2.2 The Impact of the Civil Procedure Rules

It is not however clear whether the approach in the *Chartered Society of Physiotherapy* case has survived the introduction of the Civil Procedure Rules (CPR) on 1 April 1999.[6] The CPR apply in both the High Court and the county court, replacing the formerly separate Rules of the Supreme Court, and County Court Rules.

Under the CPR, appeals are governed by Part 52, and the associated Practice Direction (PD 52). Under these provisions, the general rule is that an appeal is limited to a review of the decision of the lower court. This process of review involves examining the text of the lower court's decision to see whether it

---

3 The Official Referee's Court is now the Technology and Construction Court (TCC). Judges of that court are known as 'Judges of the Technology and Construction Court'. The question whether it is still possible to transfer an appeal to the High Court is considered at para **10.3**.
4 [1995] 1 EGLR 155, at 157 H.
5 [1995] 1 EGLR 155, 158 F–G.
6 SI 1998/3132 made under the Civil Procedure Act 1997 (1997 C12). The CPR have been amended from time to time. See, for the up-to-date test of the CPR, the current *Civil Court Service* (Jordan Publishing Limited, 2003).

contains errors of law. Other material will not normally be relevant.[7] The court has power to hold a re-hearing in the circumstances of an individual appeal.[8] This re-hearing does not involve the reception of fresh evidence, but rather a review of the evidence which was before the lower court. The general rule is that the Appeal Court will not receive oral evidence or evidence which was not available to the lower court.[9] Evidence not available to the lower court may be admitted only in exceptional circumstances, These are firstly, where events subsequent to the hearing are relevant to the appeal and secondly, where the evidence fulfils the following criteria:

(1) It could not have been obtained with reasonable diligence for use at the trial;
(2) It must be such that, if given, it could probably have an important influence on the result of the case, though it need not be decisive; and
(3) It must be such as is presumably to be believed; it must be apparently credible though it need not be incontrovertible.[10]

If CPR Part 52 were held to apply to appeals to the county court under s 10, the following consequences follow:

(a) The *Chartered Society of Physiotherapy* case could no longer be good law in so far as it establishes that fresh evidence may be adduced before the county court, at any rate, except in exceptional cases falling within the criteria laid down by *Ladd v Marshall.*
(b) The county court's task will normally be confined to a review of the surveyor's decision appealed against. Extraneous material, including evidence and submissions to the surveyors will be irrelevant, except in so far as necessary to interpret the award. (This is subject to PD 52 para 9.1, which provides for a rehearing in certain circumstances on some types of appeal.)
(c) The possibility of appealing from the county court is severely restricted, since such an appeal would be a "second appeal" for the purposes of CPR r 52.13. Such appeals will not be permitted unless they raise important points of principle or there are other compelling reasons for permission to appeal being given.[11]

---

7   CPR r 52.11(1).
8   CPR r 52.11(1)(b).
9   CPR r 52.11(2).
10 *Ladd v Marshall* [1954] 1 WLR 1489.
11 *Clark (Inspector of Taxes) v Perks and other applications* [2002] 4 All ER 1; *Prentice v Hereward Housing Association* (unreported QBD, 29 April 1999).

(d) Surveyors making awards would have to give reasons, sufficient to enable the county court to understand why the award was made. Failure to give adequate reasons would be a breach of Art 6 of the European Convention on Human Rights and Fundamental Freedoms.[12]

(e) Surveyors making awards would have to have observed the rules of natural justice, and to have complied with Art 6(1) of the Convention. The criteria which would apply would presumably be similar to those governing the conduct of arbitrators;[13] arbitrators can be removed for example: (a) if they fail to give each party a fair opportunity to put their case, and controvert that of their opponent; (b) if they rely on material not placed before them by the parties, without giving the parties an opportunity to deal with it;[14] (c) if they decide matters not put in issue by the parties.[15]

If appeals to the county court are governed by CPR Part 52, an appeal to the county court will be a statutory appeal, governed by PD52 Section II. Thus the general provisions of this section of the Practice Direction would apply, although there are no specific provisions relating to appeals under the Act. One particular point is that there is no requirement for permission to be obtained for an appeal to the county court.[16]

10.2.3 Outside CPR

The alternative view is that appeals to the county court are not within CPR Part 52 at all. On this view, although the Act speaks of an appeal, the process is in fact more in the nature of a first instance reconsideration and review of an expert determination. Accordingly, the appeal to the county court is in effect a first instance hearing. An appeal would on this basis be started by ordinary proceedings, under CPR Part 7 or 8. There would be no restrictions on the grounds of appeal, or the evidence that could be adduced in support of it, subject only to the general rules governing claims.

This view has strong attractions. Firstly, the nature of the jurisdiction of party wall surveyors is that of experts. Their role is essentially technical, to design, approve, and check the quality of the work with which they are concerned under s 10. They are in no sense a tribunal. They are employed by the parties, or in the case of the third surveyor appointed by the party-appointed surveyors. It has never been considered that they are bound to act judicially or obliged to hold any sort of hearing before reaching a decision, or to give reasons. This view is reflected in the *Chartered Society of Physiotherapy* case.

---

12 For the need to give reasons, see *Tanfern Ltd v Cameron Macdonald* [2000] 1 WLR 1311, and *English v Emery Reimbold & Strick Ltd* [2002] 3 All ER 385. for failure to give reasons as a breach of Art 6(1) of the Convention, see *Ruiz v Spain* (2001) 31 EHRR 589.

13 See generally *Lovell Partnerhips (Northern) Ltd v AW Construction plc* 81 BLR 83; *Miller Construction v James Moore Earthmoving* [2001] BLR 322.

14 See *Mount Charlotte Investments plc v Prudential Assurance Co* [1995] 1 EGLR 15.

15 See eg *Strachan & Henshaw Ltd v Stein Industrie (UK) Ltd (No 7)* (1996) 13 Const LJ 418.

16 See *Colley v Council for Licensed Conveyancers* [2001] 4 All ER 998.

In contrast, Part 2 of the CPR, and the provisions for statutory appeals in PD 52 Section II all relate to situations where there is a formal determination, often (though not invariably) involving a hearing, and resulting in a reasoned decision. The surveyors appointed under the Act, however, perform in principle a quite different set of roles.

The jurisdiction of the county court is apparently wide. Its powers on appeal include remaking the award. This is difficult to reconcile with its functions being limited to those laid down in CPR Part 52, and PD52.

10.2.4 Conclusion

It is tentatively suggested that the better view is that an appeal to the county court is not governed by CPR Part 52, but is effectively a first instance hearing, so that the practice described in the *Chartered Society of Physiotherapy* case continues to apply. In at least one reported case subsequent to the introduction of CPR Part 52, *Frances Holland School v Wassef*[17] both the form of the proceedings and the hearing, followed the previous practice. Whilst this point remains unresolved, it is suggested that surveyors may be well advised to observe the rules of natural justice, and to give properly reasoned decisions, to minimise any difficulties in the county court reviewing the decision. The parties would be well advised to maintain careful records of the evidence submitted to the surveyors. In conducting the appeal itself, the question whether one or both of the parties should apply to the court to hold a rehearing, or even to admit fresh evidence will require careful consideration.

10.3 VENUE

Section 10(17) provides for an appeal to the county court. This removes the dual procedures for appeal to High Court and county court formally embodied in s 55(n) and (o) of the 1939 Act.

Under ss 41 and 42 of the County Courts Act 1984 the High Court and the county court have power to transfer cases proceeding in the county court to the High Court, in defined circumstances. The question is whether the powers of transfer are compatible with the wording of the Act, or whether on the other hand, the Act evinces an intention that appeals thereunder can only be dealt with by the county court.

In *Chartered Society of Physiotherapy v Simmons Church Smiles*[18] the appeal had been transferred from the county court to the High Court under s 42 of the County Courts Act 1984. However, the relevant legislation (the 1939 Act) allowed for an appeal either to the county court or to the High Court.

---

17 [2001] 2 EGLR 88.
18 See **10.2.1**.

It is clear that as a matter of principle, where a statute provides that certain proceedings may only be taken in a certain court, proceedings taken in the wrong court will be a nullity, as they will have been taken without jurisdiction[19]. Therefore, there is no doubt that the Act requires an appeal to be *commenced* in the county court.

Whether there is a right to transfer under ss 41 or 42 of the County Courts Act 1984 is not entirely clear. The *Chartered Society of Physiotherapy* case supports the view that this is possible, although as noted above the 1939 Act, which was then in force, allowed appeals to either the High Court or the county court. Nevertheless, the appeal in that case had been transferred from the county court. On the other hand, in *Yorkshire Bank Plc v Hall*[20] it was held that the provisions of the County Courts Act 1984 relating to transfer did not allow transfer to the High Court of claims falling under s 21 of that Act, which provides that:

> 'If a County Court has jurisdiction by virtue of this section to hear and determine an action in which the mortgagee under that mortgage claims possession of the mortgaged property, no court other than a County Court shall have jurisdiction to hear and determine that action.'

Despite this, it is thought that there is jurisdiction to transfer an appeal to the High Court. Section 10(17) of the Act is not in the same terms as the provision considered in the *Yorkshire Bank* case, and in particular there is no provision that only a county court can deal with an appeal. This view is supported by the *Chartered Society of Physiotherapy* case. Where a case is transferred to the High Court, frequently this will be so that it can be dealt with by a Judge of the Technology and Construction Court.

10.4 APPEAL TO THE COURT OF APPEAL

If (as tentatively suggested above) an appeal is in effect a first instance hearing, an appeal lies (with permission of the trial court or the Court of Appeal) to the Court of Appeal. The criterion for permission is: (a) that the appeal could have a real prospect of success; or (b) that there is some other compelling reason why the appeal should be heard.[21] If, however, the appeal to the county court is itself to be regarded as an appeal, any further appeal is governed by CPR r 52.13, which imposes more restrictive criteria. The procedure for appeal is laid down in CPR Part 52, the text of which can be found in the current edition of the *Civil Court Service*, published by Jordan Publishing.[22]

---

19 See eg *Horner v Franklin* [1905] 1 KB 479; *Stickey v Hooke* [1906] 2 KB 20.
20 [1999] 1 All ER 879, CA.
21 See CPR r 52.3(b).
22 Rt Hon Lord Justice Laws, Stevens and Vincent, Civil Court Service 2003 (Jordan Publishing Ltd, 2003).

10.5 TIME-LIMITS

Section 10(17) lays down a 14-day time-limit for an appeal, running from the date of service of the award. Section 15 of the Act regulates service. It is considered that the 14-day time-limit is mandatory and, subject as set out below, incapable of extension either by the surveyors or the court, so that failure to enter an appeal in time results in the right of appeal being lost. The general rule is that where a time-limit is laid down by statute, it cannot be extended either by the court or by agreement.[23] The statutory period includes any bank holidays occurring within it.[24] Where the appellant has done everything required of him, his appeal will be 'made' when received at the court office even though the court delays in issuing the process.[25] If the last day for making the appeal falls on a day when the court office is closed, the application may be filed on the next day it is open.[26] Where an appeal is made to the wrong court, but within time, and the documents are forwarded to the correct Court for entry, the appeal can be proceeded with although the time for appeal has meanwhile expired.[27]

10.6 EFFECT OF APPEAL

The Act is silent on the question whether, pending appeal, the award binds the parties, or whether it is in effect suspended, so that neither party can act on it. Principle strongly favours the latter solution, at any rate in relation to those parts of the award subject to appeal, because once work has been done it may be impractical or very expensive to undo. If, therefore, an appeal is successful, the position of both building and adjoining owner may be unsatisfactory. It is submitted that the effect of the machinery for appeal laid down by the Act is that the award is suspended by appeal; this is supported by the following:

(a) section 10(16) refers to the position where the award is not appealed. By implication, the award will *not* be 'conclusive' if it *is* appealed.
(b) the wide power of review given to the court is inconsistent with the parties' rights being fixed until an appeal is heard;
(c) The short time-limit for appeal suggests some urgency, more consistent with suspension of action until the appeal is decided.[28]

---

23 *Hodgson v Armstrong* [1967] 1 All ER 307, CA; *Kammin's Ballrooms Co Ltd v Zenith Investments (Torquay) Ltd* [1970] 2 All ER 871; *Smith v East Elloe Rural District Council* [1956] AC 736.
24 Compare *Stainer v Secretary of State for the Environment and Shepway District Council* [1993] EGCS 130.
25 *Aly v Aly* (1984) 128 SJ 65.
26 Compare *Hodgson v Armstrong* [1967] 1 All ER 307, CA.
27 *Sharma v Knight* [1986] 1 WLR 757, CA.
28 Support for this view can be found in *Standard Bank of British South America v Stokes* (1878) 9 Ch D 68 at 77, although the specific point considered there was whether the award took effect before the decision of the third surveyor.

10.7 OTHER METHODS OF CHALLENGING AN AWARD

It is considered that an award could not be challenged by way of judicial review. The words of the Act purporting to make an award conclusive are probably not enough to preclude judicial review.[29] But a dispute regarding an award is concerned solely with private rights, and in the absence of any public law element no question could arise of judicial review.[30] A further obstacle to judicial review would lie in the existence of an alternative remedy by way of appeal.[31]

An award which is ultra vires may be challenged on that ground, notwithstanding that it has not been appealed.[32]

10.8 SEVERABILITY

The fact that the award is invalid in part will not invalidate the whole award, provided the invalid part is severable, and not 'inextricably connected' with the remainder.[33] In applying this test the court would probably have to have regard to two questions (derived from other contexts).

(a) Whether the void part of the award is capable of being excised without substantially affecting the sense and grammar of the remainder of the award.[34]
(b) Whether the excision of the invalid part radically alters the nature of the remainder of the obligations in question, or the award as a whole.[35] If the void part of the award cannot be removed without fundamentally altering its effect, or without substantially rewriting it, the whole award will be invalid.

---

29 See for example *Smith v East Elloe Rural District Council* [1956] 1 All ER 855; *Anisminic v Foreign Compensation Commission* [1967] 2 All ER 986, CA; *R v Cornwall County Council ex parte Huntington* [1994] 1 All ER 694.
30 Compare *Poplar Housing Association v Donoghue* [2001] 4 All ER 604; *R v Leonard Cheshire Foundation* [2002] 2 All ER 936.
31 Compare *R v Birmingham City Council ex parte Ferrero Ltd* [1993] 1 All ER 530, CA.
32 See *Re Stone and Hastie* [1903] 2 KB 463; *Gyle-Thompson v Wall Street Properties Ltd* [1974] 1 All ER 295; *Woodhouse v Consolidated Property Corp* [1993] 1 EGLR 174, CA.
33 *Selby v Whitbread & Co* [1917] 1 KB 736 at 748.
34 Compare *T Lucas & Co Ltd v Mitchell* [1974] Ch 129, a case on an invalid restraint of trade.
35 Compare *Amoco Australia Pty Ltd v Rocca Bros Motor Engineering Co Pty Ltd* [1975] AC 561.

Chapter 11

FINANCIAL MATTERS

11.1 INTRODUCTION

Work carried out in pursuance of the Act has a financial impact in three areas. First, there is the cost of the work carried out by a building owner pursuant to an award under the Act. Secondly, there are the costs involved in operating the dispute resolution procedure under the Act, including such matters as the fees of the surveyors and costs incurred by the parties in relation to an award. Thirdly, the Act envisages contingent liabilities which may arise in the future, for example where the adjoining owner makes greater use of the works than originally anticipated. The provisions are of great importance in practice, and need to be carefully scrutinised by building and adjoining owners and their advisers when any work to which the Act applies is under consideration.

11.2 THE MEANING OF 'COSTS' AND 'EXPENSES'

Confusion can result if the terminology used by the Act is not appreciated. The Act distinguishes between 'costs' and 'expenses', but without defining either term.

11.2.1 Costs

Costs are mentioned several times in s 10 in contexts which make it clear that the term means much the same as it does when used in relation to litigation.[1] Thus, it will include:

(a) the fees of any surveyor appointed to discharge functions under the Act; and
(b) legal and other professional costs incurred by the parties in relation to operating the procedures of the Act.

These costs would include, for example, those incurred in relation to service of notices, fees of engineering and other consultants, and fees for legal advice related to the procedures of the Act. Although the machinery for making an award does not prescribe a formal hearing by the surveyors, the possibility of an informal hearing is clearly envisaged by the Act. For example in *Chartered Society of Physiotherapy v Simmonds Church Smiles*,[2] the parties' surveyors having disagreed, the third surveyor held a hearing at which he was addressed by the parties' surveyors, and subsequently made his award. The costs of such a hearing would qualify as 'costs'.

---

1 See s 10(12), (13), (15), (17).
2 [1995] 1 EGLR 155.

11.2.2 Expenses

The terms 'expense' and 'expenses' occur frequently in the Act (ss 1(3)(b), 1(4)(a), 1(7), 11, 12, 13, 14). It is clear that they refer to the actual cost of carrying out work. Presumably (although this is not spelt out in the Act), expenses would include not only the prime cost of work but also reasonable incidental professional fees, fees paid to statutory authorities, and insurance related to the work.

Where, as often happens, work to which the Act applies is carried out as part of a wider project, it is presumably necessary to separate out the expenses relating to the work to which the Act applies from the global cost of the project. In the case of the prime cost of the work, this exercise may be straightforward, simply extracting the relevant elements from the bills of quantities or specification. But there may be arguments as to the apportionment of preliminaries, for example whether they should be apportioned directly proportional to the cost of the relevant work, or in some other way, if for example a large element of the preliminaries is directly related to the need to provide temporary protection and support to the party wall. The surveyors will have to consider what is fair and reasonable in the circumstances.

Costs of matters too remote from the work will not fall within the definition of expenses. This would exclude feasibility studies, environmental assessments, and costs related to the obtaining of planning permission.

11.3 EXPENSES: GENERAL RULE

The general rule is that except as provided under s 11, expenses of work under the Act are to be defrayed by the building owner (s 11(1)). Section 11 then sets out a number of cases where the general rule is not to apply. These include a number of contingent liabilities, which may occur some time in the future, which are considered more fully in Chapter 14.

In addition to the general rule of s 11(1), reference should be made to the following provisions of the Act which expressly cast liability for expenses on the building owner.

(a) Section 1(4), where the adjoining owner does not consent to the building of a party wall or party fence wall.
(b) Section 1(7), where the building owner desires to build on the line of junction a wall placed wholly on his own land (ie a fence wall: see **3.4.3**).
(c) Section 6(3), where the building owner bears the expense of underpinning or otherwise strengthening or safeguarding the foundations of the building or structure of the adjoining owner.

11.4 LIABILITIES OF ADJOINING OWNER

There is a medley of separate provisions, the unifying theme of which is that where the expense in question confers a benefit on the adjoining owner, or is incurred at his request, he ought to bear part of it. However, only certain cases are covered, and there is no general principle that wherever work benefits an adjoining owner (eg by improving the stability or fabric of his building) he is automatically liable to contribute to the expense. The circumstances where the adjoining owner may be called upon to contribute to the expenses are as follows.

11.4.1 Section 11(3)

Where a new party wall is constructed with the agreement of the adjoining owner, ss 1(3)(b) and 11(3) require the expense to be apportioned, having regard to the use made or to be made of the wall, by each of the building and adjoining owner respectively and to the cost of labour and materials prevailing at the time when that use is made by each. Thus, for example, if a party wall is built which is an external wall of the building owner's building, and the adjoining owner derives no benefit from it except in its function as a boundary wall, the building owner will be obliged to bear the majority of the expenses at that time. If the adjoining owner later constructs a building of his own against the wall, thus making greater use of it, he will become liable to a 'clawback' by the building owner, representing a fair contribution in respect of his increased use of the wall. The clawback will reflect costs current at the time the adjoining owner constructs his building, not costs actually incurred by the building owner when the wall was built originally.

11.4.2 Section 11(4)

Where work of underpinning, thickening or raising a party structure, party fence wall or an external wall which belongs to the building owner and is built against a party structure or party fence wall, is necessitated by a defect or want of repair of the structure or wall concerned, ss 2(2)(a) and 11(4) enable the building owner to recoup part of the expenses which result from him having to carry out works of repair as opposed to new works. The expenses have to be apportioned, and the factors to be taken into account are:

(a) the use which the owners respectively make or may make of the structure or wall concerned; here it is clear (from the words 'or may make') that anticipated future use is material as well as present, and no doubt past, use;
(b) responsibility for the defect or want of repair, if more than one owner makes use of the structure or wall concerned: here the focus is on past use. The responsibility seems to be related to the degree of use rather than legal liability. In other words the question seems to be not so much which owner is legally responsible, but which owner's use has contributed more to the disrepair.

11.4.3 Section 11(5)

Where work is carried out to make good, repair or demolish and rebuild a party structure or party fence wall, in a case where such work is necessitated by a defect or want of repair of the structure or wall, ss 2(2)(b) and 11(5) require an apportionment of the same kind as under s 11(4).

11.4.4 Section 11(7)

Where the building owner wishes to reduce the height of a party (fence) wall under s 2(2)(m), and the adjoining owner serves a counter-notice requiring the existing height of the wall to be maintained, s 11(7) requires the adjoining owner to bear a due proportion of the cost of the wall so far as it exceeds two metres in height, or the height currently enclosed upon by his own building.

11.4.5 Section 11(9)

Where the adjoining owner requests or requires work to be done, and it is carried out by the building owner, s 11(9) provides that the adjoining owner must pay for what he has requested or required. A request could presumably be made at any time before the work is carried out: a requirement would be by counter-notice under s 4. But if the adjoining owner requires underpinning under s 6(3), that section requires the building owner to pay, and overrides s 11(9).

11.4.6 Section 11(11)

Where use is subsequently made by the adjoining owner of work carried out solely at the expense of the building owner, s 11(11) provides for a clawback payment to the building owner, representing a due proportion of the expense. As under s 11(3), the apportionment is assessed by reference to current values at the time when the adjoining owner makes use of the work (see further **14.10**).

11.5 COSTS

Costs are within the surveyors' discretion.[3] No principles are prescribed upon which they should be awarded, but the usual form of award requires the building owner to pay the adjoining owner's surveyor's fees in connection with the award and the inspection of the works.[4] This seems consistent with the general principle that the building owner, for whose benefit the work is being carried out, should bear the costs, except where there is a specific provision to the contrary.

---

3   See s 10(13).
4   See Appendix 4 for a precedent award.

In arbitration, the principle is that the successful party receives his costs, except where a substantial part of the time and costs of the arbitration are expended on issues on which the successful party fails.[5] It might be argued that by this analogy the building owner who is permitted by an award under the Act to do work, is the successful party, and should be entitled to his costs. It is considered, however, that an analogy with arbitration would be misleading. The right to carry out the work is conferred by the Act itself, which authorises certain things which would otherwise be an infringement of the property rights of the adjoining owner. The Act provides safeguards for the adjoining owner, most importantly by the provision of impartial resolution of the disputes under s 10. It would be inconsistent with the general scheme of the Act for the adjoining owner to be, in effect, obliged to pay for the very protection which the Act confers on him.

There may, however, be cases where the usual practice should be departed from. This could occur where, for example, the cost of the procedure was increased by unreasonable conduct by the adjoining owner or his surveyor, or where proposals were put forward on behalf of the adjoining owner that were completely unreasonable, but required the building owner's surveyor to carry out extensive work. A further point is that the liability is only for reasonable costs, and hence if the costs claimed are unreasonable in amount, the building owner ought not to be required to pay them.

The categories of costs within s 10(13) include not only costs of making the award and of reasonable inspections, but also costs of 'any other matter arising out of the dispute' (s 10(13)(c)). The process of making the award may require the surveyors to determine difficult questions of law such as entitlement to easements and support.[6] It is considered that it is within their discretion to take their own legal advice on such questions, and that the cost of such advice will be within s 10(13).

11.6 OTHER LIABILITIES OF BUILDING OWNER

In addition to his liabilities for expenses and costs, the building owner is under obligations to make payments under s 11(6) and (8), and to pay compensation under s 7. These matters have already been covered in Chapter 6.

---

5   *Lewis v Haverfordwest Rural District Council* [1953] 1 WLR 1486; *Demolition & Construction Co Ltd v Kent River Board* [1963] 2 Lloyd's Rep 7; *The Rozel* [1994] 2 Lloyd's Rep 161; *Metro-Cammell Hong Kong Ltd v FKI Engineering Plc* (1996) 77 BLR 84; *Shirley v Caswell* (2001) Costs LR 1; *English v Emery Reimbold* [2002] 3 All ER 385, CA, cf CPR r 44.3(2).
6   See eg **15.4**.

11.7 RECOVERING EXPENSES FROM ADJOINING OWNER

Sections 13 and 14 contain provisions enabling the building owner to recover any expenses for which the adjoining owner is liable under s 11 by the following procedure.

11.7.1 Account

The building owner must serve an account on the adjoining owner under s 13(1). The requirements are as follows:

(a) It must be served within a 2-month period beginning on the day when the work, whose expenses the adjoining owner must (wholly or partially) pay, is completed. It might be thought that such a time-limit is merely directory, but in *Spiers and Son Ltd v Troup*,[7] time was held to be of the essence, so that a late account was ineffective.[8]
(b) It must be in writing, and must show:
   (i) particulars and expenses of the work;
   (ii) any deduction to which the adjoining owner or any other person is entitled in respect of old materials or otherwise.
(c) The work must be estimated and valued at fair average rates and prices according to the nature of the work, the locality, and the cost of labour and materials prevailing at the time when the work is executed.

11.7.2 Notice of objection

Within one month beginning with the date of service of the account the adjoining owner may serve a notice on the building owner stating any objection he has to the account. If he does so, a dispute is deemed to have arisen (s 13(2)), which must be resolved under s 10. If he does not, he is deemed to have no objection to the account (s 13(3)). This is the only area in which the Act imposes liability on the adjoining owner for failure to serve a notice. Whether time is of the essence with regard to this time-limit does not appear ever to have been decided. It may be doubted whether the adjoining owner would be prevented from asserting an objection of substance out of time, although he might be condemned in costs.

11.8 SECTION 14

Once the account has been duly served, and any dispute about it resolved, the adjoining owner is liable to pay the sum due (s 14(1)). Further, by way of an

---

7   (1915) 84 LJKB 1986.
8   That was a decision on s 96 of the 1894 Act, where the period was one month, but the language does not otherwise appear to be distinguishable.

unusual form of security, the property in the works to which the expenses (ie for which the adjoining owner is liable) relate vests solely in the building owner until the adjoining owner pays him (s 14(2)). For example, the adjoining owner may consent to a party wall under s 1(3), and it may be agreed or determined that he will pay half the expense, because he will make equal use of it. When the wall is built, half on the adjoining owner's land, it will nevertheless vest solely in the building owner until the adjoining owner pays his share, and until then it will be a trespass, which could be restrained by injunction, for the adjoining owner to make any use of his half of the wall. The following further points may be noted.

(a) Upon payment of the adjoining owner's contribution, the building owner's interest in the adjoining owner's half of the wall will presumably lapse, leaving the adjoining owner absolutely entitled to it, because it is on his side of the boundary, and part of his land. This is the force of the word 'until'. The building owner's interest is probably best regarded as a form of charge, securing the monetary liability, which is redeemed by payment.[9]

(b) Presumably, the building owner's interest will also lapse if he fails to serve any account under s 13, and thereby loses his right to enforce the adjoining owner's contribution.

(c) If the adjoining owner later makes greater use of the wall than was originally contemplated, he will become liable to an additional contribution under s 1(3)(b).[10] It is clear, however, that s 14(2) will not operate to vest any part of the wall in the building owner again, as security for this clawback, since the section applies only where an account has been served under s 13 (see s 14(1)).[11]

(d) It is considered that the interest conferred on the building owner is a property interest capable of binding successors in title of the adjoining owner.[12]

---

9 See *Mason v Fulham Corp* [1910] 1 KB 631.
10 The same will apply under s 11(11).
11 Dicta to the contrary in *Mason v Fulham Corp* [1910] 1 KB 631, where s 99 of the 1894 Act was considered, are no longer applicable since that section was not restricted in this way.
12 This was assumed in *Carlish v Salt* [1906] 1 Ch 335, where it was held to be a latent defect in title. See **14.1**.

Chapter 12

SECURITY FOR EXPENSES

12.1 INTRODUCTION

Section 12 of the Act confers on both the building owner and the adjoining owner the right in certain circumstances to require the other to give security for expenses. The provisions derive from s 57 of the 1939 Act, save that under the 1939 Act disputes with regard to security were determined by the county court. Under the Act, disputes must be resolved in accordance with s 10.

Section 12(1) gives the adjoining owner a right to claim security from the building owner. The need for this is self-evident. The statutory rights given to the building owner may authorise him to embark on extensive and radical works intimately affecting the adjoining property, but his entitlement is not conditional on financial substance, or even solvency. Without any provision for some kind of monetary security the adjoining owner might find himself having to fund from his own pocket expensive repairs to his own property, caused by insolvency of the building owner supervening in the middle of his operations. The adjoining owner's right is to call for security to be provided *before the works are begun*, and if it is awarded, the building owner will have to provide it before beginning.

Section 12(2) gives reciprocal rights to the building owner. The need for this is less obvious, but since the adjoining owner can impose additional works upon the building owner in his counter-notice (s 4(1)), and there are several other ways in which he may incur liability under the Act (Chapter 11), such liabilities can be substantial enough to justify requiring security from him. What is somewhat strange is that the building owner is also given a right (which is not new) to claim security merely because the adjoining owner has claimed it from him (tit-for-tat).

Section 12(3) spells out rigorous consequences for the adjoining owner if he fails to respond to a security notice, or to provide any security awarded against him, within a month. Contrary to the Act's usual practice these are automatic consequences, which follow merely from inaction. No such penalty is imposed on the building owner; his risk is that he will not be able to proceed.

These rights are claimed by serving notices before works are started. In default of agreement the issue has to be determined by surveyors under s 10, but there is no deemed dispute, so the party claiming must make a positive application to the surveyors for an award.

12.2 SECURITY BY THE BUILDING OWNER (section 12(1))

The object of the adjoining owner's right is to enable him to ensure that sufficient funds are available before any work is begun, and accordingly his notice under s 12(1) must be served[1] before any work pursuant to the Act is carried out. Once such work starts, unless it is *de minimis*, the right to seek security in respect of it is lost. However, the carrying out, before the service of the notice, of work which does not need to be authorised by the Act will not exclude the adjoining owner's rights. In the typical case of work to a party wall authorised by an award under s 10, therefore, work carried out on the building owner's building which is not subject to the provisions of the award will not count, even if it is part of a rebuilding scheme that will also involve the work to which the award relates.

The right to claim security is not expressly limited in any way. It is considered that it extends not only to the works which will be carried out, but to any claim to which their execution may give rise under the Act (including compensation under s 7(2) and allowance for disturbance under s 11(6)), or otherwise. But works not carried out under the Act, or claims arising from such works, would be beyond the scope of s 12. In the normal case of work authorised by an award, it will be necessary only to see what work the award covers in order to determine the extent of the matters in respect of which security can be required.

12.3 FACTORS

As to the matters to be taken into account, it is suggested that these can be grouped into two categories. First, those related to the work, and, secondly, those related to the building owner.

12.3.1 Related to work

In the first category are all those costs and losses related to the work which may potentially have to be borne by the adjoining owner. They will include the following:

(a) costs which may fall on the adjoining owner if the building owner, having commenced the work, either proves unable to complete it, or carries it out defectively and does not remedy the defects;
(b) amounts to which the adjoining owner may be entitled under any award made under s 10, insofar as unpaid at the date of the adjoining owner's notice;
(c) amounts to which the adjoining owner may be or become entitled by reason of works carried out, eg by way of compensation under s 7;

1　Ie under s 15; see Chapter 13.

(d) amounts to which the adjoining may be or become entitled under s 1(7);

(e) disturbance allowance to which the adjoining owner may be or become entitled under s 11(6).

It is suggested, however, that the contingent entitlement of the adjoining owner under s 11(10), where the adjoining owner subsequently erects a building which is found to be more expensive by reason of special foundations on the adjoining owner's land, will not be taken into account in ordering security. The right of the adjoining owner will only arise once he has erected his building, established the increased costs, and delivered the necessary account and invoices. Accordingly, these future expenses are, it is suggested, too remote from the work to be taken into account.

The weight to be accorded to these factors is bound to vary from case to case. Relevant considerations will include:

(a) the extent and complexity of the works;
(b) the degree of detailed preparation by the building owner (eg has he a competent design and supervisory team, a detailed method statement, adequate structural calculations, etc?);
(c) the terms of any building contract.

12.3.2 Related to building owner

The second group of factors are those relating to the building owner. Primary among these will be financial standing. It would clearly be inappropriate in normal cases for a local authority, government department or substantial public company to be required to give security. On the other hand, a building owner who is bankrupt (or a company in liquidation) ought generally to be required to give security. The appointment of administrative receivers inevitably casts doubt on the future solvency of a company. The appointment of an administrator, or the existence of an individual voluntary arrangement or corporate voluntary arrangement, would likewise be relevant factors. The building owner's country of residence may also be material, since residence outside England and Wales may complicate enforcement, and therefore be a factor favouring security.[2]

12.4 AMOUNT

The amount of security (if any) must be determined by balancing all relevant factors. The starting point may well be the realistic total of potential claims for which the building owner may be liable. This figure must, however, be

---

2   This is, however, subject to the position of individual EU residents, see *Fitzgerald v Williams* [1996] 2 All ER 171, CA.

discounted as appropriate, because the security, rather analogous to that afforded by a bond under a building contract, is to guard against the *risk* that the building owner will not fulfil his obligations. It is then necessary to consider the factors relating to the building owner himself. There will be a spectrum of situations, ranging from the well-funded building owner with a carefully planned programme of works involving little risk of damage to the adjoining owner's building, to cases where extensive and hazardous work is proposed on the basis of limited documentation by a building owner of doubtful financial worth. In the case of security under the Companies Act 1985 (s 726(1)), it is a general principle that security should not be oppressive so as to stifle a genuine claim. It is submitted that, whilst security should not be used indirectly as a way of placing unreasonable obstacles in the way of work which the Act entitles the building owner to carry out, it may not necessarily be unreasonable to order security in an amount which de facto prevents the particular building owner from proceeding.

12.5 MANNER OF GIVING SECURITY

In court proceedings, security is normally provided by way of payment into court. Under the 1939 Act this would have been the normal procedure, since questions as to security were dealt with by a county court judge. Under the Act, no guidance is given as to how security should be provided. The options appear to be:

(a) Depositing a sum in a bank account in the joint names of the surveyors. This has the advantage that the money is under the control of impartial experts who are familiar with the work and competent to assess the validity of any claim of recourse against security. It is suggested that this will be the most convenient course.
(b) Security by bond, the condition of which is that if the building owner fulfils his obligations the bond shall become void, but otherwise remain in force. It may be necessary to consider whether the bond should be an 'on demand' bond or only one giving rise to liability on proof of loss. It is thought that in general the latter will be appropriate.[3]
(c) Parent company (or other suitable) guarantee.

12.6 SECURITY BY ADJOINING OWNER (section 12(2))

Under s 12(2) the building owner is given a right in two cases to require the adjoining owner to give security. Again the right must be exercised by service of a notice, and again the notice must be served before he starts work. The

---

3 For the distinction see *Trafalgar House Construction (Regions) Ltd v General Surrey Ltd & Guarantee Co Ltd* [1996] AC 199, HL.

requirement can be agreed, and in default must be determined under s 10. A valid notice will give rise to similar discretionary considerations in relation to the adjoining owner (*mutatis mutandis*) as have been suggested above in relation to the building owner. The two cases are as follows.

12.6.1 Works required by adjoining owner

The first, unsurprising, case (s 12(2)(a)) is where the adjoining owner has put the building owner to additional expense, and has thereby become liable for some part of his resulting costs. This may have been by a requirement in his counter-notice (under s 4(1); see also s 11(7)), or even by an informal request to which the building owner has agreed, since this too will impose liability on the adjoining owner (under s 11(9)(b)). The scope of the security must therefore be limited to expenses within these categories.

12.6.2 Tit-for-tat

The second case is more surprising. Section 12(2)(b) enables the building owner to serve a notice requiring security merely because the adjoining owner has served such a notice on him. The principle behind this right, seems to be nothing better than tit-for-tat, which sits uncomfortably with the general principle of s 11(1) that expenses are to be borne by the building owner. It is true that there are several cases in which the Act requires the adjoining owner to contribute to the expense of works,[4] and some of these cases are not covered by s 12(2)(a). It is reasonable that the building owner should be entitled to claim security in all such cases, so that there is that legitimate scope for this right. What is surprising, however, is that this limited scope is not spelled out, so that the impression may be given that the building owner is entitled not merely to claim, but to receive, security simply because the adjoining owner has claimed it. It would clearly be inappropriate and unreasonable for any security to be granted to the building owner except in one of the specific cases where the Act imposes some liability on the adjoining owner, and it is regrettable that the right to claim is not so limited. An unfortunate consequence is that an unwary adjoining owner may, by failing to respond, lose his right to security even though none could have been ordered against him (see **12.8.1**). It would be even more unfortunate if a mistaken practice was to develop of imposing security upon adjoining owners merely on tit-for-tat grounds.

12.7 PROCEDURE: TIME LIMIT

In all cases the parties are free to agree over security, and in default the issue must be determined by the surveyors under s 10. Apart from the implied requirement that any notice must be served before the building owner starts

---

4 See **11.4**.

work, no time-limit is prescribed. This can cause difficulty. The building owner may be ready to proceed under an award, only to be delayed by a security notice, which then has to be determined. It is considered that in such a case the security award can extend any time-limit arising from the date of the original initiating notice.

12.8 FAILURE TO RESPOND OR COMPLY

What happens if the recipient of a security notice fails to respond, or to comply with an award of security made against him?

12.8.1 Adjoining owner: section 12(3)

In the case of the adjoining owner the consequences are provided for in s 12(3). In the first place he must respond to any security notice served on him within one month of its service. That is to say, he must either comply with the notice, by providing the security asked for, or initiate a dispute by referring it to the surveyors for determination; there is no provision for silence to give rise to an automatic dispute. In default he will suffer two consequences:

(a) any requirement for additional works in his counter-notice will cease to have effect;[5] and
(b) any security notice which he has served will also cease to have effect.

These are draconian consequences to be visited (contrary to the Act's normal practice) on a month's silence. It is particularly objectionable that they can apparently flow from a tit-for-tat notice, served when there was no liability to justify it. Faced with these consequences a court might hold that such a notice was an abuse and a nullity, but adjoining owners and their advisers must be alert to the dangers.

In the second place, when there has been a determination by the surveyors, the adjoining owner must provide any security awarded against him, again within a month of the award. In default the same two consequences will follow. There is nothing unreasonable in this, since the process of determination will have shown up the emptiness of any tit-for-tat notice which is not underpinned by liability on the part of the adjoining owner. One month may be a short time for providing substantial security, and in times of financial stringency the surveyors may have to take this into account in determining the amount of the security.

12.8.2 Building owner

No penalty is expressly imposed on a building owner who fails to respond to a security notice, or to comply with an award of security against him, nor does the

---

5 Note that there is no reference here to works requested (contrast s 11(9)) and agreed; s 12(3) does not in terms affect any such agreement.

Act provide any time-limit for his compliance. It is clear, however, from the wording of s 12(1) that the adjoining owner is entitled to require that security be given before work is started, and once that award is made it is his statutory duty to observe it.[6] It must follow that he could be restrained from starting, as soon as the issue has been raised by the service of a notice under s 12(1). This consequence is no doubt sufficient to induce building owners to comply with directions for security. It remains anomalous that only the adjoining owner is penalised for silence by losing the benefit of notices he has served.

---

6   See **9.4.2**.

Chapter 13

SERVICE OF NOTICES

13.1 INTRODUCTION

The Act requires notices to be served in many contexts. These are covered on the individual topics dealt with by the Act. A check-list of the notices for which the Act provides is contained in Appendix 3. This chapter considers the formal requirements of the notices required by the Act, the methods of service, and the effect of non-service.

13.2 FORMAL REQUIREMENTS OF NOTICES

Although the Act does not specifically say so, it is clear that all notices required to be given under its provisions must be in writing since they invariably have to be 'served'. The Act, like the 1939 Act, does not prescribe any particular form of notice. Therefore, any notice which contains the particulars required by the relevant provision of the Act will be sufficient.[1]

Whether a document constitutes a proper notice under the provisions of the Act falls to be decided, therefore, on general principles. In order to satisfy the relevant provisions of the Act the notice must be in terms that are sufficiently clear and intelligible to bring home to the ordinary recipient the fact that the building owner or adjoining owner, as the case may be, is purporting to exercise a right under the Act, and to enable him to see what counter-notice he should give or what other action he should take.[2] Having regard to the strictness with which courts have approached interpretation of the 1939 Act,[3] it is suggested that the notice must specify with reasonable precision what action the giver of the notice proposes to take, and the provision of the Act which authorises him to take it. For example, a notice under s 3 should, it is submitted, specify within which paragraphs of s 2(2) the work proposed by the building owner falls. The details of the work should be such as to enable a fair idea to be gathered of the extent and nature of the proposals, but it will be unnecessary to include a full analysis of the work, for example by way of a bill of quantities, structural calculations, and drawings relating to details. The information must be sufficient to enable the recipient of the notice both to know what is proposed, and to decide what action is necessary in order to protect his interests, and (where necessary) to instruct a surveyor.

---

1 For forms of notice see Appendix 4.
2 Compare *Hobbs Hart & Co v Grover* [1899] 1 Ch 11 (a decision on s 91 of the London Building Act 1894); *Nunes v Davies Laing & Dick Ltd* [1986] 1 EGLR 106.
3 As in *Gyle-Thompson v Wall Street (Properties) Ltd* [1974] 1 All ER 295.

However, a notice wil be upheld if it contains an obvious error if the real intent could be clear to the recipient so that he would not be mislead by it.[4]

13.3 AMENDMENT OF NOTICE

The Act makes no provision for amendment of notices. It is considered that no amendment is possible, unless both parties concur in treating the amendment as included in the original notice. But the surveyors ought to give notices a reasonably liberal construction, so as to avoid delay and expense arising from the need to serve fresh notices.

13.4 MODE OF SERVICE

Section 15 of the Act provides for service. Section 15(1) provides three primary methods of service. Section 15(2) provides two alternatives where the Act requires or authorises a notice or other document to be served on a person as owner of premises. These alternatives will not apply to all the notices required by the Act, since some have to be served on occupiers (eg under s 8). These prescribed methods are not compulsory or exhaustive, and do not preclude proof of service by other means.

The three primary methods of service authorised by s 15(1) are:
(a) delivery to the recipient in person;
(b) service by post to the recipient's usual or last known residence or place of business in the UK;
(c) in the case of a body corporate, delivery to the secretary or clerk of the body corporate at its registered or principal office or service by post to the secretary or clerk of that body corporate at that office.

13.4.1 Personal delivery

By analogy with the rules governing personal service of writs, it is suggested that:

(a) handing the notice to an agent of the recipient will not be sufficient, unless this is at the request of the recipient;[5]
(b) the document must be left with and not merely shown to the recipient.

13.4.2 Postal service on an individual

Service by post requires that the letter containing the notice be properly addressed, pre-paid and posted to the proper address of the person to be

---

4 *Mannou Investments Co Ltd v Eagle Star Life Assurance Co Ltd* [1997] AC 749.
5 *Montgomery, Jones & Co v Liebenthal & Co* [1898] 1 QB 487.

served. If the letter is returned through the post office as undelivered, it will not be treated as having been served.[6] By s 7 of the Interpretation Act 1978, it is provided that where an Act authorises or requires any document to be served by post, service is deemed to be effective by properly addressing, pre-paying, and posting a letter containing the document, and unless the contrary is proved, to have been effected at the time at which the letter would be delivered in the ordinary course of post. It has been held that where a notice has to be served by a certain time, it is open to a party on whom it is served by post to prove either that he in fact received it later than the ordinary course of post, or that he did not receive the document at all.[7]

13.4.3 Postal address

The address to which the letter is posted must be the 'usual or last-known residence or place of business in the United Kingdom'. The United Kingdom includes England, Wales, Scotland and Northern Ireland, but not the Republic of Ireland, or the Channel Islands. 'Sending' a document by post involves the whole process of transmission from server to recipient, so that if a letter is incorrectly addressed, but subsequently re-directed by the post office to the correct address it will be validly served by post.[8] 'Last known' has been held to mean 'last known to the giver of the notice'.[9] It has also been held that 'last known address' are words in ordinary usage in English;[10] the test is what would the ordinary person regard as the last known address of the person in question.[11] The last known address of a company is its registered office, not its managing agent's office.

13.4.4 Service on a body corporate

Section 15(1)(c) provides two alternative methods of service, which apply not only to limited companies but also to other bodies corporate such as local authorities. In regard to limited companies, s 725 of the Companies Act 1985 provides for service of documents by leaving the document at the registered office of the company, or sending it to the registered office by post. The document can be validly served by recorded delivery.[12]

---

6 *R v London County Quarter Sessions Appeals Committee ex parte Rossi* [1956] 1 All ER 670.
7 *R v London County Quarter Sessions Appeals Committee ex parte Rossi* [1956] 1 All ER 670; *Maltglade Ltd v St Albans Rural District Council* [1972] 3 All ER 129.
8 *Austin Rover Group Ltd v Crouch Butler Savage Associates (A Firm) and Others* [1986] 3 All ER 50, CA.
9 Ibid.
10 See *National Westminster Bank Ltd v Betchworth Investments Ltd* [1975] 1 EGLR 57, CA.
11 Ibid.
12 *TO Supplies (London) Ltd v Jerry Creighton Ltd* [1951] 2 All ER 992. Recorded Delivery Service Act 1962, s 1.

13.5 OTHER METHODS OF SERVICE

The reference in s 15(1)(b) to 'post' includes registered post and recorded delivery as well as the ordinary post. Further, it is possible for irregularities of service to be waived by the recipient of the notice taking action on it. It is also possible for the parties to agree an alternative method of service of notices, for example by agreeing that notices shall be exchanged between their respective surveyors.

13.6 SERVICE ON THE OWNER OF PREMISES

Section 15(2) makes additional provision where a notice or other document is authorised or required to be served on a person as owner of premises. It provides for the notice to be addressed to 'the owner' (ie without naming him) of the premises (which must be named), and for delivery of it to a person on the premises, or if no person to whom it can be delivered is found there, fixing it to a conspicuous part of the premises.[13] This provision appears to apply to almost all the notices required by the Act, since building and adjoining owners are required to be served as owners of their respective premises. But it does not apply where service is required on an occupier (eg under s 8(3)).

13.7 PERSONS ON WHOM NOTICES MUST BE SERVED

The Act clearly contemplates the need to serve multiple notices. There may be numerous persons who satisfy the description of adjoining owner. All of them must be served with notice, even if the work proposed will not affect them directly. There can also be more than one building owner, but the adjoining owner's task is simplified: he need only respond to the notice served on him, and need not (and indeed has no right to) seek to serve any counter-notice on other persons who might satisfy the definition of building owner. However, it is open to the recipient of a notice to question the validity of it on the basis that it has not been served by all those persons by whom it should have been served, as for example where two persons together constituted the 'building owner', but the notice was served by only one of them.[14]

---

13 Compare Law of Property Act 1925, s 196(3).
14 *Lehmann v Herman* [1993] 1 EGLR 172.

13.8 JOINT OWNERS

Where there are joint building owners, notices must be served by or on behalf of all of them.[15] But where there are joint adjoining owners, it has been held sufficient to serve only one.[16]

13.9 FAILURE TO SERVE NOTICES

It is an essential precondition of a building owner's exercise of rights under the Act that he has served the relevant notices under ss 1, 3 or 6. Failure to do this cannot be cured by any subsequent 'award' purporting to authorise the work to be done, which will itself be a nullity.[17] Failure by an adjoining owner to serve a counter-notice consenting to works proposed by the building owner will not in general prejudice the adjoining owner's position, and indeed in the case of s 1(3) of the Act he would seem positively ill-advised to serve such a notice because of the onerous responsibilities which will then be placed on him. In general, the adjoining owner, if in doubt, is probably best advised simply not to respond to a notice served by the building owner, provided he wishes to protect his position and instruct a surveyor. Since the building owner is normally obliged to pay for the works and the surveyor's costs and expenses, the adjoining owner usually has little incentive to serve a notice consenting to the works. But if he is content to accept the building owner's party structure notice subject only to the modifications contemplated by s 4, the service of a counter-notice can reduce the area of dispute, and so save costs. Only s 13(2) (notice of objection to an account) imposes liability on an adjoining owner for failure to serve notice, but note also the penalties under s 12(2) if he fails to respond to a notice for security served by the building owner (see **12.8.1**).

13.10 WAIVER OF TIME-LIMITS OR IRREGULARITIES IN NOTICES

It is considered that the timetable laid down by the Act is capable of being enlarged by agreement between the parties, or their surveyors with their authority. The time-limits are inserted for the protection of the recipient of the notice, and are therefore capable of being waived. There is no public interest involved which would require the court to adopt a stricter approach.[18] The same principle would apply to other irregularities in notices. The policy of the

---

15   *Lehmann v Herman* [1993] 1 EGLR 172.
16   *Crosby v Alhambra Co Ltd* [1907] 1 Ch 295.
17   *Gyle-Thompson v Wall Street (Properties) Ltd* [1974] 1 All ER 295; *Lehmann v Herman* [1993] 1 EGLR 172.
18   Compare *Kammin's Ballrooms Co Ltd v Zenith Investments (Torquay) Ltd* [1970] 2 All ER 871 (statutory time-limit capable of being waived).

Act is to facilitate dispute resolution. If the parties accept that irregular notices are to be treated as valid, the surveyors would, it is suggested, be entitled to proceed on this basis, since the parties would be estopped by convention from denying that the relevant notices were valid.[19]

Equally, if one party made a clear and unequivocal representation to the other that it would accept or notice as valid notwithstanding that it was irregular, and the other party relied on that representation, the representor would be precluded from resiling from it. But mere silence would not be sufficient.[20]

---

19 *Amalgamated Investment and Property Co Ltd v Texas Commerce International Bank Ltd* [1981] 3 All ER 577.
20 *Central London Property Trust Ltd v High Trees House Ltd* [1947] KB 130, *Woodhouse AC Israel Cocoa SA and another v Nigerian Produce Marketing Co Ltd* [1972] AC 741, *Dun and Bradstreet Software Services (England) Ltd and another v Provident Mutual Life Assurance Association and another* [1998] 2 EGLR 175, *HH Casualty and General Insurance Ltd v New Hampshire Insurance Co* [2003] Lloyds Rep IR 1.

Chapter 14

SUCCESSORS IN TITLE

14.1 INTRODUCTION

The Act is concerned with owners of pieces of adjoining land. It gives them rights, and imposes on them liabilities, some of which are contingent on the occurrence of events at an indefinite time in the future. Yet the Act contains no general provision explaining how successors in title are affected, if at all. So long as the adjoining lands remain in the same hands as when the initiating notice is served, the effect of the Act is relatively clear. But as soon as one or both of the adjoining parcels of land change hands, difficult questions arise which the Act does not expressly answer. This can happen before or after the award.

14.2 DEFINITIONS

Granted that the Act deals fully with the rights and liabilities of the original building owner and adjoining owner, the questions which arise, however, concern the rights and liabilities of their successors in title. The material available for answering the questions consists of: (a) the Act itself; and (b) the general principles of property law. So far as the Act is concerned, the starting point is the definitions of 'building owner' and 'adjoining owner'. These have already been outlined (see **2.5**). They give rise to a number of points.

(a) 'Building owner' means an owner of land 'who is desirous of exercising rights under the Act'. Thus he is defined not by the land which he owns, but by his desire, a personal attribute, which will not necessarily be shared by his successor in title.
(b) 'Adjoining owner' means an owner of land adjoining that of the building owner. This is a definition which assumes the existence of a neighbouring building owner, and therefore depends not only on the land owned, but also on the personal attribute of the neighbour.
(c) The personal nature of these definitions can be illustrated by reference to the building owner who ceases to desire to build (eg because he has completed his operations). He thereupon ceases to be a building owner. And because there is no longer a building owner, there is no longer an adjoining owner. The definitions do not run with the land.
(d) It follows that whenever the Act gives rights to, or imposes liabilities on, the building owner or the adjoining owner as such, it is at least arguable, as a matter of language, that those rights and liabilities accrue only to the persons (if any) answering the definitions at the material time, and not to any successors of theirs. This is what the Act does, except in a single context (s 11(10)).

(e) On the other hand, it must be kept in mind that the definitions in s 20 apply 'unless the context otherwise requires'. If the 'personal' construction above produces a result which is wholly unreasonable or capricious, it may therefore be permissible to adopt another, reasonable, construction.

(f) In particular contexts, these approaches can give rise to an acute conflict. For example, under s 11(10) a contribution may become payable to the adjoining owner long after the original building owner has ceased to satisfy the definition. The personal construction suggests that only the original adjoining owner can benefit, since his successors are not within the definition. But the policy behind that section suggests that such a narrow construction would defeat its object.[1]

14.3 ASSIGNABILITY: BENEFIT AND BURDEN

Property law suggests a supplementary approach. The rights and liabilities created by the Act may be considered in terms of their assignability.

(a) Rights and liabilities may be real (ie annexed to land) or personal. As has been shown, the nature of the definitions of building owner and adjoining owner means that rights and liabilities conferred and imposed on them by those descriptions are likely to be personal. There is only one context in which the Act confers a right by reference to a land-based description (s 11(10)). And apart from the rights of entry under s 8, there is only one context where the Act clearly imposes a liability which is annexed to land (s 14(2)).

(b) Real rights and liabilities run with the land to which they are annexed, affecting its successive owners according to the principles of real property law.

(c) Personal rights do not normally run with the land automatically but are usually assignable expressly. Rights created by statute can usually be assigned either at law[2] or in equity. A few rights are not assignable at all.[3]

(d) Personal liabilities, however, are in general not assignable.

14.4 BEFORE AWARD: DISPUTE PROCEDURE

We can now turn to the specific problems posed by changes of ownership at particular times. The first time span is the period during which the machinery of the Act is being operated, ie from the service of the initiating notice by the building owner until the date of the resulting award.

---

1 See **5.8.2(b)**.
2 Under the Law of Property Act 1925, s 136.
3 For example a bare cause of action: see *Trendtex Trading Corp v Credit Suisse* [1982] AC 679.

14.5 AGREEMENT

It is always open to the parties to reach agreement outside the Act's procedures. If this happens the effect on successors must depend on the application of ordinary common law principles (see above) to the contract. In general, benefits will be assignable but not burdens, and so on. If the agreement is by deed, it may also grant rights in the land (eg easements) which will bind successors. If the agreement arises from the service of a notice of consent under s 5, it is considered that a binding contract arises for the works to be carried out in the manner provided by the Act: the benefit will be assignable to a new building owner, and the adjoining owner's successor (who will satisfy the definition of adjoining owner until the work is complete) will be bound by the statutory rights of entry.[4]

14.6 DISPUTE

If the parties cannot agree, a dispute ensues and surveyors are appointed. What if one party sells his land before they have made an award? What is the new owner's standing in the dispute? Is he entitled to step into his predecessor's shoes? Can he insist on the procedure starting again from the beginning? There are no authoritative answers to these questions. The extreme view is that the personal nature of the rights under the Act means that any succession technically requires the procedure to be started again, and that any new party can insist on this. This view is inconvenient, and open to abuse (eg by an adjoining owner who wishes at all costs to delay the start of works). It is also, it is considered, incorrect. The personal nature of the Act's definitions does not affect the procedure leading to an award, because until then there is always a building owner desiring to build, and therefore an adjoining owner, within the definitions. This suggests further consequences.

(a) Since they satisfy the definitions, it is considered that it is open to new owners to step in and adopt the proceedings taken by their predecessors, at any rate provided they are prepared to accept the burdens (eg payment of expenses and costs) as well as the benefits.
(b) Even if that is wrong, the rights created by notices served under the Act are, it is considered, capable of assignment, so that the new owner can be put in a position to adopt the proceedings by express assignment. The right to have a dispute determined in accordance with all the provisions of the Act is a benefit to both parties, and although the burdens may not be technically assignable, the assignment will be subject to the accrued rights of the other party,[5] as will adoption of the proceedings. The assignment is not of a bare cause of action, since it affects the assignee's land.

---

4   Consent under s 1(3) leaves further matters undecided, which may still lead to a dispute.
5   See Snell, *Principles of Equity* 30th edn (Sweet & Maxwell, 1991) p 81.

14.7 DISSENTING SUCCESSOR

The question remains whether a successor who does not wish to adopt the proceedings can be bound by them.

14.7.1 Building owner

The question is unlikely to affect an incoming building owner, because the remedy is in his own hand. He can insist that his vendor withdraws his notice, or otherwise determines the existing proceedings, and then serve his own notice.

14.7.2 Adjoining owner

The question arises acutely in the case of an incoming adjoining owner who does not cooperate. If he refuses to take part in the existing proceedings, can they lead to an award binding on him? Or is the building owner bound to start afresh by serving a new notice on him? Policy considerations pull both ways. On the one hand, it may seem unjust for an adjoining owner to be bound by deliberations between surveyors he has not chosen, and who have not heard him. On the other, the building owner may be severely prejudiced by the delay, especially if an unscrupulous adjoining owner is able to keep moving his land from one person to another. It is submitted that, provided the new owner purchased with notice of the dispute, this is a mere procedural question, which ought to be dealt with by analogy with proceedings in court. The new adjoining owner satisfies the definition in the Act, and is therefore a proper party to the dispute. The transfer of the land to him does not affect the building owner's claim: it is no more than the devolution of the original adjoining owner's interest. In litigation, it would be a matter of course for the new owner to be substituted as a party.[6] Subject to directions protecting his interest as far as necessary (eg notification of all that has happened in the dispute; opportunity to make representations; decision to be made by third surveyor, if he wishes), there seems to be no reason why the new owner should not be substituted as a party to the dispute under the Act. On that footing no new notice need be served, and the award will bind him whether he participates in the procedure or not. This, however, may not apply to a purchaser who has purchased without any notice of the dispute.[7]

14.8 AFTER AWARD

An award gives rise to a series of rights and liabilities which are immediate, in the sense that they are immediately defined (although monetary liabilities will not be payable until they are quantified, which will not be until the works are

---

6 See CPR r 19.
7 See **14.13.1**.

completed). There are other rights and liabilities which may subsequently arise under the Act, but which are contingent on the occurrence of defined circumstances in the future. It is convenient to distinguish between these categories of immediate and contingent rights and liabilities.

14.9 IMMEDIATE RIGHTS AND LIABILITIES

The principal immediate rights and liabilities are the right of the building owner to carry out works defined by the award, and the liability of the adjoining owner (under s 8) to allow entry for the purpose. Since the works will take a certain amount of time, and more time will pass before the consequential financial liabilities are quantified, there is plenty of leeway for either party's land to change hands before the rights are exhausted and liabilities discharged. Which rights and liabilities will devolve on the successors?

14.9.1 Rights (benefit)

Just as contractual benefits are, in general, assignable, so it is considered that the rights conferred by an award are assignable, so that a building owner can assign to his successor his rights of entry, and his rights to any payments due from the adjoining owner on completion of the works. Indeed, *Mason v Fulham Corp*[8] suggests that rights will pass automatically with a conveyance of the building owner's land unless expressly reserved. But *Re Stone and Hastie*[9] suggests there is no such automatic assignment on the grant of a lease.

14.9.2 Liabilities (burden)

Contractual burdens cannot be assigned. Nor can a building owner's immediate liability under an award: it is personal to him, and he cannot escape it by conveying to a man of straw.[10] It is considered that the same applies to the immediate financial liabilities of the adjoining owner. But his successor will be bound by the liabilities which affect the land itself (ie the rights of entry under s 8, and the vesting of the works under s 14(2)).

14.10 CONTINGENT RIGHTS AND LIABILITIES

There are three sections under which contingent financial liabilities may arise at some indefinite time in the future. They are as follows.

---

8   [1910] 1 KB 631. This case actually concerns an agreement, not an award, and a contingent, not immediate, right.
9   [1903] 2 KB 463. This case concerns an award, but again a contingent right.
10 See *Selby v Whitbread & Co* [1917] 1 KB 736.

(a) Section 1(3)(b), which provides for the allocation of expenses where the adjoining owner has consented. The two owners are to bear them 'from time to time' in a proportion which pays regard to the use they make of the wall. Thus, either owner may at any time or times become liable for an additional contribution whether or not he paid anything in the first instance.
(b) Section 11(11) deals with similar subject matter. It applies where an adjoining owner makes use of work originally paid for entirely by the building owner. It imposes liability only on the adjoining owner, and only where he made no contribution in the first instance.
(c) Section 11(10) is concerned with special foundations, and requires 'the owner of the building to which the foundations belong' to make a contribution to later building expenses of the adjoining owner, if they impede him. This provision has been considered above (see **5.8.2**).

It cannot be every increase in use, however trivial, which will trigger liability for clawbacks under ss 1(3)(b) and 11(11). No doubt, there will need to be works requiring a notice under the Act to be served. The award will then take into account the allocation of expenses on the earlier occasion.[11] There is no uniformity of benefit and burden between the cases. Under s 1(3)(b), either party may serve the notice, and the contingent liability will fall upon him; under s 11(11) only the former adjoining owner will serve the notice and incur the liability; under s 11(10), again the notice will be by the former adjoining owner, but the liability will fall on his neighbour.

14.10.1 Rights (benefit)

There are two leading cases concerned with the devolution of the contingent right to a clawback payment (under the equivalent of s 11(11)).

In *Re Stone and Hastie* (above) the original building owner had leased his property on a 21-year term, and an award upon a later notice by the adjoining owner directed payment of a clawback to the lessee. It was held that the lessee was not entitled to it, and that the award was to that extent void.

On the other hand, in *Mason v Fulham Corp* (above), the original building owner sold his property and a clawback payment was later made to the purchaser. The original building owner thereupon claimed that the payment should have been made to him, but it was held that the right had passed (without mention) to his successor in title. If the reasoning is less than satisfactory (since it ignored the difficulties that the purchaser did not satisfy the definition of building owner, and the right was not annexed to the land), the result is realistic.

---

11 As happened in *Re Stone and Hastie* (above).

The principle to be deduced from these decisions is that, in the absence of express reservation[12] or assignment, the benefit of a contingent right will pass with the freehold, but not with a derivative interest. It is thought unlikely that this principle will be disturbed. It will presumably apply also to clawbacks under s 1(3)(b). The special difficulties posed by the wording of s 11(10) are considered elsewhere (see **5.8.2(b)** and **14.2(f)**): if (as is suggested there) the benefit is capable of passing, this principle will presumably apply to it.

14.10.2 Liabilities (burden)

Under s 11(10), the wording is deliberately designed to make the burden of the contingent liability fall on successors of the building owner. But there is a serious question as to whether the contingent liability for clawbacks under ss 1(3)(b) and 11(11) is capable of binding successors.[13] One further argument may be noticed here. It is established that the benefit of the clawback under s 11(11) can pass,[14] so that the reference to the building owner in that section is treated as including successors.[15] It would be surprising, therefore, if the reference to the adjoining owner in the same section should not be treated in the same way, and s 1(3)(b) is a shortened provision which must take its colour from s 11(11). No authority has been found in which this question has been considered.[16] On the assumption that the contingent liabilities are not restricted to the original parties, the following features may be noted.

(a) They will fall upon the relevant owner at some future date. There is no provision of the Act which charges them on the land,[17] but they are incidents which affect the owner because of his ownership.

(b) Normally, they will arise when the owner wishes to build, and serves a notice under the Act. At that stage they become immediate liabilities of the new building owner, to be determined by the award, and no doubt they are personal to him like his other immediate liabilities.[18]

---

12 See *Mason v Fulham Corp* (above), at p 639.
13 See **14.2**.
14 See *Mason v Fulham Corp* (above).
15 See the headnote in the *Mason* case, which expresses the sense, rather than the words, of the judgments.
16 In *Re Stone and Hastie* (above), the adjoining owner against whom a clawback was awarded was holding under a long lease which appears to have been granted by the original adjoining owner (see p 468): but there was no appeal on the ground that the liability had not passed to him, and no discussion of this issue.
17 Section 14(2) applies only to immediate liabilities: see **11.8(c)**.
18 See **14.9.2**.

14.11 CONVEYANCING IMPLICATIONS

The standard works on conveyancing[19] contain no material reference to the party walls legislation. No doubt this is partly because of its local application. But it is clear from the Act's effect on successors in title that conveyancers will have to pay more attention to it, now that its application is countrywide.

14.12 LIABILITIES AFFECTING A PURCHASER

The foregoing survey has considered what liabilities arising under the Act will bind a purchaser. They can be categorised as follows.

14.12.1 Purchaser from building owner

If a building owner sells, whether before or after award, the purchaser from him is in relatively little jeopardy. He will in principle be liable for works which he undertakes, but not for those already undertaken by his vendor. Contingent liabilities affecting him can arise only in the unusual cases of s 1(3)(b) (where the original notice was consented to) and s 11(10) (where works included special foundations).

14.12.2 Purchaser from adjoining owner

The exposure of a purchaser from an adjoining owner is considerably greater. If the sale is before award, he is buying a dispute to which he may become an unwilling party. If the sale is after award, he may be bound by:

(a) the building owner's rights of entry;
(b) the vesting of works in the building owner (s 14(2));
(c) the contingent clawback provisions (ss 1(3)(b) and 11(11)).

14.13 REGISTRATION AS LAND CHARGE

Are any of these liabilities registrable as land charges, so as to be discoverable by normal conveyancing processes?

14.13.1 Dispute

The dispute arising from the service of a notice, although analogous to a pending land action, is not within the statutory definition because it is not 'pending in court'.[20] It therefore appears that a purchaser who purchases without notice of the dispute may be entitled to insist that the procedure be

---
19 *Emmett on Title* (Sweet & Maxwell) and Ruoff and Roper *Registered Conveyancing* (Sweet & Maxwell, 1991).
20 See Land Charges Act 1972, s 17(1).

started afresh by service of a new notice on him. On the other hand, if an award is appealed into the county court, the proceedings thereon satisfy the definition and should be registered immediately, or a purchaser without express notice will not be bound by them.[21]

14.13.2 Rights under an award

An award is unlikely to grant any interest in land to either party capable of being registered (with the possible exception of immediate rights of entry: see **14.13.3**). In *Observatory Hill Ltd v Camtel Investments SA*[22] an award provided that the building owner should at his own expense make good any damage done to the adjoining owner's land, and that in default the adjoining owner could carry out the work himself on the building owner's land. The adjoining owner thereupon lodged a caution against the building owner's registered title in respect of the award. At its highest the adjoining owner's interest amounted to no more than a future contingent right of entry. This was held insufficient to justify the caution, which was therefore ordered to be vacated.[23]

14.13.3 Rights of entry

Rights of entry under s 8 are not legal interests in the normal sense,[24] and it is considered that they are probably not registrable as equitable easements (although the contrary is arguable) in view of the restrictive construction given to that term.[25] Be that as it may, there appears to be no incentive to register them, since non-registration will not enable a purchaser to escape them. They are not like rights originating in a private grant which, if registrable, will be lost once and for all by non-registration. Even if a purchaser can technically take free of the rights of entry triggered by a notice served on his vendor, the most the building owner need do is serve a fresh 14-day notice on him. The right of entry is then exercisable against the land by force of s 8.

14.13.4 Vesting of works

If the adjoining owner has not paid his immediate liabilities under an award, the works on his side of the boundary will still be vested in the building owner under s 14(2). It is considered that this gives the building owner (without any

---

21 See Land Charges Act 1972, s 5(7).
22 [1997] 1 EGLR 140.
23 But subject to a cross-undertaking in damages. This was offered, no doubt by analogy with a practice instituted in *Clearbrook Properties Ltd v Verrier* [1974] 1 WLR 243, as a condition of vacating a caution. The modern practice is the opposite: ie to maintain the caution but impose a cross-undertaking on the cautioner, see *Tucker v Hutchinson* (1987) 54 P & CR 106. But those practices applied to properly cautionable interests (estate contracts); it is not thought that they could be insisted on where there is no such interest.
24 Since they do not fall within the Law of Property Act 1925, s 1(2)(e). But rights under the Act are not mere equitable rights: see *Selby v Whitbread & Co* [1917] 1 KB 736, at 747.
25 See *Ives (ER) Investment Ltd v High* [1967] 2 QB 379; *Poster v Slough Estates Ltd* [1969] 1 Ch 495; *Shiloh Spinners Ltd v Harding* [1973] AC 691.

application by him) a charge for expenses incurred by him under the Act, which is therefore within the definition of a Class B land charge.[26] The building owner should therefore register such a charge as soon as he serves his account, or it will be void against the purchaser.[27]

14.13.5 Contingent liabilities

The contingent liabilities are mere personal liabilities which attach to the owner (if at all: see **14.10.2**) because of his ownership of the land at the material time. They are not charged on the land, and are therefore not registrable, although their potential existence will be deducible from the award.

14.14 ACTION FOR CONVEYANCERS

It is evident that the Act may give rise to liabilities affecting a purchaser which fall outside the modern systems of registration. It is beyond the scope of this book to attempt a detailed analysis of the consequences for conveyancers. The following steps are suggested.

14.14.1 Before contract

The purchaser will wish to know whether there is about to be, or ever has been, an award which will affect him. Preliminary enquiries should be directed to the following issues:

(a) Whether there is currently a dispute on foot, and if so:
 - what notices have been served (including consent notices);
 - what appointments of surveyors have been made;
 - has any security been awarded to, or given by, either party;
 - what stage the surveyors have reached in their deliberations.
(b) Whether any award has been made at any time which affects the property, and if so:
 - is it an old award, in the sense that all the works have been carried out, and immediate liabilities discharged; or
 - is it a new award, in the sense that the works have not yet been completed.
(c) If there is an old award:
 - did the work include special foundations;
 - were the expenses borne solely by the building owner.[28]
(d) If there is a new award:
 - are there any expenses to be borne by the adjoining owner;[29]

---

26 See Land Charges Act 1972, s 2(2), (3).
27 For registered land see **14.14.5**.
28 These enquiries go to contingent liabilities under ss 11(10), (11).
29 If there are, they will constitute a latent defect in title which an adjoining owner who is selling is bound to disclose: see *Carlish v Salt* [1906] 1 Ch 335.

- has any account been served for them.
(e) Whether any works have ever been carried out under the Act by consent, and if so:
- what notices were served (including any counter-notice);
- were any expenses borne by the adjoining owner.

14.14.2 Contract

(a) If there is a dispute in progress, or work still proceeding under a new award:
- the parties will have to consider how immediate liabilities are to be shared between them, and to agree upon appropriate indemnities;
- the purchaser should consider insisting on the express assignment of the benefit of all notices served, or of the award.
(b) If there is an old award:
- the vendor should sell subject to the award;
- the purchaser should seek to acquire the benefit of the award expressly.[30]

14.14.3 Completion

(a) Subject to contrary agreement, the property should be conveyed subject to and with the benefit of: (i) any current notices under the Act; and (ii) any award.
(b) If the land is registered, it will be more appropriate to embody this transaction in a separate document.

14.14.4 Land charges

The following matters appear to be registrable under the Land Charges Act 1972[31] (although it is not the current practice of conveyancers to register them).

(a) An appeal against an award will be registrable as a pending land action.
(b) The vesting of works in the building owner appears to be a Class B land charge.
(c) It is perhaps arguable that the rights of entry arising from an award are registrable as equitable easements (Class D(iii)).

14.14.5 Registered land

If the land is registered, it should be possible to protect interests under (a) and (b) above, either by unilateral notice under s 34(2)(b) of the Land Registration Act 2002, or by an appropriate restriction under s 42(1)(c), or even by both. Equitable easements, however, are no longer overriding interests.

---

30 These provisions go to the contingent rights and liabilities.
31 See **14.13**.

14.15 SHORTCOMINGS

It is regrettable that the Act has not taken the opportunity to clear up the ancient ambiguity about the standing of successors in title. What is more disturbing is the failure to adapt the machinery of the Act to the registration regimes of modern conveyancing. Registration ensures, so far as reasonably possible, that purchasers of land do not find themselves saddled with liabilities that they could not have discovered. Detailed enquiries are all very well, but not an adequate substitute. It may be that a purchaser from an adjoining owner is sure to learn of a current dispute under the Act, and can only be kept in ignorance of it by misrepresentation. But the same is not true of an award which is some years old. Unregistered documents fall out of sight quickly, and a vendor who knows nothing of an award made before his time will, without fault, give unhelpful answers to enquiries. But the purchaser's ignorance will not, of itself, protect him from contingent liabilities which may arise from the provisions of a forgotten award.

Chapter 15

RELATIONSHIP WITH OTHER AREAS OF LAW

15.1 INTRODUCTION

The rights conferred by the Act impinge on various other areas of the law relating to the relationship between building and adjoining owners. In general, it may be said that the provisions of the Act are not intended to affect other rights except to the extent necessary in order to give effect to the purposes of the Act. On second reading the Earl of Lytton said:[1]

> 'The Bill will have no effect on title. The wall owned by one party or another is not a party wall, nor does it cut across provisions for easements contained in titles. It is not designed to affect common law rights of support or conflict with other statutory requirements ... the Bill dovetails in with the Access to Neighbouring Land Act. I am satisfied that there is no conflict with that. Statutory consents such as planning, listed buildings and Building Regulations will be unaffected ...'

In general, this intention is achieved by s 9(a), but there are nevertheless a number of important subsidiary points that require clarification.

15.2 COMMON LAW RIGHTS IN PARTY WALLS

This book is concerned with the new law of party walls, which is to be found in the Act. If it becomes necessary to refer to the extra-statutory common law affecting party walls, as it may in some circumstances,[2] the only convenient source is *Halsbury's Laws* 5th ed, vol (4)1, paras 964–975. It is as well, however, to be aware of the following.

At common law, the expression 'party wall' had no precise meaning. It included four categories of wall:

(a) a wall owned by both owners as tenants in common;
(b) a wall divided into longitudinal halves, one half being owned by each owner;
(c) a wall belonging entirely to one owner, subject to an easement in favour of the other owner, to have it maintained as a dividing wall;
(d) a wall longitudinally divided, each half being subject to an easement of support in favour of the other half.[3]

---

1 *Hansard*, HL Deb, vol 568, cols 1536, 1540 (31 January 1996).
2 For example, it may be necessary for the purposes of compensation to show that a work authorised by the Act could not have been carried out at common law: see **6.6.4** and also **6.4**.
3 See *Watson v Gray* (1880) 14 Ch D 192.

The Law of Property Act 1925, abolished legal tenancies in common, and contained provisions which had the effect of subjecting walls in category (a) to a trust for sale, and moving them into category (d).[4] Thus, at common law the extent to which either owner could carry out work affecting the whole of a party wall without either trespassing upon the other's property, or interfering with his easement, was likely to be severely restricted.

15.3 SECTION 9

The machinery of the Act enables the building owner to carry out work affecting the whole of a party wall, notwithstanding the adjoining owner's rights at common law. But s 9 provides that:

> 'Nothing in this Act shall—
>
> (a) authorise any interference with an easement of light or other easements in or relating to a party wall; or
> (b) prejudicially affect any right of any person to preserve or restore any right or other thing in or connected with a party wall in case of the party wall being pulled down or rebuilt.'

15.3.1 Section 9(a)

This subsection expressly protects an adjoining owner's rights of light, and also his other easements relating to the party wall, of which the most obvious is the easement of support. These rights are considered separately below. What may be noted here is that this provision does not prohibit temporary interference with such rights during the carrying out of works. The works which the Act authorises to be carried out necessarily involve physical interference with the party wall, often removal of support, and sometimes interference with the access of light. The common law rights of the adjoining owner to prevent these invasions are necessarily overridden temporarily, so that the authorised work can be carried out. What this subsection ensures is that the invasion is only temporary, and that the adjoining owner's established easements must continue once the works are complete (see 15.5(a)).

15.3.2 Section 9(b)

It is difficult to attach any sensible meaning to the words 'prejudicially affect any right... to preserve or restore any *right* or other thing in or connected with a party wall'. A right is not a thing: nor is it clear what right there can be to preserve or restore any right in a party wall. The phrase has an intriguing statutory history, which partly illuminates the mystery.

---

4   See s 38 and First Sch, Pt V para 1.

(a) In s 101 of the 1894 Act the wording was 'take away abridge or prejudicially affect any right of any person to preserve or restore any *light* or other thing ...'. In this context, it is clear that 'light' means an aperture to receive light (as in the expression 'leaded lights'), ie a thing.
(b) Section 127 of the 1930 Act dropped the words 'take away abridge or', but made no other change. It retained the word 'light'.
(c) Section 54 of the 1939 Act made no change, except to substitute 'right' for 'light'. The resulting nonsense suggests that this was a simple error.
(d) The Act has unfortunately repeated the error of 1939.

In view of this history, it is considered that the court's power to correct obvious misprints in a statute[5] enables 'right' to be read as 'light'. The subsection then gives the adjoining owner a right to insist on retaining or restoring windows, or other physical features of the wall (eg eaves with an established right of eavesdrop). If the word 'right' has to remain, it may be possible to support the same result by the word 'thing' alone.

15.4 RIGHT TO LIGHT

The right to light is an easement, capable of being acquired by grant or prescription. It is acquired in favour of buildings, and cannot exist in favour of land in its unbuilt state. The basic measure of light to which a building is entitled is that which is sufficient for the ordinary use of the building.[6] The test of an infringement, therefore, is not how much light was taken away by the obstruction in question, but whether sufficient is left for ordinary enjoyment of the dominant premises.

Section 9(a) of the Act specifically protects easements of light. It is clear, therefore, that for example the right to raise a party wall under s 2(2)(l) could not be used so as to interfere with an existing easement of light.[7] The need to protect easements of light may involve the surveyors in difficult questions of law.

(a) It may be doubtful whether there is any easement. If the origin is prescriptive, 20 years' enjoyment provides a starting point, but the law of prescription relating to rights of light is notoriously complex and capricious.[8] Often, rights of light are regulated between neighbours by deeds whose precise legal effect is unclear. They may grant easements, expressly or by implication, but it is quite usual for them to operate only by covenants. Only easements are protected by s 9(a).

---

5   See *R v Wilcock* (1845) 7 QB 317; *Eton College v Minister of Agricultural Fisheries and Food* [1964] Ch 274.
6   *Colls v Home and Colonial Stores Ltd* [1904] AC 179.
7   Giving statutory effect to *Crofts v Haldane* (1867) LR 2 QB 194.
8   See Megarry and Wade *Law of Real Property* (Sweet & Maxwell, 6th edn, 1995).

(b) If there was once an easement, it may be claimed that it has come to an end by, for example, abandonment. This is another difficult question. Even the bricking up of a window may not amount to abandonment of the easement: there must be evidence of an intention to abandon the right permanently.[9]

The surveyors making an award may therefore have to determine difficult questions of law. It is considered that it is within their discretion to take their own legal advice on such questions, and that the costs of such advice will fall within s 10(13).[10]

15.5 RIGHT OF SUPPORT

There is no natural right to the support of a building, but a right may be acquired by grant or prescription.[11] The right can be acquired by 20 years' user as of right. Thus, a building can acquire the right of support from an adjoining building provided such support has been enjoyed for at least 20 years. Where two buildings are in common ownership, and one of them is sold off, the purchaser will normally acquire a right of support under s 62 of the Law of Property Act 1925. It appears that it is not an interference with the right of support to withdraw water from the foundations of the building supported.[12] However, where the demolition of the neighbouring house caused shrinkage to the clay underlying the foundation of the plaintiff's house this was held actionable.[13] Withdrawal of support is only actionable once damage occurs.[14] The recent expansion of the concept of nuisance (see **15.7**) has extended to nuisance by loss of support,[15] but since this is nuisance arising from long neglect, it is unlikely to affect works under the Act.

Work carried out pursuant to s 2 of the Act clearly includes acts which would ordinarily be an interference with rights of support. The execution of such work is expressly authorised by the Act, but liability to make good damage caused by the work is expressly imposed by various provisions of the Act, in particular ss 2(3)(a), (4)(a), (5), (6) and 7(2), and the adjoining owner whose right of support is affected by work carried out under the Act is protected by these provisions. If there is a dispute, an award made under s 10 will make

---

9 Compare *Tapling v Jones* (1865) 11 HLC 290; *News of the World Ltd v Allen Fairhead & Sons Ltd* [1931] 2 Ch 402; *Marine & General Mutual Life Assurance Society v St James' Real Estate Co Ltd* [1991] 2 EGLR 178.
10 See **11.5**.
11 *Dalton v Angus* (1881) 6 App Cas 740.
12 *Langbrook Properties Ltd v Surrey County Council* [1970] 1 WLR 161.
13 *Brace v South East Regional Housing Association Ltd and Another* [1984] 1 EGLR 144, CA.
14 *Midland Bank Plc v Bardgrove Property Services Ltd and John Willmott (WB)* [1992] 65 P & CR 153, CA, considered and followed in *Yorkshire Water Services Ltd v Sun Alliance & London Insurance plc & Others* [1998] EnvLR 204.
15 See *Holbeck Hall Hotel Ltd v Scarborough Borough Council* [2000] QB 836, CA.

provision for the carrying out of such works as are necessary to ensure that the adjoining owner's property is adequately supported. A question arises as to the effect of the work on the right of support. Does the right continue, or does the carrying out of the work, resulting in the adjoining owner's property being supported by a new structure, mean that the previously enjoyed easement comes to an end? What is the effect of s 9(a) here? There are two apparently conflicting authorities to be considered.

(a) In *Selby v Whitbread & Co*,[16] an award authorised the defendant to take down a building, thereby removing support from the flank wall of the plaintiff's building. A second award required the defendant to support the flank wall (validly, it was held) by erecting a substantial pier, but this was not done. The plaintiff sued, inter alia, for wrongful withdrawal of support. McCardie J rejected this claim, holding that the statutory rights superseded the common law right of support, but he nevertheless granted damages for failure to build the pier. Despite the width of the judge's words (at p 752) about the statute 'repealing' the common law, this decision is not inconsistent with the analysis suggested above (see **15.3.1**). The first award authorised the removal of support, and thereby necessarily overrode the existing right of support to that extent. The upholding of the second award demonstrates that the adjoining owner's principal protection lies in securing adequate provision for continuing support in the award. The fact that the pier had not been built meant that no question could arise as to whether the plaintiff had a right of support from it. It is considered that the force of s 9(a) is that he would have had such a right as soon as the pier was built, without having to prescribe for it afresh.

(b) In *Brace v South East Regional Housing Association Limited and Another*,[17] the Court of Appeal held that the plaintiff's existing right of support was not determined by an agreement allowing the defendant to demolish the adjoining house. The conflict with the *Selby* decision, however, is superficial. The agreement, although modelled on an award under the 1939 Act, was not an award, and indeed the Act did not apply. The only relevant question before the court was whether the plaintiff had abandoned her right of support, and as a matter of construction of the agreement it was held that she had not. The decision casts no light on the effect of s 9(a).

15.6 PROTECTION FROM THE WEATHER

In principle there is no easement of protection from the weather, so that a building owner is entitled to remove his neighbouring wall or building notwithstanding that the result is to expose his neighbour's external wall to the

---

16 [1917] 1 KB 736.
17 [1984] 1 EGLR 144.

full blast of the elements.[18] In recent years, however, this principle has been somewhat eroded. Even at common law the building owner may be liable in damages for the removal if it exposes an internal wall for the first time, or an external or any wall to serious wind suction.[19] Under the Act damage of this kind will be the subject of compensation under s 7(2),[20] and ought to be the subject of special precautions in the award. Note also that it has been held that an award can validly impose on the building owner an obligation to maintain a party wall after completion of the works, thereby in effect requiring him to keep the wall weatherproof.[21]

15.7 NEGLIGENCE

The mere undertaking of work authorised by the Act cannot constitute negligence. But the Act does not affect any cause of action for negligence in executing such work. The Act does nothing to relieve the building owner of his duty of care, which is non-delegable.[22] Nor does it authorise work to be carried out carelessly. It is also clear that an owner of a supporting building or land is liable in negligence for his failure to take positive steps to maintain that support.[23]

15.8 NUISANCE

In recent years the law of nuisance has taken substantial strides in imposing liability on landowners for neglect of natural forces which proceed to cause damage to neighbouring land; in such circumstances the concept of a 'measured duty of care' is continuing to develop.[24] This has implications in respect of removal of support and protection from the weather, of which surveyors and building owners will need to be aware. In general, however, liability for neglect of natural forces will be of only peripheral relevance to the positive building works undertaken pursuant to the Act.

The execution of building work may constitute a nuisance to adjoining or nearby occupiers, by the creation of excessive noise, vibration and dust which disturbs the reasonable enjoyment by such occupiers of their premises.

---

18 *Phipps v Pears* [1965] 1 QB 76.
19 *Rees v Skerrett* [2001] 1 WLR 1541, CA.
20 See **6.6.4**.
21 See *Marchant v Capital & Counties Plc* [1983] 2 EGLR 156, a decision reached by the Court of Appeal notwithstanding the earlier decision in *Leadbetter v Marylebone Corporation* [1904] 2 KB 893, CA.
22 See *Hughes v Percival* (1883) 8 App Cas 443, *Jolliffe v Woodhouse* (1894) 10 TLR 553.
23 *Holbeck Hall Hotel Ltd v Scarborough Borough Council* [2000] QB 836, CA.
24 See *Leakey v National Trust* [1980] QB 485, CA; *Holbeck Hall Hotel Ltd v Scarborough Borough Council* [2000] QB 836; *Rees v Skerrett* [2001] 1 WLR 1541, CA.

Liability attaches to the person creating the nuisance, and to his employer, if the act done is one which in its very nature involved a special danger of nuisance.[25] In the case of physical damage to property, all damage is actionable. But no cause of action arises in respect of operations insofar as they cause disturbance through noise, if the works are carried on reasonably and all reasonable and proper steps are taken to ensure that no undue inconvenience is caused to neighbours.[26] How far is a building owner vulnerable to this common law claim?

15.8.1 Adjoining owners and occupiers

The Act authorises works which may constitute an nuisance, which gives rise to the well known question whether it exempts such works from the law of nuisance.[27] A material provision in the Act is s 6(10), which provides that:

> Nothing in this section shall relieve the building owner from any liability to which he would otherwise be subject for injury to any adjoining owner or any adjoining occupier by reason of work executed by him.'[28]

The liabilities referred to here must include liability in nuisance. Thus, the building owner, it seems, remains technically exposed to the possibility of liability in nuisance in respect of work carried out under s 6. But the implication is that work carried out under the enabling sections (1 and 2) *are* protected against liability in nuisance. More persuasive, perhaps, is the point that s 7 expressly prohibits unnecessary inconvenience and makes wide provision for loss and damage caused by any works under the Act to be compensated (see Chapter 6). The criterion of unnecessary inconvenience under s 7(1) is certainly stricter than the nuisance test of unreasonable interference with the enjoyment of land, and there is no reason to suppose that the compensation recoverable for loss or damage under s 7(2) will be less than the damages available at common law. In these circumstances it is considered that for works under ss 1 and 2 liability in nuisance is technically excluded, and that for work under s 6, although not technically excluded, there is no practical scope for such liability.

It is not thought that the passing reference to nuisance by McCardie J in *Selby v Whitbread & Co*[29] seriously undermines the analysis suggested above. After holding that the 1894 Act excluded any common law claim for withdrawal of support, he proceeded:

> 'In so holding I in no way negative the proposition that a plaintiff may bring his action for damages if he can establish that the defendant has exerted his statutory

---

25 *Matania v National Provincial Bank Ltd* [1936] 2 All ER 633, CA.
26 *Andreae v Selfridge & Co Ltd* [1937] 3 All ER 255, CA.
27 See *Allen v Gulf Oil Refining Ltd* [1981] AC 1001.
28 This reproduces s 50(4) of the 1939 Act.
29 [1917] 1 KB 736, at 753.

priviliges so as to inflict injury on the plaintiff by negligence, improper obstructiveness, *avoidable nuisance*, or unreasonable delay ...' [emphasis added]

The long and careful judgment deals with many points, but not the question whether liability in nuisance is technically excluded by the statute. The italicised words appear to be coloured by the statutory concept of unnecessary inconvenience.[30]

15.8.2 Third parties

The foregoing paragraph applies to claims by adjoining owners and adjoining occupiers, who are the only beneficiaries of the provisions of s 7. The Act does nothing to regulate the building owner's relations with third parties, nor to deprive them of any common law rights they may have against him. Anyone not within the definitions of adjoining owner or adjoining occupier will, if work under the Act gives him a claim in nuisance, be entitled to pursue his common law remedy.

15.9 TRESPASS

The Act authorises the carrying out of work that would otherwise constitute a trespass, and further confers express rights of entry (s 8). Insofar as the procedures laid down by the Act are followed, no claim for trespass can arise. However, if entry is desired for purposes not related to work authorised by the Act, recourse must be had to the Access to Neighbouring Land Act 1992.

15.10 BREACH OF STATUTORY DUTY

It has already been suggested (see **9.4.2**) that breach of a term of an award gives rise to a cause of action for breach of statutory duty. It cannot be doubted that the same applies if a building owner (without the consent of the adjoining owner) carries out works covered by the Act without serving the notice required by the Act. All the provisions requiring the service of notice (ss 1(2),(5), 3(1), 6(5)) are mandatory in form; they are passed for the benefit of adjoining owners and occupiers, and the cause of action is necessary to prevent the statute being relegated to the level of a pious aspiration.[31] In the case of works under ss 1 or 2, however, this cause of action is liable to fall out of sight, because there is likely to be a more obvious cause of action in tort, such as trespass.[32] But this does not apply to failure to serve a s 6 notice, since in the normal s 6 case the building owner will be operating only within his own boundaries; there will be no question of trespass, and no demonstrable nuisance, or not until damage by

---

30 See also *Halsbury's Laws*, 5th ed, vol 38, para 561, text and footnote 29.
31 See *Cutler v Wandsworth Stadium Ltd* [1949] AC 398, at 407 per Ld Simonds.
32 See *Louis v Sadiq* [1997] 1 EGLR 136, and other authorities referred to in para 3.1.

withdrawal of support actually occurs.[33] Here therefore the nature of the statutory duty needs to be considered with more care.

15.10.1 Existence of Duty

The *dictum* of Lord Simonds cited above does not provide the sole criterion for finding the existence of a statutory duty. It is also established that the class protected must be a limited class, and the duty must be of a limited and specific nature, rather than a general administrative function.[34] Further, breach of the duty must be calculated to cause loss of a kind for which the law normally awards damages.[35] It is considered that the duty under s 6 clearly passes these further tests: adjoining owners and occupiers are a limited class, the requirement of notice is limited and specific, and the primary damage likely to be suffered is in the nature of nuisance.

15.10.2 Scope of Duty

More problematical is the scope of the duty, and the relief which is available for its breach. Damages for actual withdrawal of support will in any event be recoverable in nuisance, since this cause of action is preserved by s 6(10). But the specific duty is to serve a notice, which must give particulars of the work intended to be carried out below ground level, and these are of considerable practical importance to the adjoining owner. If there is no notice, there will be no award, and he will have no assurance that the work is suitable, or will be carried out to a satisfactory standard. Before the work is completed the adjoining owner must be entitled to an injunction to stop work until the formalities have been complied with. But if the work has actually been completed, the adjoining owner's plight will be worse, because he cannot even investigate what has been done. The breach and the uncertainty it produces are factors which may sound in damages by affecting the value of the adjoining property, but such damage is hard to prove, and is unlikely to provide an adequate remedy. What will be needed is specific relief; at the very least delivery of full particulars of the work done, but also a right to verify the particulars, and to investigate the suitability and quality of the work, if necessary by entry and inspection. It has already been pointed out that specific relief by injunction is available as a remedy for breach of statutory duty (see **9.4.4**). It may be that the arm of equity is long enough to provide the adjoining owner with what he needs.

---

33 See *Midland Bank Ltd v Bardgrove Property Services and John Willmott (WB)* [1992] 65 P & CR 153.
34 See *X and others (Minors) v Bedfordshire County Council* [1995] 2 AC 633.
35 See *Cullen v Chief Constable of the Royal Ulster Constabulary (Northern Ireland)* [2003] 1 WLR 1763, *Pickering v Liverpool Daily Post and Echo Newspapers Plc and others* [1991] 2 AC 370.

15.11 ACCESS TO NEIGHBOURING LAND ACT 1992 ('THE 1992 ACT')

The 1992 Act was passed to remedy the impasse which arises where a building stands on or close to a boundary, and it becomes necessary to carry out work to the building that cannot be carried out without access to the neighbouring land, permission for which is refused.

The 1992 Act enables the court to make an 'access order' if and only if it is satisfied:

(a) that works to land are reasonably necessary for the preservation of the whole or any part of the dominant land (ie the building owner's land, to use the 1996 Act's terminology); and
(b) that they cannot be carried out, or would be substantially more difficult to carry out, without the entry upon the servient land (ie the adjoining owner's land).[36]

Certain works ('basic preservation works') are automatically considered to be reasonably necessary for the preservation of the land. The basic preservation works are:

(a) maintenance, repair or renewal of any part of a building or other structure comprised in or situate on the dominant land;
(b) the clearance, repair or renewal of any drain, sewer, pipe or cable so comprised or situate;
(c) the treatment, cutting back, felling, removal or replacement of any hedge, tree, shrub or other growing thing which is so comprised and which is or is in danger of becoming damaged, diseased, dangerous, insecurely rooted, or dead;
(d) the filling in, or clearance, of any ditch so comprised.[37]

Section 2 of the 1992 Act enables the court to settle the terms of an access order, including terms for regulating the time and manner of execution of the work, and provision for compensation for loss suffered by the owner of the servient land. The access order may also (s 2(5)) require the applicant to pay the respondent a sum for the privilege of entering the servient land, calculated by reference to the financial advantage of the order to the applicant and connected persons, and the degree of inconvenience likely to be caused to the respondent or other person by the entry. This, however, does not apply where the application relates to residential land.

As has been seen (**15.1**), it was claimed during the passage of the Bill that the provisions of the Act dovetail with the 1992 Act. The first reported case under

---

36 See s 1(2).
37 See s 1 (4).

the 1992 Act has shown this claim to be mistaken. In *Dean v Walker*[38] the applicant needed to repoint a free-standing external wall which marked the boundary with his neighbour's property. His application under the 1992 Act was resisted on the ground that that Act applied only to works to the dominant land,[39] and that either the whole wall, or at least the neighbour's side of it, was part of the servient land. The Court of Appeal held that the 1992 Act's reference to works 'to land' was not confined to the dominant land, but applied to any building, by force of the definition in the Interpretation Act 1978 (Sch 1). It was therefore unnecessary to determine the ownership of the wall, which was assumed to be severed vertically. There was no question there of the Act applying, because the land was outside London, and the Act was not yet in force. But the decision demonstrates that there is now an overlap between the two Acts. The wall was assumed to be a party fence wall (see **2.3**), so that today the 1992 Act would be neither necessary nor sufficient for the building owner's purpose. An order under the 1992 Act cannot override the compulsory requirements of the 1996 Act, and conversely an award under the 1996 Act carries rights of entry which afford access without any need for an order under the 1992 Act. Thus the result of the overlap is that within the overlapping area (ie wherever the works which are needed fall within the 1996 Act), the 1992 Act is a dead letter. This must seriously restrict the scope and usefulness of the 1992 Act, contrary to what was said in Parliament.

There may nevertheless be circumstances in which the building owner will need to invoke the 1992 Act as well as the 1996 Act. These will occur where he needs access for work of repair or maintenance to his own property which do not fall within the Act. An award under the Act cannot authorise entry for the purpose of works which are not carried out pursuant to the Act (see **7.2(d)**).

15.12 OTHER STATUTORY REQUIREMENTS

An award cannot authorise works which infringe a statute, nor dispense with any need for statutory consent (s 7(5)(a)). For example, it could not require that building work be carried out without complying with appropriate safety requirements, or using materials not permitted by the building regulations. Difficulties may, however, sometimes arise where it appears to the surveyors desirable that the work proposed by the building owner be carried out in a modified way for technical reasons, where this may necessitate a further application for planning permission or listed building consent, or relaxation of building regulations, under the powers conferred by the Building Act 1984 on local authorities. There is nothing in the Act to pevent the surveyors awarding works which will require planning permission, or any other statutory consent,

---

38 (1996) 73 P&CR 366, CA. This case is notable also for the invention of the novel category of 'party and party wall' in the judgment of–Wall J.
39 This view was adopted in the 1st edn of this book (**15.10**).

and even if there is some existing permission or consent, their discretion cannot be restricted to awarding works which fall within its terms. Other things being equal, they will no doubt wish to avoid putting the building owner to additional delay and expense, but such a consideration is merely one among many, and should not be treated as carrying decisive weight.

Nothing in the Act affects the need for planning permission and (where appropriate) listed building consent under the Town and Country Planning Act 1990 and the Planning (Listed Buildings and Conservation Areas) Act 1990. Nor does the Act affect the requirements of building regulations or the regulations concerning work on construction sites.

15.13 HUMAN RIGHTS ACT 1988

15.13.1 General

The Human Rights Act 1998[40] ('the 1998 Act') incorporates into domestic law most of the provisions of the European Convention for the Protection of Human Rights and Fundamental Freedoms agreed by the Council of Europe at Rome on 4 November 1950 ('the Convention'). Section 3 of the 1998 Act requires legislation to be interpreted and given effect to so far as possible in a way compatible with the Convention. Section 6 prohibits public authorities acting in a way incompatible with a Convention right, unless required so to act by primary legislation, or where the authority is acting to give effect to, or enforce, provisions of, or made under primary legislation which cannot be read or given effect to in a way which is compatible with the Convention rights. A public authority, by s 6(3) includes a court or tribunal.

15.13.2 Relevant provisions of the Convention

The 1998 Act incorporates the Convention in Schedule 1. Part 1 of Schedule 1 contains the Convention and Part 2 contains the First Protocol. The Convention and Protocol are divided into Articles, each of which embodies a separate right.

Article 8 of the Convention provides that everyone has the right to respect for his private and family life, home and correspondence. This must not be interfered with except in accordance with law and to the extent necessary in a democratic society in the interests of national security, public safety or the economic well-being of the country.

Article 1 of the First Protocol provides that every person is entitled to the peaceful enjoyment of his possessions. No one shall be deprived of his possessions except in the public interest and subject to the conditions provided for by law and by the general principles of international law.

---

40   1998 C 42.

These are the Convention rights most likely to arise for consideration in connection with the Act. Their possible impact will be examined separately.

15.13.3 Article 8

The operation of the provisions of ss 2 and 6 of the Act can evidently involve interference with home and family life, since work to a party wall or in excavation or underpinning is potentially disruptive in terms of noise, dust, vibration etc.[41] The persons whose right would be in issue would be the adjoining owner and adjoining occupiers. They have no choice but to submit to the activities of the building owner, subject in the case of the adjoining owner to the provisions of an award under s 10.

Two questions arise. Firstly, whether the whole scheme of the Act is incompatible with Article 8: secondly, whether circumstances could arise in which a particular exercise of the powers under these provisions could involve a breach of the Article.

On the first point it is thought that the relevant provisions of the Act can be read in a way which does not clash with the Article 8 right. It is submitted that the following factors are relevant:

(i) The circumstances in which interference can occur are in practice limited.
(ii) The rights of the building owner are closely defined and circumscribed.
(iii) Compensation is payable on exercise of those rights.
(iv) In the case of an adjoining owner, he must be notified of the works proposed and is entitled to an award from an independent surveyor or tribunal of surveyors.
(v) The interference is transitory, lasting only as long as the works in question.
(vi) The provisions are justified on the basis of economic well-being, and are proportionate.

On the second point, it is in practice unlikely that the position of an adjoining owner under the Act would ever give rise to a claim that Article 8 was engaged by the exercise of the rights under ss 2 or 6. Occupiers might be in a different position, since they have no right to participate in the procedure. Building owners need to ensure that such occupiers are not subject to noise, pollution or discomfort to an unreasonable extent by exercise of their rights under the Act.

The rights of entry under s 8 give rise to the possibility of fairly radical physical intrusion into a person's home without any procedural safeguards, such as a warrant. Nevertheless it is thought that the provisions would not be held incompatible with Article 8, given that:

(i) they are of long standing;

---

41 It is well established that noise and pollution may infringe Article 8: *Lopes-Ostra v Spain* (1994) 20 EHRR 277, *S v France* App. No 13728/88 65 DR 250, *Baggs v United Kingdom* App. No 9310/81 52 DR 29.

(ii) they facilitate the rapid resolution of party wall disputes, a desirable objective;

(iii) they are purely facultative, and thus do not require to be exercised in any particular way, or at all.

In *Wilson v First County Trust Limited*[42] the House of Lords emphasised that the fact that a statutory provision may have harsh consequences in a particular case, will not in itself result in it being declared incompatible with a Convention right. The provision must be read in context, and the question is whether the overall package of measures is a proportionate response by Parliament to the problem in question.

An over-zealous exercise of the powers in s 8 might nevertheless in a particular case breach Article 8. It is not entirely clear what practical effect this would have on the resolution of the dispute, since under the 1998 Act, ss 7–9 the rights of the victim lie against public authorities, not private individuals. It is thought unlikely that surveyors appointed under s 10 of the Party Wall etc Act would be held to be a public authority. They are appointed purely to decide a private dispute. Hence there would be no free-standing claim against them under the 1988 Act. The general remedy of the aggrieved party lies against the state, for damages or a declaration as appropriate.[43] However, it might be possible to persuade a court to refuse to enforce exercise of s 8 rights of entry by injunction, on the ground that to grant such an injunction would involve the court acting incompatibly with Article 8.

15.13.4 Article 1 of the First Protocol

Works under the Act may involve interference with possessions. However, the scheme of the Act almost certainly complies with Article 1 of the first protocol, given the various safeguards already referred to, in particular the short duration of the interferences allowed, and the provisions for compensation.[44] In addition, the Act has as its aim public benefit, a concept which extends to facilitating transfer of rights in private property for example.[45]

---

42 [2003] UKHL 40.
43 Compare *South Bucks District Council v Porter* [2003] 3 All ER 1 HL.
44 *Stran Refineries v Greece* (1995) 19 EHRR 293, *Matos e Silva v Portugal* (1996) 24 EHRR 573.
45 *James v United Kingdom* (1986) 8 EHRR 123.

Chapter 16

CRIMINAL OFFENCES

16.1 SECTION 16(1): REFUSAL OF ENTRY

Section 16 of the Act creates two criminal offences. First, under s 16(1), if an occupier of land or premises refuses to permit a person to do anything which he is entitled to do with regard to the land or premises under s 8(1) or (5), he commits an offence. Section 8(1) is the provision which entitles a building owner to enter and remain on any land or premises for the purpose of executing any work in pursuance of the Act. Section 8(5) is the provision entitling a surveyor appointed or selected under s 10 of the Act to enter or remain on any land or premises for the purpose of carrying out the object for which he is appointed or selected.

16.2 VICARIOUS LIABILITY

The offence can only be committed by an occupier. The occupier can be vicariously liable for acts committed by his servants or agents, and, indeed, if the occupier is a corporation, it can only act through its servants or agents. The principles of criminal liability of corporations for the acts of their servants or agents are well established.

The act or default of a subordinate employee who is not part of the controlling mind or will of the corporation will not make the corporation liable (unless the subordinate employee is following instructions given by the controlling mind or will).[1] It follows that a corporate occupier will only be liable to conviction if the refusal emanates either from those who control the mind and will of the corporation, such as directors, or from subordinate employees acting on their instructions.

It is an essential ingredient of the offence under s 16(1) that the occupier knows or has reasonable cause to believe that the person concerned is entitled to enter the land or carry out the work (s 16(1)(b)). In the case of a corporation the relevant knowledge or reasonable cause to believe will be that of a servant or agent. The guilty mind of a director or manager would render the corporation itself guilty, but not necessarily that of a subordinate employee who is not in a managerial position.[2]

---

1 *Tesco Supermarkets Ltd v Nattrass* [1971] 2 All ER 127, HL; *R v British Steel Plc* [1995] 1 WLR 1356, CA.
2 See *Director of Public Prosecutions v Kent & Sussex Contractors Ltd* [1944] 1 All ER 119; *R v ICR Haulage* [1944] 1 All ER 691; *John Henshall Quarries v Harvey* [1965] 1 All ER 725.

16.3 REFUSAL

The offence involves a refusal to permit entry etc. What amounts to refusal will be a question of fact. It is considered that the following circumstances, (among others) will not amount to refusal.

(a) Where a person is excluded only for sufficient time to verify his identity and business. It is submitted that it is incumbent on the person requiring entry to demonstrate to the occupier that he has a prima facie right to do so, and until this is done there is no refusal.[3] It follows that it would be prudent for persons seeking to exercise their rights to make an appointment with the occupier and to establish their credentials and to agree times for subsequent visits.
(b) Where the person seeking admittance is kept waiting for a short period.
(c) Where the occupier remonstrates with the person seeking admittance, but without refusing entry.[4]
(d) Where the occupier simply fails to make access available, for example because no-one is at the premises when the person seeking entry calls. Mere inaction or failure to give entry is not the same as refusal.[5]

16.4 REASONABLE CAUSE

The words 'has reasonable cause to believe' clearly involve something less than knowledge. Probably, the words are intended to import the idea of the occupier being in possession of information from which a reasonable person in his position would believe that the person is so entitled. The test is no doubt objective: does the occupier have material which viewed objectively would give a reasonable person grounds for believing that the person claiming entry was entitled to that right? For this reason, a notice of entry under s 8 should explicitly state the entitlement of the person entering.[6]

16.5 ENTRY PURSUANT TO THE ACT

The offence is only committed where rights of entry pursuant to the Act are being exercised. If, therefore, the statutory procedures have not been followed, or a purported award is a nullity, refusal to permit entry would not constitute an offence, because no rights under the Act will have been conferred. For example, the exclusion of a surveyor attempting to exercise rights under s 8(5) will not give rise to an offence if he has not been properly appointed under s 10.

---

3   Compare *Duncan v Dowding* [1897] 1 QB 575.
4   Compare *Caswell v Worcestershire Justices* (1889) 53 JP 820.
5   Compare *Lowson v Percy Main & District Social Club and Institute* [1979] ICR 568.
6   See Appendix 4, Precedent 7.

16.6 OCCUPIERS

The term 'occupier' is not defined by the Act, although s 20 defines 'adjoining occupier', without defining occupation. It is not thought that any useful inference can be derived from the definition of 'owner', nor from extraneous fields such as rating.[7]

There appears to be no reason to exclude any person who maintains sufficient presence on the land to enable him to frustrate the statutory right of entry. It is considered that the offence can be committed not only by owner-occupiers and tenants, but also by licensees and even squatters.

16.7 SECTION 16(2): HINDERING ENTRY

Section 16(2) of the Act creates an offence of hindering or obstructing a person exercising rights under s 8(1) or (5). It is not provided that the acts complained of must amount to physical restraint, and it seems that verbal abuse or other intimidation could be sufficient to constitute the offence. It is, however, considered that the acts complained of must be accompanied by the necessary criminal intent. Although s 16(2) does not use the word 'intentionally',[8] it is well established that, in general, proof of *mens rea* is required for a criminal offence. Accordingly, acts done without an intention to hinder or obstruct will not constitute an offence, even if they in fact have that effect.

It is further considered that mere inaction will not constitute the offence. If, for example, access to the premises can only be gained in a dangerous and difficult way, the occupier will not be liable for failing to make the access safe.[9]

16.8 PROCEDURE

The offences created by s 16 are summary offences, and can only be tried in the magistrates' court. They cannot be the subject of imprisonment. The reference to a fine of level 3 on the standard scale is to the scale fixed pursuant to s 37 of the Criminal Justice Act 1982 as amended by s 17 of the Criminal Justice Act 1991.

Both offences are of a continuing nature for the purposes of the 6-month time-limit for laying informations under the Magistrates' Court Act 1980, s 127.[10]

---

7 But see *Northern Ireland Commissioner of Valuation v Fermanagh Protestant Board of Education* [1969] 3 All ER 352; *Trustees of Methodist Schools v O'Leary* (1993) 25 HLR 364.
8 Contrast, for example, the Banking Act 1987, s 40(3).
9 Compare *R v Ahmad (Zafar)* (1987) 84 Cr App R 64, CA, (1986) 18 HLR 416.
10 Compare *Camden London Borough Council v Marshall* [1996] EGCS 104.

Chapter 17
REFORM

17.1 INTRODUCTION

It would be impossible for any commentator, however indulgently disposed, to regard the Act as a satisfactory piece of modern legislation. It poses many technical questions, as earlier chapters have shown, and although it has not yet given rise to much in the way of reported litigation, it would be complacent to imagine that this position will continue indefinitely, now that its scope is countrywide. A review of the Act is being conducted by the Office of the Deputy Prime Minister, and in addition concerns have been expressed by interested professionals.

17.2 ODPM REVIEW

It is understood that the principal concerns which have been raised are as follows.

17.2.1 Summary procedures

No summary procedure is provided to enable an adjoining owner to restrain a building owner who fails to observe the formalities required by the Act. The normal remedy of injunction is, of course, available, but it is thought that a significant body of aggrieved householders are deterred from going to law by the expense and risks involved. The reintroduction of direct criminal liability[1] is thought to be inappropriate. Another suggestion is to give local authorities power to interfere by some form of notice procedure, like for example the procedure for dangerous structures.

17.2.2 Section 7(2)

Another suggestion is that s 7(2) is too sweeping, and that compensation should revert to the piecemeal provisions of the 1939 Act, thus putting the clock back to *Adams v Marylebone BC*.[2] The authors see no justification for this retrograde step. The Act enlarges the building owner's common law rights and enables him to compel the adjoining owner, however unwilling, to submit to his wishes (subject to the control of the surveyors). If this process causes loss to the adjoining owner it is only right that the building owner should compensate him for it. Further, the removal of compensation would raise questions under the Human Rights Act (see **15.13**). The *Adams* decision, though understandable in

---

1　As formerly under the 1939 Act, s 148.
2　[1907] 2 KB 822.

its day, is out of tune with modern concepts of property rights, and s 7(2) is one of the few unequivocal benefits introduced by the Act.

17.2.3 Deemed dispute

The question is raised whether the Act's policy of deeming a dispute to arise in default of any response by the adjoining owner should be reversed. The view of the authors is that it should not. The law of contract has set its face against the creation of rights and liabilities through silence, and long usage has hallowed the same approach in the area of party walls. To reverse the presumption would tend to bring the Act into disrepute by imposing unforeseen intrusions. After all, what the Act provides is an arm's length procedure; in most cases good neighbours are able to proceed with active consent, and without resorting to the Act.

17.2.4 Small works

More meritorious is the suggestion that the Act might be disapplied or modified in relation to small works. But there is an obvious difficulty over defining what is meant by small. The following categories have been put forward:

(a) extensions not exceeding 10% of gross floor area, up to a fixed limit;
(b) works not requiring planning consent;
(c) single-storey conversions of existing roof structures.

These are selective and arbitrary, and it is not easy to suggest anything more convincing. Cost or value would provide a universally applicable yardstick, but it would be difficult to name the limit.

If small works could be defined, they would not necessarily have to be taken outside the Act. Another suggestion is that they could be put under the jurisdiction of a single surveyor. This would require a new procedure for appointing the surveyor; in default of agreement between the parties, some independent appointor would have to be found.

17.3 PYRAMUS AND THISBE CLUB

This is an active organisation[3] with a countrywide membership drawn from surveyors interested in party walls. Its working party has put forward the following detailed amendments, to cure perceived shortcomings in the Act. These proposals are currently being considered by the ODPM.

(a) Section 1(5): change 'on' the line of junction to 'at'.[4]

---

3 Founded by the late John Anstey, the principal promoter of the Act, who was a surveyor with a wide practice in party walls.
4 The authors disagree: see **3.2.1** and **3.4**.

(b) New s 1(9): to add the s 3(1) requirements to notices under s 1.
(c) Section 2(2)(f): to be extended to party fence walls.
(d) Section 2(2)(j): to be extended to permit flashing over an adjoining owner's wall at a lower level.
(e) Section 2(3)(a), (4)(a), (5): 'finishings' to be restored in place of 'furnishings'.[5]
(f) Section 3(3)(a): omit 'and of the adjoining occupiers'.[6]
(g) Section 4(1)(a): to extend the counter-notice procedure to cover the raising of party walls, underpinning and foundations, where the adjoining owner requires them (thus imposing the cost on him by virtue of s 11(9)).
(h) Section 6: subsections to be reordered more logically; further particulars to be required in notices; underpinning to be subject to counter-notice procedure (again throwing the cost on the adjoining owner).
(i) Section 8(2): to be extended to apply where the adjoining owner or occupier is obstructing access.[7]
(j) Section 9(a): add 'permanent' before 'interference' and 'or land of the adjoining owner' after 'party wall'.[8]
(k) Section 11(5): to be extended to apply also to expenses incurred under s 2(2)(c) and (d).[9]
(l) Section 12(2)(b): to be removed, since it has no clear rationale.[10]
(m) Section 20: Here several modifications are proposed:
- in 'appointing officer' change 'appointments' to 'selections';[11]
- in 'building owner' change 'exercising rights under this Act' to 'carrying out works in pursuance of this Act' (in order to embrace s 6, which limits rights rather than granting them);
- 'building owner' to be extended to accommodate local authorities carrying out works under statutory default powers;
- 'owner' to exclude licensees, in (b) to add 'lawful' before 'possession', and to clarify the position of option holders.

---

5 See **3.7(a)(i), 3.7(e)**.
6 The authors disagree: see **3.8.3**.
7 Although this will be an offence under s 16(2) if proper steps have been taken to bring the right of entry to the occupier's notice.
8 The object of clarifying the section, and extending it to prohibit interference with rights of way is sensible, so far as it goes, but the proposed wording is not considered appropriate.
9 The authors disagree. Section 11(5) addresses costs occasioned by disrepair. The additional sections are concerned with disconformity with statute, which may have nothing to do with disrepair: if there is also disrepair, s 2(2)(b) can be used, and s 11(5) will apply.
10 The author's view is that this right, if it is to remain at all, should be expressly limited to cases where the adjoining owner has some prospective liability for expenses; see **12.6.2**.
11 The author's agree: see **8.4(a)**.

17.4 AUTHORS' VIEWS

A comment prompted by the points mentioned in the last two paragraphs is that they are somewhat one-sided. They appear to be directed more to easing the position of the building owner than to protecting adjoining owners and occupiers against unwelcome intrusion. It must remain the policy of the Act to strike a fair balance between these two objectives, and proposals for reform must not lose sight of this policy.

There is no doubt that the Act is full of unnecessary infelicities, inconsistencies, misconceptions and plain errors, many of which have been noticed in the last two paragraphs. Some have been taken uncritically from the 1939 Act, others have been misguidedly introduced for the first time. A list of those which are most obvious, and most amenable to simple verbal amendment, can be found in Appendix 6.

Most intractable are the areas where there is conceptual inaccuracy or imprecision. These are inherited from the past legislation, and have survived because London surveyors had grown used to them, and managed to work round them in their own ways. But what was accepted in London should not be regarded as adequate for countrywide legislation. The difficulties are real, and for the most part are not amenable to simple verbal correction. In these areas there is no substitute for hard thought and radical surgery, without which recourse to the courts will become inevitable. The principal areas identified in this book are as follows.

(a) The inherent contradiction in s 1: see **3.2.1**.
(b) Uncertainties over the degree to which consent can authorise the Act's procedures to be dispensed with, a question approached only by ss 3(3)(a) and 7(4) and (5): see **3.8.3, 5.7**.
(c) Doubts over the effects of the formulae and concepts restricting adjacent excavation and construction (s 6), and their adequacy in modern circumstances: see Chapter 6.
(d) Doubts over the scope and relationship of the compensation provisions: see Chapter 6.
(e) The questionable policy of singling out s 2(2)(e) for special treatment in s 11(6), when other subsections of s 2(2) seem to be equally deserving: see **6.5.2**.
(f) Doubts over the extent of the surveyors' jurisdiction, and how far it is exclusive: see **6.8, 9.5**.
(g) Doubts over the standing of the surveyors: see **8.19, 8.20**.
(h) The questionable policy of tit-for-tat security in favour of the building owner: see **12.6.2**.
(i) The questionable policy of imposing penalties on the adjoining owner for silence, even in exceptional cases (ss 12(2) and 13(2)): see **12.8.1, 13.9**.
(j) The difficulties posed by the various contingent liabilities: see **5.8.2, 14.10**.

(k) The complete failure of the Act to address the difficulties affecting successors in title, and generally to relate to modern conveyancing machinery: see Chapter 14, especially **14.15**.
(l) The unintended overlap with the Access to Neighbouring Land Act 1992 (see **15.11**); and uncertainties about the Act's relationship with some other areas of law: see Chapter 15.
(m) Doubts whether the Act does enough to protect the adjoining occupier (as opposed to owner), who has no access to the s 10 procedure, see **3.5**, **3.8.3**.

These are all matters which require serious attention from interested bodies.

Appendix 1

PARTY WALL ETC ACT 1996

(1996 c 40)

ARRANGEMENT OF SECTIONS

Construction and repair of walls on line of junction

Section		Page
1	New building on line of junction	152
2	Repair etc. of party wall: rights of owner	153
3	Party structure notices	155
4	Counter notices	156
5	Disputes arising under sections 3 and 4	157

Adjacent excavation and construction

6	Adjacent excavation and construction	157

Rights etc.

7	Compensation etc.	158
8	Rights of entry	159
9	Easements	160

Resolution of disputes

10	Resolution of disputes	160

Expenses

11	Expenses	163
12	Security for expenses	164
13	Account for work carried out	165
14	Settlement of account	166

Miscellaneous

15	Service of notices etc	166
16	Offences	166
17	Recovery of sums	167
18	Exception in case of Temples etc	167

19 The Crown	167
20 Interpretation	167
21 Other statutory provisions	168

General

22 Short title, commencement and extent	169

An Act to make provision in respect of party walls, and excavation and construction in proximity to certain buildings or structures; and for connected purposes.

[18th July 1996]

Construction and repair of walls on line of junction

1   New building on line of junction

(1) This section shall have effect where lands of different owners adjoin and—

- (a) are not built on at the line of junction; or
- (b) are built on at the line of junction only to the extent of a boundary wall (not being a party fence wall or the external wall of a building),

and either owner is about to build on any part of the line of junction.

(2) If a building owner desires to build a party wall or party fence wall on the line of junction he shall, at least one month before he intends the building work to start, serve on any adjoining owner a notice which indicates his desire to build and describes the intended wall.

(3) If, having been served with notice described in subsection (2), an adjoining owner serves on the building owner a notice indicating his consent to the building of a party wall or party fence wall—

- (a) the wall shall be built half on the land of each of the two owners or in such other position as may be agreed between the two owners; and
- (b) the expense of building the wall shall be from time to time defrayed by the two owners in such proportion as has regard to the use made or to be made of the wall by each of them and to the cost of labour and materials prevailing at the time when that use is made by each owner respectively.

(4) If, having been served with notice described in subsection (2), an adjoining owner does not consent under this subsection to the building of a party wall or party fence wall, the building owner may only build the wall—

- (a) at his own expense; and
- (b) as an external wall or a fence wall, as the case may be, placed wholly on his own land,

and consent under this subsection is consent by a notice served within the period of fourteen days beginning with the day on which the notice described in subsection (2) is served.

(5) If the building owner desires to build on the line of junction a wall placed wholly on his own land he shall, at least one month before he intends the building work to start, serve on any adjoining owner a notice which indicates his desire to build and describes the intended wall.

(6) Where the building owner builds a wall wholly on his own land in accordance with subsection (4) or (5) he shall have the right, at any time in the period which—

(a) begins one month after the day on which the notice mentioned in the subsection concerned was served, and
(b) ends twelve months after that day,

to place below the level of the land of the adjoining owner such projecting footings and foundations as are necessary for the construction of the wall.

(7) Where the building owner builds a wall wholly on his own land in accordance with subsection (4) or (5) he shall do so at his own expense and shall compensate any adjoining owner and any adjoining occupier for any damage to his property occasioned by—

(a) the building of the wall;
(b) the placing of any footings or foundations placed in accordance with subsection (6).

(8) Where any dispute arises under this section between the building owner and any adjoining owner or occupier it is to be determined in accordance with section 10.

Commentary in text—paragraphs **3.2–3.5**.

2 Repair etc. of party wall: rights of owner

(1) This section applies where lands of different owners adjoin and at the line of junction the said lands are built on or a boundary wall, being a party fence wall or the external wall of a building, has been erected.

(2) A building owner shall have the following rights—

(a) to underpin, thicken or raise a party structure, a party fence wall, or an external wall which belongs to the building owner and is built against a party structure or party fence wall;
(b) to make good, repair, or demolish and rebuild, a party structure or party fence wall in a case where such work is necessary on account of defect or want of repair of the structure or wall;
(c) to demolish a partition which separates buildings belonging to different owners but does not conform with statutory requirements and to build instead a party wall which does so conform;

(d) in the case of buildings connected by arches or structures over public ways or over passages belonging to other persons, to demolish the whole or part of such buildings, arches or structures which do not conform with statutory requirements and to rebuild them so that they do so conform;

(e) to demolish a party structure which is of insufficient strength or height for the purposes of any intended building of the building owner and to rebuild it of sufficient strength or height for the said purposes (including rebuilding to a lesser height or thickness where the rebuilt structure is of sufficient strength and height for the purposes of any adjoining owner);

(f) to cut into a party structure for any purpose (which may be or include the purpose of inserting a damp proof course);

(g) to cut away from a party wall, party fence wall, external wall or boundary wall any footing or any projecting chimney breast, jamb or flue, or other projection on or over the land of the building owner in order to erect, raise or underpin any such wall or for any other purpose;

(h) to cut away or demolish parts of any wall or building of an adjoining owner overhanging the land of the building owner or overhanging a party wall, to the extent that it is necessary to cut away or demolish the parts to enable a vertical wall to be erected or raised against the wall or building of the adjoining owner;

(j) to cut into the wall of an adjoining owner's building in order to insert a flashing or other weather-proofing of a wall erected against that wall;

(k) to execute any other necessary works incidental to the connection of a party structure with the premises adjoining it;

(l) to raise a party fence wall, or to raise such a wall for use as a party wall, and to demolish a party fence wall and rebuild it as a party fence wall or as a party wall;

(m) subject to the provisions of section 11(7), to reduce, or to demolish and rebuild, a party wall or party fence wall to—

   (i) a height of not less than two metres where the wall is not used by an adjoining owner to any greater extent than a boundary wall; or
   (ii) a height currently enclosed upon by the building of an adjoining owner;

(n) to expose a party wall or party structure hitherto enclosed subject to providing adequate weathering.

(3) Where work mentioned in paragraph (a) of subsection (2) is not necessary on account of defect or want of repair of the structure or wall concerned, the right falling within that paragraph is exercisable—

(a) subject to making good all damage occasioned by the work to the adjoining premises or to their internal furnishings and decorations; and

(b) where the work is to a party structure or external wall, subject to carrying any relevant flues and chimney stacks up to such a height and in such materials as may be agreed between the building owner and the adjoining owner concerned or, in the event of dispute, determined in accordance with section 10;

and relevant flues and chimney stacks are those which belong to an adjoining owner and either form part of or rest on or against the party structure or external wall.

(4) The right falling within subsection (2)(e) is exercisable subject to—

(a) making good all damage occasioned by the work to the adjoining premises or to their internal furnishings and decorations; and
(b) carrying any relevant flues and chimney stacks up to such a height and in such materials as may be agreed between the building owner and the adjoining owner concerned or, in the event of dispute, determined in accordance with section 10;

and relevant flues and chimney stacks are those which belong to an adjoining owner and either form part of or rest on or against the party structure.

(5) Any right falling within subsection (2)(f), (g) or (h) is exercisable subject to making good all damage occasioned by the work to the adjoining premises or to their internal furnishings and decorations.

(6) The right falling within subsection (2)(j) is exercisable subject to making good all damage occasioned by the work to the wall of the adjoining owner's building.

(7) The right falling within subsection (2)(m) is exercisable subject to—

(a) reconstructing any parapet or replacing an existing parapet with another one; or
(b) constructing a parapet where one is needed but did not exist before.

(8) For the purposes of this section a building or structure which was erected before the day on which this Act was passed shall be deemed to conform with statutory requirements if it conforms with the statutes regulating buildings or structures on the date on which it was erected.

Commentary in text—paragraphs 3.6–3.7.

3 Party structure notices

(1) Before exercising any right conferred on him by section 2 a building owner shall serve on any adjoining owner a notice (in this Act referred to as a 'party structure notice') stating—

(a) the name and address of the building owner;

- (b) the nature and particulars of the proposed work including, in cases where the building owner proposes to construct special foundations, plans, sections and details of construction of the special foundations together with reasonable particulars of the loads to be carried thereby; and
- (c) the date on which the proposed work will begin.

(2) A party structure notice shall—

- (a) be served at least two months before the date on which the proposed work will begin;
- (b) cease to have effect if the work to which it relates—
  - (i) has not begun within the period of twelve months beginning with the day on which the notice is served; and
  - (ii) is not prosecuted with due diligence.

(3) Nothing in this section shall—

- (a) prevent a building owner from exercising with the consent in writing of the adjoining owners and of the adjoining occupiers any right conferred on him by section 2; or
- (b) require a building owner to serve any party structure notice before complying with any notice served under any statutory provisions relating to dangerous or neglected structures.

Commentary in text—paragraph **3.8**.

4 Counter notices

(1) An adjoining owner may, having been served with a party structure notice serve on the building owner a notice (in this Act referred to as a 'counter notice') setting out—

- (a) in respect of a party fence wall or party structure, a requirement that the building owner build in or on the wall or structure to which the notice relates such chimney copings, breasts, jambs or flues, or such piers or recesses or other like works, as may reasonably be required for the convenience of the adjoining owner;
- (b) in respect of special foundations to which the adjoining owner consents under section 7(4) below, a requirement that the special foundations—
  - (i) be placed at a specified greater depth than that proposed by the building owner; or
  - (ii) be constructed of sufficient strength to bear the load to be carried by columns of any intended building of the adjoining owner,

  or both.

(2) A counter notice shall—

- (a) specify the works required by the notice to be executed and shall be accompanied by plans, sections and particulars of such works; and

(b) be served within the period of one month beginning with the day on which the party structure notice is served.

(3) A building owner on whom a counter notice has been served shall comply with the requirements of the counter notice unless the execution of the works required by the counter notice would—

(a) be injurious to him;
(b) cause unnecessary inconvenience to him; or
(c) cause unnecessary delay in the execution of the works pursuant to the party structure notice.

Commentary in text—paragraph **3.9**.

5 Disputes arising under sections 3 and 4

If an owner on whom a party structure notice or a counter notice has been served does not serve a notice indicating his consent to it within the period of fourteen days beginning with the day on which the party structure notice or counter notice was served, he shall be deemed to have dissented from the notice and a dispute shall be deemed to have arisen between the parties.

Commentary in text—paragraph **3.10**.

Adjacent excavation and construction

6 Adjacent excavation and construction

(1) This section applies where—

(a) a building owner proposes to excavate, or excavate for and erect a building or structure, within a distance of three metres measured horizontally from any part of a building or structure of an adjoining owner; and
(b) any part of the proposed excavation, building or structure will within those three metres extend to a lower level than the level of the bottom of the foundations of the building or structure of the adjoining owner.

(2) This section also applies where—

(a) a building owner proposes to excavate, or excavate for and erect a building or structure, within a distance of six metres measured horizontally from any part of a building or structure of an adjoining owner; and
(b) any part of the proposed excavation, building or structure will within those six metres meet a plane drawn downwards in the direction of the excavation, building or structure of the building owner at an angle of forty-five degrees to the horizontal from the line formed by the intersection of the plane of the level of the bottom of the foundations of the building or structure of the adjoining owner with the plane of the external face of the external wall of the building or structure of the adjoining owner.

(3) The building owner may, and if required by the adjoining owner shall, at his own expense underpin or otherwise strengthen or safeguard the foundations of the building or structure of the adjoining owner so far as may be necessary.

(4) Where the buildings or structures of different owners are within the respective distances mentioned in subsections (1) and (2) the owners of those buildings or structures shall be deemed to be adjoining owners for the purposes of this section.

(5) In any case where this section applies the building owner shall, at least one month before beginning to excavate, or excavate for and erect a building or structure, serve on the adjoining owner a notice indicating his proposals and stating whether he proposes to underpin or otherwise strengthen or safeguard the foundations of the building or structure of the adjoining owner.

(6) The notice referred to in subsection (5) shall be accompanied by plans and sections showing—

(a) the site and depth of any excavation the building owner proposes to make;
(b) if he proposes to erect a building or structure, its site.

(7) If an owner on whom a notice referred to in subsection (5) has been served does not serve a notice indicating his consent to it within the period of fourteen days beginning with the day on which the notice referred to in subsection (5) was served, he shall be deemed to have dissented from the notice and a dispute shall be deemed to have arisen between the parties.

(8) The notice referred to in subsection (5) shall cease to have effect if the work to which the notice relates—

(a) has not begun within the period of twelve months beginning with the day on which the notice was served; and
(b) is not prosecuted with due diligence.

(9) On completion of any work executed in pursuance of this section the building owner shall if so requested by the adjoining owner supply him with particulars including plans and sections of the work.

(10) Nothing in this section shall relieve the building owner from any liability to which he would otherwise be subject for injury to any adjoining owner or any adjoining occupier by reason of work executed by him.

Commentary in text—Chapter 4.

Rights etc.

7   Compensation etc.
(1) A building owner shall not exercise any right conferred on him by this Act

in such a manner or at such time as to cause unnecessary inconvenience to any adjoining owner or to any adjoining occupier.

(2) The building owner shall compensate any adjoining owner and any adjoining occupier for any loss or damage which may result to any of them by reason of any work executed in pursuance of this Act.

(3) Where a building owner in exercising any right conferred on him by this Act lays open any part of the adjoining land or building he shall at his own expense make and maintain so long as may be necessary a proper hoarding, shoring or fans or temporary construction for the protection of the adjoining land or building and the security of any adjoining occupier.

(4) Nothing in this Act shall authorise the building owner to place special foundations on land of an adjoining owner without his previous consent in writing.

(5) Any works executed in pursuance of this Act shall—

(a) comply with the provisions of statutory requirements; and
(b) be executed in accordance with such plans, sections and particulars as may be agreed between the owners or in the event of dispute determined in accordance with section 10;

and no deviation shall be made from those plans, sections and particulars except such as may be agreed between the owners (or surveyors acting on their behalf) or in the event of dispute determined in accordance with section 10.

Commentary in text—Chapter 6.

8 Rights of entry

(1) A building owner, his servants, agents and workmen may during usual working hours enter and remain on any land or premises for the purpose of executing any work in pursuance of this Act and may remove any furniture or fittings or take any other action necessary for that purpose.

(2) If the premises are closed, the building owner, his agents and workmen may, if accompanied by a constable or other police officer, break open any fences or doors in order to enter the premises.

(3) No land or premises may be entered by any person under subsection (1) unless the building owner serves on the owner and the occupier of the land or premises—

(a) in case of emergency, such notice of the intention to enter as may be reasonably practicable;
(b) in any other case, such notice of the intention to enter as complies with subsection (4).

(4) Notice complies with this subsection if it is served in a period of not less than fourteen days ending with the day of the proposed entry.

(5) A surveyor appointed or selected under section 10 may during usual working hours enter and remain on any land or premises for the purpose of carrying out the object for which he is appointed or selected.

(6) No land or premises may be entered by a surveyor under subsection (5) unless the building owner who is a party to the dispute concerned serves on the owner and the occupier of the land or premises—

- (a) in case of emergency, such notice of the intention to enter as may be reasonably practicable;
- (b) in any other case, such notice of the intention to enter as complies with subsection (4).

Commentary in text—Chapter 7.

9   Easements

Nothing in this Act shall—

- (a) authorise any interference with an easement of light or other easements in or relating to a party wall; or
- (b) prejudicially affect any right of any person to preserve or restore any right or other thing in or connected with a party wall in case of the party wall being pulled down or rebuilt.

Commentary in text—paragraphs **15.3–15.6**.

Resolution of disputes

10   Resolution of disputes

(1) Where a dispute arises or is deemed to have arisen between a building owner and an adjoining owner in respect of any matter connected with any work to which this Act relates either—

- (a) both parties shall concur in the appointment of one surveyor (in this section referred to as an 'agreed surveyor'); or
- (b) each party shall appoint a surveyor and the two surveyors so appointed shall forthwith select a third surveyor (all of whom are in this section referred to as 'the three surveyors').

(2) All appointments and selections made under this section shall be in writing and shall not be rescinded by either party.

(3) If an agreed surveyor—

- (a) refuses to act;
- (b) neglects to act for a period of ten days beginning with the day on which either party serves a request on him;
- (c) dies before the dispute is settled; or
- (d) becomes or deems himself incapable of acting,

the proceedings for settling such dispute shall begin *de novo*.

(4) If either party to the dispute—

(a) refuses to appoint a surveyor under subsection (1)(b), or
(b) neglects to appoint a surveyor under subsection (1)(b) for a period of ten days beginning with the day on which the other party serves a request on him,

the other party may make the appointment on his behalf.

(5) If, before the dispute is settled, a surveyor appointed under paragraph (b) of subsection (1) by a party to the dispute dies, or becomes or deems himself incapable of acting, the party who appointed him may appoint another surveyor in his place with the same power and authority.

(6) If a surveyor—

(a) appointed under paragraph (b) of subsection (1) by a party to the dispute; or
(b) appointed under subsection (4) or (5),

refuses to act effectively, the surveyor of the other party may proceed to act *ex parte* and anything so done by him shall be as effectual as if he had been an agreed surveyor.

(7) If a surveyor—

(a) appointed under paragraph (b) of subsection (1) by a party to the dispute; or
(b) appointed under subsection (4) or (5),

neglects to act effectively for a period of ten days beginning with the day on which either party or the surveyor of the other party serves a request on him, the surveyor of the other party may proceed to act *ex parte* in respect of the subject matter of the request and anything so done by him shall be as effectual as if he had been an agreed surveyor.

(8) If either surveyor appointed under subsection (1)(b) by a party to the dispute refuses to select a third surveyor under subsection (1) or (9), or neglects to do so for a period of ten days beginning with the day on which the other surveyor serves a request on him—

(a) the appointing officer; or
(b) in cases where the relevant appointing officer or his employer is a party to the dispute, the Secretary of State,

may on the application of either surveyor select a third surveyor who shall have the same power and authority as if he had been selected under subsection (1) or subsection (9).

(9) If a third surveyor selected under subsection (1)(b)—

(a) refuses to act;

(b) neglects to act for a period of ten days beginning with the day on which either party or the surveyor appointed by either party serves a request on him; or
(c) dies, or becomes or deems himself incapable of acting, before the dispute is settled,

the other two of the three surveyors shall forthwith select another surveyor in his place with the same power and authority.

(10) The agreed surveyor or as the case may be the three surveyors or any two of them shall settle by award any matter—

(a) which is connected with any work to which this Act relates, and
(b) which is in dispute between the building owner and the adjoining owner.

(11) Either of the parties or either of the surveyors appointed by the parties may call upon the third surveyor selected in pursuance of this section to determine the disputed matters and he shall make the necessary award.

(12) An award may determine—

(a) the right to execute any work;
(b) the time and manner of executing any work; and
(c) any other matter arising out of or incidental to the dispute including the costs of making the award;

but any period appointed by the award for executing any work shall not unless otherwise agreed between the building owner and the adjoining owner begin to run until after the expiration of the period prescribed by this Act for service of the notice in respect of which the dispute arises or is deemed to have arisen.

(13) The reasonable costs incurred in—

(a) making or obtaining an award under this section;
(b) reasonable inspections of work to which the award relates; and
(c) any other matter arising out of the dispute,

shall be paid by such of the parties as the surveyor or surveyors making the award determine.

(14) Where the surveyors appointed by the parties make an award the surveyors shall serve it forthwith on the parties.

(15) Where an award is made by the third surveyor—

(a) he shall, after payment of the costs of the award, serve it forthwith on the parties or their appointed surveyors; and
(b) if it is served on their appointed surveyors, they shall serve it forthwith on the parties.

(16) The award shall be conclusive and shall not except as provided by this section be questioned in any court.

(17) Either of the parties to the dispute may, within the period of fourteen days beginning with the day on which an award made under this section is served on him, appeal to the county court against the award and the county court may—

(a) rescind the award or modify it in such manner as the court thinks fit; and
(b) make such order as to costs as the court thinks fit.

Commentary in text—Chapters 8, 9, 10.

Expenses

11 Expenses

(1) Except as provided under this section expenses of work under this Act shall be defrayed by the building owner.

(2) Any dispute as to responsibility for expenses shall be settled as provided in section 10.

(3) An expense mentioned in section 1(3)(b) shall be defrayed as there mentioned.

(4) Where work is carried out in exercise of the right mentioned in section 2(2)(a), and the work is necessary on account of defect or want of repair of the structure or wall concerned, the expenses shall be defrayed by the building owner and the adjoining owner in such proportion as has regard to—

(a) the use which the owners respectively make or may make of the structure or wall concerned; and
(b) responsibility for the defect or want of repair concerned, if more than one owner makes use of the structure or wall concerned.

(5) Where work is carried out in exercise of the right mentioned in section 2(2)(b) the expenses shall be defrayed by the building owner and the adjoining owner in such proportion as has regard to—

(a) the use which the owners respectively make or may make of the structure or wall concerned; and
(b) responsibility for the defect or want of repair concerned, if more than one owner makes use of the structure or wall concerned.

(6) Where the adjoining premises are laid open in exercise of the right mentioned in section 2(2)(e) a fair allowance in respect of disturbance and inconvenience shall be paid by the building owner to the adjoining owner or occupier.

(7) Where a building owner proposes to reduce the height of a party wall or party fence wall under section 2(2)(m) the adjoining owner may serve a counter notice under section 4 requiring the building owner to maintain the

existing height of the wall, and in such case the adjoining owner shall pay to the building owner a due proportion of the cost of the wall so far as it exceeds—

(a) two metres in height; or
(b) the height currently enclosed upon by the building of the adjoining owner.

(8) Where the building owner is required to make good damage under this Act the adjoining owner has a right to require that the expenses of such making good be determined in accordance with section 10 and paid to him in lieu of the carrying out of work to make the damage good.

(9) Where—

(a) works are carried out, and
(b) some of the works are carried out at the request of the adjoining owner or in pursuance of a requirement made by him,

he shall defray the expenses of carrying out the works requested or required by him.

(10) Where—

(a) consent in writing has been given to the construction of special foundations on land of an adjoining owner; and
(b) the adjoining owner erects any building or structure and its cost is found to be increased by reason of the existence of the said foundations,

the owner of the building to which the said foundations belong shall, on receiving an account with any necessary invoices and other supporting documents within the period of two months beginning with the day of the completion of the work by the adjoining owner, repay to the adjoining owner so much of the cost as is due to the existence of the said foundations.

(11) Where use is subsequently made by the adjoining owner of work carried out solely at the expense of the building owner the adjoining owner shall pay a due proportion of the expenses incurred by the building owner in carrying out that work; and for this purpose he shall be taken to have incurred expenses calculated by reference to what the cost of the work would be if it were carried out at the time when that subsequent use is made.

Commentary in text—Chapter 11.

12 Security for expenses

(1) An adjoining owner may serve a notice requiring the building owner before he begins any work in the exercise of the rights conferred by this Act to give such security as may be agreed between the owners or in the event of dispute determined in accordance with section 10.

(2) Where—

(a) in the exercise of the rights conferred by this Act an adjoining owner requires the building owner to carry out any work the expenses of which are to be defrayed in whole or in part by the adjoining owner; or

(b) an adjoining owner serves a notice on the building owner under subsection (1),

the building owner may before beginning the work to which the requirement or notice relates serve a notice on the adjoining owner requiring him to give such security as may be agreed between the owners or in the event of dispute determined in accordance with section 10.

(3) If within the period of one month beginning with—

(a) the day on which a notice is served under subsection (2); or
(b) in the event of dispute, the date of the determination by the surveyor or surveyors,

the adjoining owner does not comply with the notice or the determination, the requirement or notice by him to which the building owner's notice under that subsection relates shall cease to have effect.

Commentary in text—Chapter 12.

13 Account for work carried out

(1) Within the period of two months beginning with the day of the completion of any work executed by a building owner of which the expenses are to be wholly or partially defrayed by an adjoining owner in accordance with section 11 the building owner shall serve on the adjoining owner an account in writing showing—

(a) particulars and expenses of the work; and
(b) any deductions to which the adjoining owner or any other person is entitled in respect of old materials or otherwise;

and in preparing the account the work shall be estimated and valued at fair average rates and prices according to the nature of the work, the locality and the cost of labour and materials prevailing at the time when the work is executed.

(2) Within the period of one month beginning with the day of service of the said account the adjoining owner may serve on the building owner a notice stating any objection he may have thereto and thereupon a dispute shall be deemed to have arisen between the parties.

(3) If within that period of one month the adjoining owner does not serve notice under subsection (2) he shall be deemed to have no objection to the account.

Commentary in text—paragraph **11.7**.

14 Settlement of account

(1) All expenses to be defrayed by an adjoining owner in accordance with an account served under section 13 shall be paid by the adjoining owner.

(2) Until an adjoining owner pays to the building owner such expenses as aforesaid the property in any works executed under this Act to which the expenses relate shall be vested solely in the building owner.

Commentary in text—paragraphs 11.8, 14.10, 14.13.

Miscellaneous

15 Service of notices etc.

(1) A notice or other document required or authorised to be served under this Act may be served on a person—

- (a) by delivering it to him in person;
- (b) by sending it by post to him at his usual or last-known residence or place of business in the United Kingdom; or
- (c) in the case of a body corporate, by delivering it to the secretary or clerk of the body corporate at its registered or principal office or sending it by post to the secretary or clerk of that body corporate at that office.

(2) In the case of a notice or other document required or authorised to be served under this Act on a person as owner of premises, it may alternatively be served by—

- (a) addressing it to 'the owner' of the premises (naming them), and
- (b) delivering it to a person on the premises or, if no person to whom it can be delivered is found there, fixing it to a conspicuous part of the premises.

Commentary in text—Chapter 13.

16 Offences

(1) If—

- (a) an occupier of land or premises refuses to permit a person to do anything which he is entitled to do with regard to the land or premises under section 8(1) or (5); and
- (b) the occupier knows or has reasonable cause to believe that the person is so entitled,

the occupier is guilty of an offence.

(2) If—

- (a) a person hinders or obstructs a person in attempting to do anything which he is entitled to do with regard to land or premises under section 8(1) or (5); and

(b) the first-mentioned person knows or has reasonable cause to believe that the other person is so entitled,

the first-mentioned person is guilty of an offence.

(3) A person guilty of an offence under subsection (1) or (2) is liable on summary conviction to a fine of an amount not exceeding level 3 on the standard scale.

Commentary in text—Chapter 16.

17 Recovery of sums
Any sum payable in pursuance of this Act (otherwise than by way of fine) shall be recoverable summarily as a civil debt.

Commentary in text—paragraph 9.4.1.

18 Exception in case of Temples etc.
(1) This Act shall not apply to land which is situated in inner London and in which there is an interest belonging to—

(a) the Honourable Society of the Inner Temple,
(b) the Honourable Society of the Middle Temple,
(c) the Honourable Society of Lincoln's Inn, or
(d) the Honourable Society of Gray's Inn.

(2) The reference in subsection (1) to inner London is to Greater London other than the outer London boroughs.

19 The Crown
(1) This Act shall apply to land in which there is—

(a) an interest belonging to Her Majesty in right of the Crown,
(b) an interest belonging to a government department, or
(c) an interest held in trust for Her Majesty for the purposes of any such department.

(2) This Act shall apply to—

(a) land which is vested in, but not occupied by, Her Majesty in right of the Duchy of Lancaster;
(b) land which is vested in, but not occupied by, the possessor for the time being of the Duchy of Cornwall.

20 Interpretation
In this Act, unless the context otherwise requires, the following expressions have the meanings hereby respectively assigned to them—
   'adjoining owner' and 'adjoining occupier' respectively mean any owner and any occupier of land, buildings, storeys or rooms adjoining those of the

building owner and for the purposes only of section 6 within the distances specified in that section;

'appointing officer' means the person appointed under this Act by the local authority to make such appointments as are required under section 10(8);

'building owner' means an owner of land who is desirous of exercising rights under this Act;

'foundation', in relation to a wall, means the solid ground or artificially formed support resting on solid ground on which the wall rests;

'owner' includes—

(a) a person in receipt of, or entitled to receive, the whole or part of the rents or profits of land;

(b) a person in possession of land, otherwise than as a mortgagee or as a tenant from year to year or for a lesser term or as a tenant at will;

(c) a purchaser of an interest in land under a contract for purchase or under an agreement for a lease, otherwise than under an agreement for a tenancy from year to year or for a lesser term;

'party fence wall' means a wall (not being part of a building) which stands on lands of different owners and is used or constructed to be used for separating such adjoining lands, but does not include a wall constructed on the land of one owner the artificially formed support of which projects into the land of another owner;

'party structure' means a party wall and also a floor partition or other structure separating buildings or parts of buildings approached solely by separate staircases or separate entrances;

'party wall' means—

(a) a wall which forms part of a building and stands on lands of different owners to a greater extent than the projection of any artificially formed support on which the wall rests; and

(b) so much of a wall not being a wall referred to in paragraph (a) above as separates buildings belonging to different owners;

'special foundations' means foundations in which an assemblage of beams or rods is employed for the purpose of distributing any load; and

'surveyor' means any person not being a party to the matter appointed or selected under section 10 to determine disputes in accordance with the procedures set out in this Act.

Commentary in text—paragraphs 2.2–2.5.

21 Other statutory provisions

(1) The Secretary of State may by order amend or repeal any provision of a private or local Act passed before or in the same session as this Act, if it appears to him necessary or expedient to do so in consequence of this Act.

(2) An order under subsection (1) may—

(a) contain such savings or transitional provisions as the Secretary of State thinks fit;
(b) make different provision for different purposes.

(3) The power to make an order under subsection (1) shall be exercisable by statutory instrument subject to annulment in pursuance of a resolution of either House of Parliament.

Commentary in text—paragraph **1.1**.

General

22 Short title, commencement and extent
(1) This Act may be cited as the Party Wall etc. Act 1996.

(2) This Act shall come into force in accordance with provision made by the Secretary of State by order made by statutory instrument.

(3) An order under subsection (2) may—

(a) contain such savings or transitional provisions as the Secretary of State thinks fit;
(b) make different provision for different purposes.

(4) This Act extends to England and Wales only.

Commentary in text—paragraph **1.1**, **1.7**.

Appendix 2

The Party Walls etc Act 1996 replaces Part VI (ss 44–59) of the London Building Acts (Amendment) Act 1939. The 1939 Act is set out below so that in considering the continuing relevance of cases decided under it, readers can compare the wording of its provisions with that of the corresponding provisions in the 1996 Act.

LONDON BUILDING ACTS (AMENDMENT) ACT 1939

(2 & 3 Geo 6 c xcvii)
ARRANGEMENT OF SECTIONS

PART VI

RIGHTS ETC OF BUILDING AND ADJOINING OWNERS

Section		Page
44	Interpretation of Part VI	172

Rights etc of owners

45	Rights of owners of adjoining lands where junction line not built on	172
46	Rights of owners of adjoining lands where junction line built on	173
47	Party structure notices	175
48	Counter notices	176
49	Dissent from notices	176
50	Underpinning	177
51	Execution of works	178
52	Notice of excavation of sites abutting on narrow streets or ways	178
53	Power of entry by building owner	179
54	Saving for easements	179

Differences between owners

55	Settlement of differences	179

Expenses

56	Expenses in respect of party structures	181
57	Security for expenses	183
58	Account of expenses	184
59	Recovery of expenses	184

Part VI

Rights etc of Building and Adjoining Owners

44 Interpretation of Part VI[1]

In this Part of this Act unless the context otherwise requires the following expressions have the meanings hereby respectively assigned to them:

'foundation' in relation to a wall means the solid ground or artificially formed support resting on solid ground on which the wall rests;
'party wall' means—
  (i) a wall which forms part of a building and stands on lands of different owners to a greater extent than the projection of any artificially formed support on which the wall rests; and
  (ii) so much of a wall not being a wall referred to in the foregoing paragraph (i) as separates buildings belonging to different owners;
'special foundations' means foundations in which an assemblage of steel beams or rods is employed for the purpose of distributing any load.

Rights etc of owners

45 Rights of owners of adjoining lands where junction line not built on

(1) Where lands of different owners adjoin and are not built on at the line of junction or are built on at the line of junction only to the extent of a boundary wall (not being a party fence wall or the external wall of a building) and either owner is about to build on any part of the line of junction the following provisions shall have effect—

---

1   Section 4 contains the following material definitions:
    '(1) In this Act save as it is otherwise expressly provided therein and unless the context otherwise requires the following expressions have the meanings hereby respectively assigned to them—
    'occupier' (except in Part V (Means of escape in case of fire) of this Act) does not include a lodger and the expressions "occupy" and "occupation" shall ne construed accordingly;
    'party fence wall' means a wall (not being part of a building) which stands on lands of diferent owners and is used or constructed to be used for separating such adjoining lands but does not include a wall constructed on the land of one owner the artificially formed support of which projects into the land of another owner;
    'party structure' means a party wall and also a floor partition or other structure separating buildings or parts of buildings approached solely by separate staircases or separate entrances from without;
    'party wall' (except in Part VI (Rights etc of building and adjoining owners) of this Act means so much of a wall which forms part of a building as is used or constructed to be used for separating adjoining buildings belonging to different owners or occupied or constructed or adapted to be occupied by different persons together with the remainder (if any) of the wall vertically above such before-mentioned portion of the wall.'

(a) If the building owner desires to build on the line of junction a party wall or party fence wall—

   (i) the building owner shall serve notice of his desire on the adjoining owner describing the intended wall;
   (ii) if the adjoining owner consents in writing to the building of a party wall or party fence wall the wall shall be built half on the land of each of the two owners or in such other position as may be agreed between the two owners and the expense of building the wall shall be from time to time defrayed by the two owners in due proportion regard being had to the use made or to be made of the wall by the two owners respectively and to the cost of labour and materials prevailing at the time when that use is made by each owner respectively;
   (iii) if the adjoining owner does not consent in writing to the building of a party wall or party fence wall the building owner shall not build the wall otherwise than at his own expense and as an external wall or a fence wall as the case may be placed wholly on his own land;

(b) If the building owner desires to build on the line of junction a wall placed wholly on his own land he shall serve notice of his desire on the adjoining owner describing the intended wall;

(c) Where in either of the cases described in paragraphs (a) and (b) of this subsection the building owner builds a wall on his own land he shall have a right at his own expense at any time after the expiration of one month but not exceeding six months from the service of the notice to place on land of the adjoining owner below the level of such land any projecting footings and foundation making compensation to the adjoining owner or the adjoining occupier or both of them for any damage occasioned thereby the amount of the compensation in the event of difference to be determined in the manner provided in this Part of this Act.

(2) Nothing in this section shall authorise the building owner to place special foundations on land of the adjoining owner without his previous consent in writing.

46 Rights of owners of adjoining lands where junction line built on

(1) Where lands of different owners adjoin and at the line of junction the said lands are built on or a boundary wall being a party fence wall or the external wall of a building has been erected the building owner shall have the following rights—

(a) A right to make good underpin thicken or repair or demolish and rebuild a party structure or party fence wall in any case where such work is necessary on account of defect or want of repair of the party structure or party fence wall;

(b) A right to demolish a timber or other partition which separates buildings belonging to different owners but is not in conformity with the London Building Acts or the Building Regulations 1985 and to build instead a party wall in conformity with those regulations;

(c) A right in relation to a building having rooms or storeys belonging to different owners intermixed to demolish such of those rooms or storeys or any part thereof as are not in conformity with the London Building Acts or the Building Regulations 1985 and to rebuild them in conformity with those regulations;

(d) A right (where buildings are connected by arches or structures over public ways or over passages belonging to other persons) to demolish such of those buildings arches or structures or such parts thereto as are not in conformity with the London Building Acts or the Building Regulations 1985 and to rebuild them in conformity with those regulations;

(e) A right to underpin thicken or raise any party structure or party fence wall permitted by this Act to be underpinned thickened or raised or any external wall built against such a party structure or party fence wall subject to—

   (i) making good all damage occasioned thereby to the adjoining premises or to the internal finishings and decorations thereof; and

   (ii) carrying up to such height and in such materials as may be agreed between the building owner and the adjoining owner or in the event of difference determined in the manner provided in this Part of this Act all flues and chimney stacks belonging to the adjoining owner on or against the party structure or external wall;

(f) A right to demolish a party structure which is of insufficient strength or height for the purposes of any intended building of the building owner and to rebuild it of sufficient strength or height for the said purposes subject to—

   (i) making good all damage occasioned thereby to the adjoining premises or to the internal finishings and decorations thereof; and

   (ii) carrying up to such height and in such materials as may be agreed between the building owner and the adjoining owner or in the event of difference determined in the manner provided in this Part of this Act all flues and chimney stacks belonging to the adjoining owner on or against the party structure or external wall;

(g) A right to cut into a party structure subject to making good all damage occasioned thereby to the adjoining premises or to the internal finishings and decorations thereof;

(h) A right to cut away any footing or any projecting chimney breast jamb or flue or other projection on or over the land of the building owner from a party wall party fence wall external wall or boundary wall in order to erect raise or underpin an external wall against such party wall party fence wall external wall or boundary wall or for any other purpose subject to making good all damage occasioned thereby to the adjoining premises or to the internal finishings and decorations thereof;

(i) A right to cut away or demolish such parts of any wall or building of an adjoining owner overhanging the land of the building owner as may be necessary to enable a vertical wall to be erected against that wall or building subject to making good any damage occasioned thereby to the wall or building or to the internal finishings and decorations of the adjoining premises;

(j) A right to execute any other necessary works incidental to the connection of a party structure with the premises adjoining it;

(k) A right to raise a party fence wall to raise and use as a party wall a party fence wall or to demolish a party fence wall and rebuild it as a party fence wall or as a party wall.

(2) For the purposes of this section a ... structure which was erected before the 6th January 1986 shall be deemed to be in conformity with the London Building Acts and a building which was erected before that date shall be deemed to be in conformity with those Acts and the Building Regulations 1985 if it is in conformity with the Acts and any byelaws made in pursuance of the Acts which regulated buildings or structures in London at the date at which it was erected.

(3) Nothing in this section shall authorise the building owner to place special foundations on land of the adjoining owner without his previous consent in writing.

47 Party structure notices

(1) Before exercising any right conferred on him by section 46 (Rights of owners of adjoining lands where junction line built on) of this Act a building owner shall serve on the adjoining owner notice in writing (in this Act referred to as a 'party structure notice') stating the nature and particulars of the proposed work the time at which it will be begun and those particulars shall where the building owner proposes to construct special foundations include plans sections and details of construction of the special foundations with reasonable particulars of the loads to be carried thereby.

(2) A party structure notice shall be served—
  (a) in respect of a party fence wall or special foundations at least one month; and
  (b) in respect of a party structure at least two months;
before the date stated therein as that on which the work is to be begun.

(3) A party structure notice shall not be effective unless the work to which the notice relates is begun within six months after the notice has been served and is prosecuted with due diligence.

(4) Nothing in this section shall prevent a building owner from exercising with the consent in writing of the adjoining owner and of the adjoining occupiers any right conferred on him by section 46 (Rights of owners of adjoining lands where junction line built on) of this Act and nothing in this section shall require him to serve any party structure notice before complying with any notice served under the provisions of Part VII (Dangerous and neglected structures) of this Act.

48   Counter notices

(1) After the service of a party structure notice the adjoining owner may serve on the building owner a notice in writing (in this Part of this Act referred to as 'a counter notice').

(2) A counter notice—

   (a)   may in respect of a party fence wall or party structure require the building owner to build in or on the party fence wall or party structure as the case may be to which the notice relates such chimney copings breasts jambs or flues or such piers or recesses or other like works as may reasonably be required for the convenience of the adjoining owner;
   (b)   may in respect of special foundations to which the adjoining owner consents under subsection (3) of section 46 (Rights of owners of adjoining lands where junction line built on) of this Act require them to be placed at a specified greater depth than that proposed by the building owner or to be constructed of sufficient strength to bear the load to be carried by columns of any intended building of the adjoining owner or may include both of these requirements; and
   (c)   shall specify the works required by the notice to be executed and shall be accompanied by plans sections and particulars thereof.

(3) A counter notice shall be served—

   (a)   in relation to special foundations within twenty-one days after the service of the party structure notice; and
   (b)   in relation to any other matter within one month after the service of the party structure notice.

(4) A building owner on whom a counter notice has been served shall comply with the requirements of the counter notice unless the execution of the works required by the counter notice would be injurious to him or cause unnecessary inconvenience to him or unnecessary delay in the execution of the works pursuant to the party structure notice.

49   Dissent from notices

If an owner on whom a party structure notice or a counter notice has been served does not within fourteen days thereafter express his consent thereto in writing he shall be deemed to have dissented from the notice and a difference shall be deemed to have arisen between the parties.

50 Underpinning

(1) Where a building owner—

(a) proposes to erect within ten feet from any part of a building of an adjoining owner a building or structure independent of the building of the adjoining owner and any part of the proposed building or structure will within the said ten feet extend to a lower level than the level of the bottom of the foundations of the building of the adjoining owner; or

(b) proposes to erect within twenty feet from any part of an independent building of an adjoining owner a building or structure any part of which will within the said twenty feet meet a plane drawn downwards in the direction of the building or structure of the building owner at an angle of forty-five degrees to the horizontal from the line formed by the intersection of the plane of the level of the bottom of the foundations of the building of the adjoining owner with the plane of the external face of the external wall of the building of the adjoining owner;

he may and if required by the adjoining owner shall subject to the provisions of this section at the expense of the building owner underpin or otherwise strengthen or safeguard the foundations of the building of the adjoining owner so far as may be necessary.

(2) In any case to which subsection (1) of this section applies the following provisions shall have effect—

(a) At least one month before beginning to erect a building or structure the building owner shall serve on the adjoining owner notice in writing of his intention so to do and that notice shall state whether he proposes to underpin or otherwise strengthen or safeguard the foundations of the building of the adjoining owner;

(b) The said notice shall be accompanied by plans and sections showing the site of the building or structure proposed to be erected by the building owner and the depth to which he proposes to excavate;

(c) Within fourteen days after service of the said notice the adjoining owner may serve notice in writing on the building that he disputes the necessity of or requires as the case may be the underpinning or strengthening or the safeguarding of the foundations of his building and if the adjoining owner serves such a notice a difference shall be deemed to have arisen between the building owner and the adjoining owner;

(d) The building owner shall compensate the adjoining owner and any adjoining occupier for any inconvenience loss or damage which may result to any of them by reason of any work executed in pursuance of this section.

(3) On completion of any work executed in pursuance of this section the building owner shall if so requested by the adjoining owner supply him with particulars including plans and sections of the work.

(4) Nothing in this section shall relieve the building owner from any liability to which he would otherwise be subject for injury to the adjoining owner or any adjoining occupier by reason of work executed by him.

51 Execution of works

(1) A building owner shall not exercise any right conferred on him by this Part of this Act in such manner or at such time as to cause unnecessary inconvenience to the adjoining owner or to the adjoining occupier.

(2) Where a building owner in exercising any right conferred on him by this Part of this Act lays open any part of the adjoining land or building he shall at his own expense make and maintain so long as may be necessary a proper hoarding shoring or fans or temporary construction for the protection of the adjoining land or building and the security of the adjoining occupier.

(3) Any works executed in pursuance of this Part of this Act shall—

(a) comply with the provisions of the London Building Acts and the Building Regulations 1985; and
(b) subject to the foregoing paragraph (a) be executed in accordance with such plans sections and particulars as may be agreed between the owners or in the event of difference determined in the manner provided in this Part of this Act and no deviation shall be made therefrom except such as may also be agreed between the parties or in the event of difference determined in manner aforesaid.

52 Notice of excavation of sites abutting on narrow streets or ways

Where a building owner proposes to erect any building or structure or carry out any work in relation to a building or structure on land which abuts on a street or way less than twenty feet in width the following provisions shall have effect if the erection of the proposed building or structure or the carrying out of the work involves excavation to a depth of twenty feet or more below the level of the highest part of the land immediately abutting on the street—

(a) Notices stating the place (being a place situate at a distance not greater than two miles of such land) at and the hours during which plans and sections of so much of the proposed building structure or work as relates to the excavation may be inspected shall be exhibited in a prominent position on the land or on any existing building or on the boundary wall fence or hoarding (if any) surrounding the said land or building and in such a manner as to be readily legible from every street or way on which the land abuts;
(b) The notices shall be exhibited at least four weeks before any such work of excavation is begun and shall be maintained and where necessary renewed by the building owner until such work of excavation is begun;
(c) The plans and sections referred to in the notices shall until the work of excavation is begun be open to public inspection without payment at the place and during such reasonable hours as are stated in the notice.

53 Power of entry by building owner

(1) A building owner his servants agents and workmen may during usual working hours enter and remain on any premises for the purpose of executing and may execute any work in pursuance of this Part of this Act and may remove any furniture or fittings or take any other action necessary for that purpose.

(2) If the premises are closed the building owner his servants agents and workmen may if accompanied by a constable or other police officer break open any fences or doors in order to enter the premises.

(3) Before entering any premises in pursuance of this section a building owner shall give to the owner and occupier of the premises—

- (a) in case of emergency such notice of his intention to enter as may be reasonably practicable;
- (b) in any other case fourteen days' notice of his intention to enter.

54 Saving for easements

Nothing in this Part shall authorise any interference with any easement of light or other easement in or relating to a party wall or prejudicially affect the right of any person to preserve any right in connection with a party wall which is demolished or rebuilt and to take any necessary steps for that purpose.

Differences between owners

55 Settlement of differences

Where a difference arises or is deemed to have arisen between a building owner and an adjoining owner in respect of any matter connected with any work to which this Part of this Act relates the following provisions shall have effect:

- (a) Either—
  - (i) both parties shall concur in the appointment of one surveyor (in this section referred to as an 'agreed surveyor'); or
  - (ii) each party shall appoint a surveyor and the two surveyors so appointed shall select a third surveyor (all of whom are in this section together referred to as 'the three surveyors');
- (b) If an agreed surveyor refuses or for ten days after a written request by either party neglects to act or if before the difference is settled he dies or becomes incapable of acting the proceedings for settling such difference shall begin de novo;
- (c) If either party to the difference refuses or for ten days after a written request by the other party neglects to appoint a surveyor under subparagraph (ii) of paragraph (a) of this section that other party may make the appointment on his behalf;
- (d) If before the difference is settled a surveyor appointed under subparagraph (ii) of paragraph (a) of this section by a party to the difference dies or becomes incapable of acting the party who appointed him may

appoint another surveyor in his place who shall have the same power and authority as his predecessor;

(e) If a surveyor appointed under subparagraph (ii) of paragraph (a) of this section by a party to the difference or if a surveyor appointed under paragraph (d) of this section refuses or for ten days after a written request by either party neglects to act the surveyor of the other party may proceed ex parte and anything so done by him shall be as effectual as if he had been an agreed surveyor;

(f) If a surveyor appointed under subparagraph (ii) of paragraph (a) of this section by a party to the difference refuses or for ten days after a written request by either party neglects to select a third surveyor under paragraph (a) or paragraph (g) of this section the superintending architect or in cases where the Council is a party to the difference the Secretary of State may on the application of either party select a third surveyor who shall have the same power and authority as if he had been selected under paragraph (a) or paragraph (g) of this section;

(g) If a third surveyor selected under subparagraph (ii) of paragraph (a) of this section refuses or for ten days after a written request by either party or the surveyor appointed by either party neglects to act or if before the difference is settled he dies or becomes incapable of acting the other two of the three surveyors shall forthwith select another surveyor in his place who shall have the same power and authority as his precedessor;

(h) All appointments and selections made under this section shall be in writing;

(i) The agreed surveyor or as the case may be the three surveyors or any two of them shall settle by award any matter which before the commencement of any work to which a notice under this Part of this Act relates or from time to time during the continuance of such work may be in dispute between the building owner and the adjoining owner;

(j) If no two of the three surveyors are in agreement the third surveyor selected in pursuance of this section shall make the award within fourteen days after he is called upon to do so;

(k) The award may determine the right to execute and the time and manner of executing any work and generally any other matter arising out of or incidental to the difference:

Provided that any period appointed by the award for executing any work shall not unless otherwise agreed between the building owner and the adjoining owner begin to run until after the expiration of the period prescribed by this Act for service of the notice in respect of which the difference arises or is deemed to have arisen;

(l) The costs incurred in making or obtaining an award under this section and the cost of reasonable supervision of carrying out any work to which the award relates shall subject to the provisions of this section be paid by such of the parties as the surveyor or surveyors making the award determine;

(m) The award shall be conclusive and shall not except as provided by this section be questioned in any court;
(n) Either of the parties to the difference may within fourteen days after the delivery of an award made under this section appeal to the county court against the award and the following provisions shall have effect—

   (i) Subject as hereafter in this paragraph provided the county court may rescind the award or modify it in such manner and make such order as to costs as it thinks fit;
   (ii) If the appellant against the award on appearing before the county court is unwilling that the matter should be decided by that court and satisfies that court that he will if the matter is decided against him be liable to pay a sum (exclusive of costs) exceeding one hundred pounds and gives security approved by the county court to prosecute his appeal in the High Court and to abide the event thereof all proceedings in the county court shall be stayed and the appellant may bring an action in the High Court against the other party to the difference;

(o) Where an appellant against an award brings an action in the High Court in pursuance of the last preceding paragraph the following provisions shall have effect—

   (i) If the parties agree as to the facts a special case may be stated for the opinion of the court and may be dealt with in accordance with or as nearly as circumstances admit in accordance with the rules of the court;
   (ii) In any other case the plaintiff in the action shall deliver to the defendant an issue whereby the matters in difference may be tried;
   (iii) The issue shall be in such form as may be agreed between the parties or in case of dispute or of non-appearance of the defendant as may be settled by the court;
   (iv) The action shall proceed and the issue be tried in accordance with or as nearly as circumstances admit in accordance with the rules of the court;
   (v) Any costs incurred by the parties in the county courts shall be deemed to be costs incurred in the action in the High Court and be payable accordingly.

Expenses

56 Expenses in respect of party structures
(1) The following provisions shall apply with respect to the apportionment of expenses as between the building owner and the adjoining owner—

(a) Expenses incurred in the exercise of the rights conferred by paragraph (a) of subsection (1) of section 46 (Rights of owners of adjoining lands where junction line built on) of this Act shall be defrayed by the building owner and the adjoining owner in due proportion regard being had to the use which the two owners respectively make or may make of the party structure or party fence wall;

(b) Expenses incurred in the exercise of the rights conferred by paragraph (b) of subsection (1) of the said section together with the expenses of building any additional party structure that may be required by reason of the exercise of those rights shall be defrayed by the building owner and the adjoining owner in due proportion regard being had to the use which the two owners respectively make or may make of the party wall or party structure and the thickness of such party wall or party structure required for support of the respective buildings of the two owners;

(c) Expenses incurred in the exercise of the rights conferred by paragraph (c) of subsection (1) of the said section shall be defrayed by the building owner and the adjoining owner in due proportion regard being had to the use which the two owners respectively make or may make of the rooms or storeys rebuilt;

(d) Expenses incurred in the exercise of the rights conferred by paragraph (d) of subsection (1) of the said section shall be defrayed by the building owner and the adjoining owner in due proportion regard being had to the use which the two owners respectively make or may make of the buildings arches or structures rebuilt;

(e) Expenses incurred in the exercise of the rights conferred by—

  (i) paragraphs (e) (g) (h) (i) and (k) of subsection (1) of the said section;

  (ii) paragraphs (f) of subsection (1) of the said section in so far as the expenses are not expenses incurred in the exercise of any rights conferred by other paragraphs of the said subsection and also a fair allowance in respect of the disturbance and inconvenience caused where the expenses have been incurred in the exercise of the rights conferred by the said paragraph (f);

shall be defrayed by the building owner.

(2) Expenses incurred in the exercise of the rights conferred by paragraph (j) of subsection (1) of the said section shall be defrayed in the same manner as the expenses of the work to which they are incidental.

(3) Any expenses reasonably incurred by the building owner in executing any works in pursuance of a counter notice served on him by an adjoining owner under section 48 (Counter notices) of this Act shall be defrayed by the adjoining owner.

(4) If at any time during the execution or after the completion of works carried out in the exercise of the rights conferred by paragraphs (e) (f) (j) or (k) of

subsection (1) of section 46 (Rights of owners of adjoining lands where junction line built on) of this Act any use of those works or any part thereof is made by the adjoining owner additional to the use thereof made by him at the time when the works began a due proportion of the expenses incurred by the building owner in the exercise of the rights conferred by any of the said paragraphs regard being had to the additional use of the works made by the adjoining owner shall be defrayed by the adjoining owner.

(5) Where in pursuance of section 45 (Rights of owners of adjoining lands where junction line not built on) or the said section 46 of this Act consent in writing has been given to the construction of special foundations on land of an adjoining owner then if the adjoining owner erects any building or structure and its cost is found to be increased by reason of the existence of the said foundations the owner of the building to which the said foundations belong shall on receiving an account with any necessary vouchers within two months after the completion of the work by the adjoining owner repay to the adjoining owner so much of the cost as is due to the existence of the said foundations.

(6) Where under this section expenses are to be defrayed in due proportion regard being had to the use made by an owner of a party structure party fence wall external wall or other work regard shall unless otherwise agreed between the building owner and the adjoining owner or provided in the award also be had to the cost of labour and materials prevailing at the time when that use is made.

57 Security for expenses

(1) An adjoining owner may by notice in writing require the building owner before he begins any work in the exercise of the rights conferred by this Part of this Act to give such security as may be agreed between the owners or in the event of dispute determined by a judge of the county court for the payment of all such expenses costs and compensation in respect of the work as may be payable by the building owner.

(2) Where in the exercise of the rights conferred by this Part of this Act an adjoining owner requires a building owner to carry out any work the expenses of which are to be defrayed in whole or in part by the adjoining owner or where the adjoining owner serves a notice on the building owner under subsection (1) of this section the building owner may before beginning the work to which the requirement or notice relates serve a notice in writing on the adjoining owner requiring him to give such security as may be agreed between the owners or in the event of dispute determined by a judge of the county court for the payment of such expenses costs and compensation in respect of the work as may be payable by him.

(3) If within one month after receiving a notice under subsection (2) of this section or in the event of dispute after the date of the determination by the judge of the county court the adjoining owner does not comply therewith the

requirement or notice by him to which the building owner's notice under that subsection relates shall cease to have effect.

58 Account of expenses

(1) Within two months after the completion of any work executed by a building owner of which the expenses are to be wholly or partially defrayed by an adjoining owner in accordance with section 56 (Expenses in respect of party structures) of this Act the building owner shall deliver to the adjoining owner an account in writing showing—

- (a) particulars and expenses of the work; and
- (b) any deductions to which the adjoining owner or any other person is entitled in respect of old materials or otherwise;

and in preparing the account the work shall be estimated and valued at fair average rates and prices according to the nature of the work the locality and the cost of labour and materials prevailing at the time when the work is executed.

(2) Within one month after delivery of the said account the adjoining owner may give notice in writing to the building owner stating any objection he may have thereto and thereupon a difference shall be deemed to have arisen between the parties.

(3) If within the said month the adjoining owner does not give notice under subsection (2) of this section he shall be deemed to have no objection to the account.

59 Recovery of expenses

(1) All expenses to be defrayed by an adjoining owner in accordance with an account delivered under section 58 (Account of expenses) of this Act shall be paid by the adjoining owner and in default may be recovered as a debt.

(2) Until an adjoining owner pays to the building owner such expenses as aforesaid the property in any works executed under this Part of this Act to which the expenses relate shall be vested solely in the building owner.

Appendix 3

CHECKLISTS OF NOTICES

1. By Building Owner on Adjoining Owner

Building Owner's Objective	Form of Notice Required	Time-Limit for Service	Authority
To build a party wall or party fence wall on the line of junction	Line of Junction Notice: *see* Precedent 1.1	At least one month before building owner intends work to start.	s 1(2)
To build on the line of junction a wall placed wholly on his own land.	Line of Junction Notice: *see* Precedent 1.2	At least one month before the building owner intends the building work to start.	s 1(5)
To carry out works to an existing party wall, party fence wall or party structure.	Party structure notice: *see* Precedent 2.	At least 2 months before the date on which the proposed work will begin.	s 3
To consent to a counter-notice	Consent Notice: *see* Precedent 5.2.	14 days beginning with the date on which the counter-notice is served.	s 5
To excavate within a distance of three metres/six metres of any part of a building or structure of an adjoining owner. **NB**: The proposed excavation must fall within s 6(1) and (2).	Three/Six-metre Notice: *see* Precedent 4.	At least one month before beginning to excavate.	s 6(5)
To require security for expenses.	Notice Requiring Security: *see* Precedent 12.2	Before beginning the work to which the requirement or notice relates. Security must be given by adjoining owner within one month of notice or determination by surveyor(s)	s 12(2)
To recover from adjoining owner expenses to be wholly or partly defrayed by adjoining owner.	Account: *see* Precedent 14.	Two months from completion of the work.	s 13(1)

2. By Building Owner on Adjoining Occupiers as well as Adjoining Owners

Building Owner's Objective	Form of Notice Required	Time-Limit for Service	Authority
To exercise rights of entry in order to execute works under the Act.	Notice of Entry: *see* Precedent 7.1	*Normally*: not less than 14 days before the proposed entry. *In emergencies*: such period as may be reasonably practicable.	s 8(3)
To enable a surveyor appointed or selected under s 10 to enter land or premises during usual working hours for the purpose of carrying out the object for which he is appointed or selected.	Notice of Entry: *see* Precedent 7.2	*Normally*: not less than 14 days before the day of the proposed entry. *In emergencies*: such period as may be reasonably practicable.	s 8(6)

3. By Adjoining Owner on Building Owner

Adjoining Owner's Objective	Form of Notice Required	Time-Limit for Service	Authority
To consent to the building of a party wall or a party fence wall. For the consequences see para **3.3.2**.	Consent Notice: *see* Precedent 5.1.	No time specified.	s 1(3)
To consent to the building of a party wall or party fence wall.	Consent Notice: *see* Precedent 5.1.	14 days beginning with the date on which the notice under section 1(2) is served.	s 1(4)
To consent to party structure notice.	Consent Notice: *see* Precedent 5.1	14 days beginning with the date on which the party structure notice is served.	s 5
To consent to party structure notice subject to requiring works as specified in s 4(1).	Counter-notice: *see* Precedent 3.	One month beginning with the date on which the party structure notice is served.	s 4(1)
To require building owner to maintain existing height of the wall.	Counter-notice under s 4(1) (*see above*).	(as above)	s 11(7)

3. **By Adjoining Owner on Building Owner**

Adjoining Owner's Objective	Form of Notice Required	Time-Limit for Service	Authority
To consent to notice by building owner under s 6(5).	Consent Notice: *see* Precedent 5.1.	14 days beginning with service of notice under section 6(5).	s 6(7)
To recover his extra cost of building on his land incurred by reason of the existence of special foundations.	Account justifying claim: any necessary invoices and other supporting documents must be supplied.	No time specified. Building owner must pay account within 2 months.	s 11(10)
To require security for expenses.	Notice Requiring Security: *see* Precedent 12.1.	Before work begins.	s 12(1)
To object to account served by building owner. Details of objection to be given.	Notice of Objections to Account: *see* Precedent 15.	One month after service of the account.	s 13(2)

Appendix 4
PRECEDENTS

1. Line of Junction Notice (s 1(2) or (5))	190
2. Party Structure Notice (s 3(1))	192
3. Counter-notice to Party Structure Notice (s 4(1))	194
4. Three/Six-metre Notice (s 6(5))	195
5. Consent Notices (ss 1(3), (4), 5 or 6(7))	197
6. Notice of Dispute (appointing surveyor)	198
7. Notice of Entry (s 8(3) or (6))	199
8. Formal Requests (s 10(4)(b), (7), (8))	201
9. Appointment of Surveyors (s 10(1)(a), (b), (4), (5))	203
10. Selection of Third Surveyor (s 10(1)(b), (8), (9))	204
11. Award (s 10(1))	205
12. Notice Requiring Security (s 12(1), (2))	208
13. Appeal to County Court (s 10(17))	210
Preliminary Note	210
13A Appellant's Notice	211
13B Part 7 claim	219
14. Account (s 13(1))	222
15. Notice of Objections to Account (s 13(2))	223

1. Line of Junction Notice[1]

Party Wall etc Act 1996 ('the 1996 Act')

To: [Name of Adjoining Owner]
of [Address]

From: [Name of Building Owner]
of [Address]

THIS is a notice under section 1(2) [1(5)] of the 1996 Act relating to the boundary between my property at   and your adjoining property at

1. I HEREBY GIVE YOU NOTICE as follows:

1.1 [If the notice is under section 1(2)]
  (a) I desire to build a party [fence] wall on the line of junction between our said properties.
  (b) If you agree to this work I request that you serve on me a notice indicating your consent within 14 days of this notice being served on you. This will lead to the consequences set out in section 1(3) of the 1996 Act.
  (c) If you do not serve such a notice, I shall be entitled to carry out the work at my own expense, wholly on my own property (apart from the footings and foundations mentioned below)

1.2 [If the notice is under section 1(5)]
  I desire to build along the line of junction between our said properties a wall which will be placed wholly on my own property, apart from the footings and foundations mentioned below.

2. (a) The work involved is described in the attached plans [specifications and drawings].[2]
  (b) The work includes the placing of projecting footings and foundations below the level of your property, which I have a right to do under section 1(6) of the 1996 Act.[3]

3. I propose to start work after the expiration of one month from the date this notice is served on you, or earlier if you agree.[4]

4. If a dispute arises between us over this work, it has to be referred to one or more Surveyors under section 10 of the 1996 Act. For the purposes of any dispute I appoint Mr   of   as my Surveyor, and invite you to concur in appointing him as an agreed Surveyor.[5]

Signed [by the Building Owner or authorised agent]

Dated:

Notes
1 This Precedent incorporates notices under both s 1(2) and (5).
2 Section 1 does not require plans, but they are sure to be advisable.
3 Projecting footings and foundations are likely (or s 1 may not apply). If special foundations are required, incorporate cl 1(c) from Precedent 2.
4 At least one month's notice is required by both sections.
5 Clause 4 is not essential, but may expedite the appointment of surveyors (for the agreed surveyor see s 10(1)(a)).

2. Party Structure Notice[1]

Party Wall etc Act 1996 ('the 1996 Act')

To: [Name of Adjoining Owner]
of [Address]

From: [Name of Building Owner]
of [Address]

THIS is a Party Structure Notice under section 3 of the 1996 Act relating to the structure on the boundary between my property at

and your adjoining property at

I HEREBY GIVE YOU NOTICE as follows:
1. (a) I propose to carry out works to or upon the said structure in exercise of my rights under section 2(2) of the 1996 Act [and in particular sub-sections (a), (b), (c), etc.[2]]
    (b) The nature and particulars of the proposed works are fully described in the attached plans, specifications and drawings ('the Plans').
    (c) The proposed works [do not] include special foundations [and the Plans include full details of them and the loads to be carried by them. I am not entitled to construct special foundations in your land without your written consent].[3]

2. I propose to begin work after the expiration of two months from the date this notice is served on you, or earlier if you agree.[4]

3. (a) If you agree to the works, I request that you serve on me a notice indicating your consent within 14 days of this notice being served on you.
    (b) If you wish to propose modifications to the works, you may be entitled to serve a counter-notice under section 4 of the 1996 Act within one month of this notice being served on you.
    (c) If you do not act under (a) or (b) a dispute is deemed to arise between us, which has to be referred to one or more Surveyors under section 10 of the 1996 Act.[5]

4. For the purposes of any dispute I appoint Mr   of
   as my Surveyor, and invite you to concur in appointing him as an agreed Surveyor.[6]

Signed [by Building Owner or authorised agent]

Dated:

Notes
1 See s 3. This notice is the essential preliminary to exercising rights under s 2, which applies when the boundary is already built on.
2 It is desirable to specify as accurately and completely as possible the subsections under which the works will be carried out.
3 Clauses 1 and 2 are required by s 3(1).
4 At least 2 months' notice of starting work is required (s 3(2)(a)).
5 Clause 3 is not essential, but helps to explain clause 4.
6 Clause 4 is not essential, but could expedite the appointment of surveyors (for the agreed Surveyor see s 10(1)(a)).

3. Counter-notice to Party Structure Notice[1]

Party Wall etc Act 1996 ('the 1996 Act')

To: [Name of Building Owner]
of [Address]
From: [Name of Adjoining Owner]
of [Address]

This is a Counter-notice under section 4(1) of the 1996 Act in response to the notice dated   and served by you on me under section 3 of the 1996 Act.

I HEREBY GIVE YOU NOTICE as follows:

1. I require:
   (a) that you build in or on the structure to which your notice relates chimney copings [breasts/jambs/flues/piers/recesses/other works] as specified in the attached plans, specifications and particulars ('the Plans'), which are works reasonably required for my convenience;[2]
   (b) that the special foundations referred to in your notice
      (i) be placed at the depth specified in the Plans, and
      (iii) be constructed of the strength specified in the Plans, which is designed to bear the load to be carried by columns of a building intended by me.[3]

2. Subject to the foregoing requirements and without prejudice to any of my rights under the 1996 Act or otherwise, I consent to the works proposed in your notice.

Signed [by Adjoining Owner or authorised agent]

Dated:[4]

Notes

1 See s 4. The point of a counter-notice is to enable the adjoining owner to consent, subject to imposing conditions of the kind permitted by s 4(1). If he wishes to dispute the party structure notice in principle, he should serve no notice, and allow a deemed dispute to arise under s 5.
2 See s 4(1)(a). The plans etc are required by s 4(2)(a).
3 See s 4(1)(b).
4 This notice must be served within one month of service of the party structure notice.

4. Three/Six-metre Notice[1]

Party Wall etc Act 1996 ('the 1996 Act')

To: [Name of Adjoining Owner]
of [Address]

From: [Name of Building Owner]
of [Address]

(1) THIS is a notice under section 6(5) of the 1996 Act relating to excavation works on my property at
which will (or may be) be within a prescribed distance from your adjoining property at

(2) I am unable to ascertain whether the works which I propose fall within a distance so prescribed or not, and this notice is served without prejudice to my contention that they do not, and will be of no effect if it is ascertained that they do not

I HEREBY GIVE YOU NOTICE as follows:

1. *For the purpose of ascertaining whether my proposed works do fall within a prescribed distance I request that you permit my agents:*

    (a) to inspect and take copies of such plans drawings specifications or other information in your possession and if necessary also

    (b) to enter you property and take such measurements and do such exploratory works (making good and damage caused)

    as may (in either case) be necessary for that purpose

    [If this is a 3-metre notice (section 6(1))]
    I propose to carry out works on my property within 3 metres of the building on your property involving excavation below the level of the bottom of its foundations.
    [If this is a 6-metre notice (section 6(2)]
    I propose to carry out works on my property within 6 metres of the building on your property involving excavation within an area defined by section 6(2) of the 1996 Act.[2]

2. (a) The proposed works, including the site and depth of the excavation and the site of the proposed building, are fully described in the attached plans and sections ('the Plans').[3]

   (b) I [do not] propose to underpin or otherwise safeguard the foundations of the building on your property [and these works are also described in the Plans].[4]

3. I propose to start excavating after the expiration of one month from the date this notice is served on you, or earlier if you agree.[5]

4. If you agree to the works, I request that you serve on me a notice indicating your consent within 14 days of this notice being served on you. If you do not, a dispute is deemed to arise between us, which has to be referred to one or more Surveyors under section 10 of the 1996 Act.[6]

5. For the purposes of any dispute I appoint Mr   of   as my Surveyor, and invite you to concur in appointing him as an agreed Surveyor.[7]

Signed [by Building Owner or authorised agent]

Dated:

Notes

1 See s 6(1) and (2). The provisions in italics should be deleted if it is certain that the proposed works will fall within either of the prescribed distances. They should be used only if there is uncertainty about this (see **4.3.5(c)**). If the works are within s 6, the notice will authorise them whether the request in cl 1 is granted or not. The adjoining owner will refuse the request at his peril (eg if it turns out that the notice is unnecessary, the notice will be void, and the surveyors will have no jurisdiction to award him any costs).
2 These summaries are not wholly accurate. The sections must be referred to in order to determine whether they apply. See Figure 3.
3 Clause 2(a) is required by s 6(6).
4 Clause 2(b) is required by s 6(5).
5 At least one month's notice must be given (s 6(5)).
6 See s 6(7).
7 Clauses 4 and 5 are not essential, but may expedite the appointment of Surveyors (for the agreed Surveyor see s 10(1)(a)).

5. Consent Notices

Party Wall etc Act 1996 ('the 1996 Act')

5.1 **Consents by Adjoining Owner**[1]

Without prejudice to any of my rights under the 1996 Act or otherwise, I [Name of Adjoining Owner] of [Address], in response to the notice under the 1996 Act dated   and served on me by [Name of Building Owner], HEREBY GIVE NOTICE that I consent to the carrying out of the works described in that notice, subject to all the provisions of the 1996 Act.

Signed: [by or on behalf of Adjoining Owner]

Dated:

5.2 **Consent by Building Owner**[2]

Without prejudice to any of my rights under the 1996 Act or otherwise, I [Name of Building Owner] of [Address], in response to the counter-notice under section 4 of the 1996 Act dated   and served on me by [Name of Adjoining Owner], HEREBY GIVE NOTICE that I consent to the requirements set out in that notice, subject to all the provisions of the 1996 Act.

Signed: [by or on behalf of Building Owner]

Dated:[3]

Notes

1. This is a general form of consent notice by the adjoining owner, which can be used under ss 1(3), (4), 5 or 6(7). It should be understood that consent under s 1(3) will involve the consequences set out in that section (which are not attractive to the adjoining owner), and that consent under s 5 may be exposing him to liability for certain expenses (see Chapter 11).
2. The only occasion for a consent notice by the building owner is under s 5, if he is content with the terms of a counter-notice. He will be giving up his right under s 4(3) to dispute the requirements in the counter-notice.
3. All consent notices should be served within 14 days of service of the notice to which they consent. (The absence of a time-limit under s 1(3) is best ignored.)

6. Notice of Dispute[1]

Party Wall etc Act 1996 ('the 1996 Act')

I, [Name of Adjoining Owner] of [Address] acknowledge receipt of a [purported][2] notice under the 1996 Act dated   and addressed to me by [Name of Building Owner] ['the Notice'], and in response HEREBY GIVE NOTICE as follows:

[1.   I dispute the validity of the Notice on the ground that   ][2]

2.   I do not consent to the carrying out of the works described in the Notice.

3.   Without prejudice to 1 and 2 above:
   [(a) I require the Building Owner at his own expense to underpin or otherwise strengthen or safeguard the foundations of the building on my land[3]].
   (b) For the purpose of the dispute I appoint Mr   of   to be my Surveyor [concur in the appointment of Mr   of   as the agreed Surveyor].

Signed: [by or on behalf of Adjoining Owner]

Dated:

Notes

1 The Act does not require any formal notice of dispute, but this Precedent will be useful: (a) under s 1, where deemed disputes do not arise; (b) in order to attack the validity of the building owner's notice: and (c) for requiring underpinning under s 6(3).

2 Clause 1 and the word 'purported' should be included or omitted together. There are many grounds for disputing the validity of a notice (eg bad service, insufficient details of works, building owner or works not qualifying).

3 Clause 3 must not give away clauses 1 and 2. For (a) see s 6(3).

7. Notice of Entry[1]

Party Wall etc Act 1996 ('the 1996 Act')

To: (1) The Owner of [Address of Adjoining Premises][2] ('the Premises')

(2) [Name] and [Name], the occupiers of the Premises[3]

From: [Name of Building Owner] of [Address]

THIS is a notice under section 8(3)[(6)] of the 1996 Act of intention to enter the Premises.

I HEREBY GIVE YOU NOTICE as follows:

1. After the expiration of 14 days[4] from the date that this notice is served on you

7.1 [If the notice is under section 8(3)]

I intend to enter the Premises with my agents and workmen [and principally my contractors, Messrs.]
for the purpose of executing the works authorised by an Award dated and made under the 1996 Act. For that purpose they are entitled under section 8(1) of the 1996 Act to enter and remain on the Premises during usual working hours, and to remove any furniture or fittings and take any other action necessary.

7.2 [If the notice is under section 8(6)]

The Surveyors appointed for the purposes of a dispute under the 1996 Act, namely Mr of and Mr of intend to enter the Premises for the purpose of carrying out the object for which they are appointed. For that purpose they are entitled under section 8(5) of the 1996 Act to enter and remain on the Premises during usual working hours.

2. Under section 16 of the 1996 Act it is an offence:

(a) for an occupier of premises to refuse to permit a person to do anything which he is entitled to do with regard to the premises under section 8(1) or (5) of the 1996 Act, if the occupier knows or has reasonable cause to believe he is so entitled;

(b) for any person to hinder or obstruct another in attempting to do anything which he is so entitled to do with regard to land, if that person knows or has reasonable cause to believe the other is so entitled.[5]

Signed: [by or on behalf of the Building Owner]

Dated:

Notes

1 This notice is an essential preliminary to exercising rights of entry for workmen (s 8(3)) or surveyors (s 8(6)). It must be served by the building owner.
2 The adjoining owner can be served by addressing him as 'the owner' and, if necessary, fixing the notice to the premises (s 15(2)).
3 Occupiers must also be served. For methods of service see s 15(1).
4 14 days is the normal minimum. In emergencies, such notice must be given as is reasonably practicable (s 8(3)(a) and (6)(a)).
5 This Precedent is designed to give enough explanation of the parties' rights of entry to pave the way for criminal sanctions under s 16. Clause 2 could be omitted if this is not thought necessary.

8. Formal Request[1]

Party Wall etc Act 1996 ('the 1996 Act')

Re Notice[2] dated from [Name of Building Owner]
to [Name of Adjoining Owner]

To: [Name of appropriate Owner or Surveyor]

of [Address]

THIS is a formal request under section 10(4)(b) [10(7)] [10(8)] of the 1996 Act made for the purpose of determining the dispute arising from the above-mentioned Notice.

I HEREBY REQUEST

8.1 [If under section 10(4)(b)][3]
that you appoint a Surveyor under section 10(1)(b) of the 1996 Act. If you fail to make an appointment in writing within 10 days of the service of this request on you, I shall be entitled to make an appointment on your behalf.

8.2 [If under section 10(7)][4]
that you act effectively in the dispute by [eg agreeing with me [my Surveyor] a timetable for determining the said dispute and proceeding in accordance with the timetable]. If you fail to do so within 10 days of the service of this request on you, I [my Surveyor] will be entitled to proceed ex parte to take those steps.

8.3 [If under section 10(8)][5]
that [in view of the [refusal to act/death/etc] of Mr   the third Surveyor] you concur with me, in selecting a third Surveyor [in his place] under section 10(1)(b) [10(9)] of the 1996 Act. I set out below the names of 3 persons whom I would approve for the purpose. If you do not approve any of them I further request that you notify me of the names of 3 persons whom you would approve. If you fail to accede to this request in writing within 10 days of its service on you, I shall be entitled to apply to the Appointing Officer [Secretary of State] to make the selection.

[List 3 names]

Signed: [by the appropriate Owner or Surveyor]

Dated:

Notes

1 Requests of this kind can readily be incorporated in a letter, provided it is written by, and served on, the appropriate person. They all have to be 'served', and must therefore be in writing. (Contrast s 10(11) where it is sufficient merely to 'call upon' the third surveyor, a process so informal that no Precedent is offered.)
2 This will be the initiating notice served by the building owner under ss 1(2), (5), 3(1) or 6(5).
3 Under this section the request must be made by or on behalf of the aggrieved owner, and served on the defaulting owner.
4 Under this section the request must be by the aggrieved owner or his surveyor, and served on the defaulting surveyor. It is the surveyor who becomes entitled to proceed ex parte, so that the request comes better from him. The alternative references to 'my surveyor' are appropriate only if the owner makes the request.
5 Under this section the request must be made by the aggrieved surveyor, and served on the defaulting surveyor. The request may arise under s 10(1)(b) (failure to select) or s 10(9) (refusal etc of third Surveyor). It is prudent to offer a choice of three names.

9. Appointment of Surveyors[1]

Party Wall etc Act 1996 ('the 1996 Act')

Re Notice[2] dated   from [Name of Building Owner]
          to [Name of Adjoining Owner]

9.1 Pursuant to section 10(1)(b) of the 1996 Act I [Name of Owner] hereby appoint Mr   of
to act as my Surveyor for the purposes of the dispute arising from the above-mentioned notice.

9.2 Pursuant to section 10(1)(a) of the 1996 Act, I [Name of Owner] hereby concur in the appointment of Mr   of
to act as the agreed Surveyor for the purposes [etc as above].

9.3 Pursuant to section 10(4) of the 1996 Act, I [Name of Owner] hereby appoint Mr   of
to act as the Surveyor of [Name of other Owner] (who has refused [neglected] to make an appointment on his own behalf) for the purposes [etc as above].

9.4 Pursuant to section 10(5) of the 1996 Act, I [Name of Owner] hereby appoint Mr   of
to act as my Surveyor for the purposes [etc as above] in place of Mr   who has [deemed himself incapable of acting].

Notes

1 These are the four forms of appointment provided for by s 10. In each case the appointment should be signed by the appropriate owner.

2 This will be the initiating notice served by the building owner under ss 1(2), (5), 3(1) or 6(5).

10. Selection of Third Surveyor[1]

Party Wall etc Act 1996 ('the 1996 Act')

Re Notice[2] dated   from [Name of Building Owner]
to [Name of Adjoining Owner]

10.1 Pursuant to section 10(1)(b) of the 1996 Act we, [Name], the Surveyor appointed by the Building Owner, and [Name], the Surveyor appointed by the Adjoining Owner, hereby select Mr   of
to act as the third Surveyor for the purposes of the dispute arising from the above-mentioned notice.

10.2 Pursuant to section 10(8) of the 1996 Act, I [Name of appointing officer], being the officer appointed for the purpose by the   Council, whose area includes the properties described in the above-mentioned notice, hereby select Mr   of
to act as the third Surveyor [etc as above].

10.3 Pursuant to section 10(9) of the 1996 Act we [Names], (the Surveyors appointed by the Building Owner and the Adjoining Owner respectively) hereby select Mr   of
to act as the third Surveyor [etc as above] in the place of [Name], who [died on the   ].

Notes

1 These are the three forms of selection of the third surveyor provided for by s 10. Under s 10(8) the selection must be made, and signed, either by the appointing officer (see s 20) or the Secretary of State. The other two selections must be made and signed by each of the parties' surveyors.

2 This will be the initiating notice served by the building owner under ss 1(2), (5), 3(1) or 6(5).

11. AWARD[1]

Party Wall etc Act 1996 ('the 1996 Act')

WHEREAS   of
('the Building Owner') the owner of the premises known as
on the [date] served upon   of
('the Adjoining Owner') the owner of the adjoining premises known as
             notice under section [1(2)/1(5)/3(1)/6(5)] of the 1996 Act
of his intention to execute works described therein

AND WHEREAS a dispute has arisen between the Building Owner and the Adjoining Owner ('the Parties')

AND WHEREAS the Adjoining Owner has appointed
of

to act as his Surveyor and the Building Owner has appointed
of

to act as his Surveyor ('the Parties' Surveyors')

AND WHEREAS the Parties' Surveyors have selected
of

to act as Third Surveyor in accordance with the provisions of the 1996 Act.

NOW WE, the Parties' Surveyors, being two of the three Surveyors so appointed, having inspected the said premises, DO HEREBY AWARD AND DETERMINE as follows:

1. We find the following facts:
   [(a) That the wall separating   and   is a party [fence] wall within the meaning of the Act.
   (b) That the said wall, although old, is sufficient for the needs of the Adjoining Owner.
   (c) That the condition of the said wall is as described in the Schedule of Condition dated   attached hereto and forming part of this Award.
   etc].

2. Fourteen days after the service of this Award on him the Building Owner shall be at liberty, but without obligation, to carry out the following works ('the Works'):

[List them]

3. No material deviation from the Works shall be made without the prior agreement of the Surveyor appointed by the Adjoining Owner.

4. The Building Owner shall:
   (a) Execute the whole of the Works at the sole cost of the Building Owner.
   (b) Take all reasonable precautions and provide all necessary shoring to retain the Adjoining Owner's land and buildings.
   (c) Make good all structural or decorative damage to the adjoining building occasioned by the Works in materials to match the existing works.
   (d) Hold the Adjoining Owner free from liability in respect of any injury or loss of life to any person or damage to property caused by or in consequence of the execution of the Works and the costs of making any justified claims.
   (e) Permit the Adjoining Owner's Surveyor to have access to the Building Owner's premises at all reasonable times during the progress of the Works.
   (f) Carry out the whole of the Works, so far as practicable, from the Building Owner's side. Where access to the Adjoining Owner's premises adjacent to the party wall is required, reasonable notice shall be given. Any scaffolding or screens will be removed as soon as possible and dust and debris cleared away from time to time as necessary.
   (g) Have the right to enter the property of the Adjoining Owner between the hours of 9.00 am and 5.30 pm, Mondays to Fridays, excluding Public Holidays, for the purpose of carrying out the following works:

   [List works requiring entry on adjoining land]

5. The Building Owner's Surveyor shall be permitted access to the Adjoining Owner's property from time to time during the progress of the works at reasonable times and after giving reasonable notice.

6. The whole of the Works shall be executed in accordance with Building Regulations and statutory requirements (including the requirements of the Control of Pollution Act 1974, the Environmental Protection Act 1990, the Health and Safety at Work etc Act 1974) and the requirements of any authority having jurisdiction over the Works, (including the Local

Authorities in whose area the work is being carried out, the Health and Safety Inspectorate and HM Inspectorate of Pollution) and to the satisfaction of the Building Control Officer or independent Certifying Officer and shall be executed in a proper and workmanlike manner in sound and suitable materials in accordance with the terms of this Award to the reasonable satisfaction of the adjoining Owner's Surveyor.

7. The Works shall be carried through with reasonable expedition after commencement and so as to avoid any unnecessary inconvenience to the Adjoining Owner and adjoining occupiers.

8. The two signed copies of the Award shall be served forthwith on the Parties by their respective Surveyors.

9. The Building Owner shall pay the fees of the Surveyor appointed by the Adjoining Owner (to be advised) plus VAT, in connection with the settling and carrying into effect of this Award.

10. The Parties' Surveyors reserve the right to make and issue one or more further Awards as may be necessary. If they cannot agree, the dispute shall be determined as provided in the 1996 Act.

11. This Award shall be null and void if the Works do not commence within twelve months from the date of service of this Award on the Building Owner.

12. Save so far as is necessary for the execution of the Works, nothing in this Award shall be construed as prejudicially affecting any right of light or air or any other easement whatever.

Signed: [by the Parties' Surveyors]

Dated:

Note
1 This Precedent is adapted from an award kindly provided by Mr A Schatunowski, FRICS. Its provisions are typical, but by way of example only.

12. Notice Requiring Security[1]

Party Wall etc Act 1996 ('the 1996 Act')

Re Notice dated   from [Name of Building Owner]
to [Name of Adjoining Owner]

To: [Name of Appropriate Owner]

of [Address]

THIS is a notice under section 12(1) [12(2)] of the 1996 Act requiring you to give security in respect of works described in the above-mentioned notice.

I HEREBY GIVE YOU NOTICE that:

12.1   [If the notice is under section 12(1)][2]

I require you to give security in respect of the said works, by [providing a bond in the sum of £   ], or in such other sum or manner as may be agreed between us or determined by the Surveyors under section 10 of the 1996 Act.

12.2   [If the notice is under section 12(2)][3]

1. I require you to give security for the expenses which will fall to be defrayed by you, by [depositing the sum of £   in a joint account in the names of the Solicitors acting for each of us], or in such other sum or manner as may be agreed between us or determined by the Surveyors under section 10 of the 1996 Act.

2. If you fail to give security within one month of the date of service of this notice on you, or of determination by the Surveyors, the notice which you served on me under section 12(1) of the 1996 Act will cease to have effect.

Signed: [by or on behalf of the Appropriate Owner]

Dated:

Notes

1 See s 12(1) (by adjoining owner) and s 12(2) (by building owner). These notices must both be served before the building owner starts work.

2 There are always likely to be expenses for which the adjoining owner would like security, for example in case the building owner leaves the work uncompleted.
3 Although s 12(2)(b) entitles the building owner to require security merely because the adjoining owner has done so, it is thought that security could only be awarded in respect of expenses which the Act imposes on the adjoining owner.

13. Appeal to county court

Preliminary Note

For reasons given in Chapter 10 there is uncertainty as to whether the correct procedure is to be governed by Part 52 of the Civil Procedure Rules on the one hand, or Parts 7 or 8 as appropriate on the other. The authors' view is that the latter is correct. To cover both eventualities two precedents appear below. The first (13A) is an appeal notice in accordance with Part 52, the second (13B) a Particulars of Claim under Part 7 for an appeal by an adjoining owner. Both have been adapted from documents served in actual cases, using fictitious names and addresses.

Precedents

13A. Part 52 Appeal

Appellant's Notice

In the **CENTRAL LONDON COUNTY COURT**

Notes for guidance are available which will help you complete this form. Please read them carefully before you complete each section.

Seal

For Court use only	
Appeal Court Reference No.	
Date filed	

Section 1 — Details of the claim or case

Name of court: **CENTRAL LONDON**

Case or claim number: **CL1234**

Names of claimants/applicants/petitioner: **SHERMAN FEIGENBAUM**

Names of defendants/respondents: **WINSTON CRUMBLE**

In the case or claim, were you the *(tick appropriate box)*

- [ ] claimant
- [ ] applicant
- [ ] petitioner
- [ ] defendant
- [ ] respondent
- [x] other *(please specify)* **ADJOINING OWNER**

Section 2 — Your (appellant's) name and address

Your (appellant's) name: **SHERMAN FEIGENBAUM**

Your solicitor's name: **HESTON, JACUZZI & CO** *(if you are legally represented)*

Your (your solicitor's) address:
**88 SOUTH FEUDAL STREET
LONDON SW1**

reference or contact name: **MR HESTON**

contact telephone number: **0207 779 0000**

DX number:

1

| Section 3 | Respondent's name and address |

Respondent's name: WINSTON CRUMBLE

Solicitor's name: NORMAN LE KRO LLP *(if the respondent is legally represented)*

Respondent's (solicitor's) contact address:

CASTLE VIEW
WINDSOR
BERKS SL1 9UA

reference or contact name: AARGH

contact telephone number: 01753 01871

DX number:

Details of other respondents are attached ☐ Yes ☐ No

| Section 4 | Time estimate for appeal hearing |

Do not complete if appealing to the Court of Appeal

How long do you estimate it will take to put your appeal to the appeal court at the hearing?

Days: 2 Hours: Minutes:

Who will represent you at the appeal hearing? ☐ Yourself ☐ Solicitor ☑ Counsel

| Section 5 | Details of the order(s) or part(s) of order(s) you want to appeal |

Was the order you are appealing made as the result of a previous appeal? Yes ☐ No ☑

Name of Judge: KARL SMITH FRICS & LEN JONES FRICS

Date of order(s): IST MARCH 2004

If only part of an order is appealed, write out that part (or those parts)

Paragraph 1 awarding the building owner the right to underpin the foundations of the party wall shown on plan 1876/9
Paragraph 6(3) (i) fixing the compensation payable whilst scaffolding is in place at £25.00 per week

Was the case allocated to a track? Yes ☐ No ☑

If Yes, which track was the case allocated to? ☐ small claims track ☐ fast track ☐ multi-track

Is the order you are appealing a case management order? Yes ☐ No ☑

| Section 6 | **Permission to Appeal** |

Has permission to appeal been granted?

        Yes ☐   complete box **A**   No ☑   complete box **B**

if you are asking for permission or it is not required

A
Date of order granting permission _____
Name of judge _____
Name of court _____

B
☑ I do not need permission
☐ I _____
appellant('s solicitor) seek permission to appeal the order(s) at **section 5** above.

Are you making any other applications?   Yes ☑   No ☐
If Yes, complete section 10

Is the appellant in receipt of legal aid certificate or a community legal service fund (CLSF) certificate?   Yes ☐   No ☑

Does your appeal include any issues arising from the Human Rights Act 1998?   Yes ☐   No ☑

| Section 7 | **Grounds for appeal** |

I (the appellant) appeal(s) the order(s) at **section 5** because:

(1) The provision of the award allowing the building owner to underpin the party wall is structurally unsound and will cause grave damage to the appellant's buidling. The wall should be taken down and rebuilt on a reinforced concrete foundation.
(2) The provision for compensation is inadequate

214   *Party Walls – Law and Practice*

| Section 8 | **Arguments in support of grounds** |

My skeleton argument is:-

☐ set out below   ☑ attached   ☐ will follow within 14 days of filing this notice

I (the appellant) will rely on the following arguments at the hearing of the appeal:-

| Section 9 | What decision are you asking the appeal court to make? |

I (the appellant) am (is) asking that:-

(tick appropriate box)

- [ ] the order(s) at **section 5** be set aside

- [✓] the order(s) at **section 5** be varied and the following order(s) substituted :-

> An award
> (1) requiring the party wall to be taken down and rebuilt on reinforced concrete foundations
> (2) Ordering the building owner to pay compensation of £250 per week whilst scaffolding is in place
> (3) Otherwise on the terms of the existing award with such consequential variations as are neccessary

- [ ] a new trial be ordered

- [ ] the appeal court makes the following additional orders :-

| Section 10 | Other applications |

I wish to make an application for additional orders   ☐ in this section

☐ in the Part 23 application form (N244) attached

Part A
I apply (the appellant applies) for an order (a draft of which is attached) that :-

1) That the appellant be allowed to adduce fresh evidence as follows

(1) The report of Cedric Bocho MICE dated 13th April 2004, attached
(2) The report of Millicent Kaefer FCA dated 1st May 2004, attached
(3) The witness statement of the Appellant attached

(2) That all the above witnesses attend court to give oral evidence

(3) That the appeal be by way of rehearing

because :-

The above evidence contains information essential to the appeal. This information should have been but was not taken into account when the award was made.

Part B
I (we) wish to rely on :

☑ evidence in Part C
☐ witness statement (affidavit)

Part C
I (we) wish to rely on the following evidence in support of this application:-

The award made by the surveyors disregarded the evidence of the structural need to demolish and rebuild the party wall, having regard to its age and the inadequacy of its foundations. The report of Mr Bocho sets out why the award was wrong in this respect.

The compensation ordered was totally inadequate, and this is dealt with in Mrs Kaefer's accountacy report and the Appellant's statement.

Statement of Truth
I believe (the appellant believes) that the facts stated in Section 10 are true.

Full name _Sherman McShane Feigenbaum_

Name of appellant's solicitor's firm _HESTON JACUZZI & CO_

signed _____ position or office held _____
Appellant ('s solicitor)   (if signing on behalf of firm or company)

Section 11	**Supporting documents**

If you do not yet have a document that you intend to use to support your appeal, identify it, give the date when you expect it to be available and give the reasons why it is not currently available in the box below.

Please tick the papers you are filing with this notice and any you will be filing later.

- [✓] Your skeleton argument *(if separate)*
- [✓] A copy of the order being appealed
- [ ] A copy of any order giving or refusing permission to appeal together with a copy of the reasons for that decision
- [✓] Any witness statements or affidavits in support of any application included in this appellant's notice
- [ ] A copy of the legal aid or CLSF certificate *(if legally represented)*
- [✓] A bundle of documents for the appeal hearing containing copies of your appellant's notice and all the papers listed above and the following:-
    - [ ] a suitable record of the reasons for the judgment of the lower court;
    - [✓] any statements of case;
    - [✓] any other affidavit or witness statement filed in support of your appeal;
    - [✓] any relevant transcript or note of evidence;
    - [ ] any relevant application notices or case management documents;
    - [✓] any skeleton arguments relied on by the lower court;
      relevant affidavits, witness statements, summaries, experts' reports and exhibits;
    - [ ] any other documents ordered by the court; (give details)

    _____

    - [ ] in a second appeal, the original order appealed, the reasons given for making that order and the appellant's notice appealing that original (first) order
    - [ ] if the appeal is from a decision of a Tribunal, the Tribunal's reasons for that decision, the original decision reviewed by the Tribunal and the reasons for that original decision

---

Reasons why you have not supplied a document and date when you expect it to be available:-

No such documents are available or required by the court.

Signed _____ Appellant ('s Solicitor)

13B. Part 7 Claim

Case No [CL 1234]

IN THE [CENTRAL LONDON] COUNTY COURT

BETWEEN:

[Abdul Mehboob]

Claimant

— and —

[William Smith]

Defendant

PARTICULARS OF CLAIM

1. The Defendant is the owner of land known as and comprising [33 Boghouse Heights, London SW11] ('the Property'). The Defendant at all material times has carried on and continues to carry on business as a property developer.

2. The Claimant is the freehold owner of property known as and comprising [31 Boghouse Heights, London SW11] ('the Adjoining Property').

3. On [date] the Defendant served upon the Claimant an award purporting to be made pursuant to the Party Walls etc Act 1996 ('the Award') by posting it in his letterbox.

4. The Award ought to be modified and the Claimant has by the proceedings herein appealed against the award.

Particulars

Clause 2: The works are described in points (i) to (iv) of the Award. There is no mention of the excavations and/or foundation work that are shown in the plans attached to the Award relating to the rear of the property. In addition the Defendant should have served a '3 metre Notice' in respect of these additional works. This was not done. The consequence of this omission is that these works, are not included in the standard indemnity given by the Defendant in the Award.

Schedule of Condition: The Schedule of Condition was incomplete at the time of signing the Award and remains so. The schedule requires amendment to include the flat roof at the rear of the Adjoining Property.

Other matters: The Award (a) makes inadequate protection for the flues serving the Adjoining Property and which were required to prevent debris falling as a result of works which were the subject-matter of the award and (b) fails adequately to address issues of security, sound and heat insulation, ventilation detailing and structural security.

Notwithstanding the time limited for appealing against the Award the Defendant commenced carrying out works at and around the boundary between the Property and the Adjoining Property. The Defendant wrongfully and without lawful authority has carried out works which were not the subject of the Award and/or to the Defendant's rights in respect of the boundary wall between the Property and the Adjoining Property. The Claimant will provide full particulars of the works which the Defendant has carried out following disclosure and/or inspection by his expert witness. Without prejudice to the foregoing, the Defendant has unlawfully carried out the following works.

Particulars

(1) commenced works with a view to underpinning and inserting deep strip foundations to the existing flank wall to the rear addition of the Adjoining Property within 3 metres of the Adjoining Property. The Claimant will provide full details of the remedial works which may be necessary following disclosure and/or further inspection of the site by the Claimant's expert.

(2) Carried out excavation works within 3 metres of the Adjoining Property which prejudice the rights of support enjoyed by the Adjoining Property and/or the party structures between the Property and the Adjoining Property.

(3) Erected scaffolding over the Adjoining Property which was not authorised in the Award or otherwise.

6. Further the Claimant has suffered loss and damage as a result of the matters aforesaid.

7. Further the Claimant seeks interest pursuant to section 69 of the County Courts Act 1984 on all sums found to be due to him.

AND the Claimant claims:

(1) An Order under Party Walls etc Act 1996 s.10(17) modifying the Award.

(2) A declaration that the works and matters specified in paragraph 5 above were unlawfully carried out by or on behalf of the Defendant.

(3) An order that the Defendant do carry out works to remedy the unlawful interference with the Claimant's rights particularised on paragraph 5(1) and (2) above. The Claimant will provide full details of the order to be sought following disclosure and/or further inspection of the site by his expert witness.

(4) An order that the damages which the Claimant has suffered as a result of the works and matters specified in paragraph 5 and carried out by the Defendant be assessed and/or there be an inquiry into such damages.

(5) Interest pursuant to section 69 of the County Courts Act 1984.

(6) Further and other relief.

(7) Costs

Statement of Truth

I believe that the facts contained in this Particulars of Claim are true.

Signed ....

Dated:

14. Account[1]

Party Wall etc Act 1996 ('the 1996 Act')

Re Award dated[2]

To: [Name of Adjoining Owner]

of [Address]

From: [Name of Building Owner]

of [Address]

THIS account is served on you under section 13(1) of the 1996 Act and has been prepared in accordance with that section to show the expenses payable by you under the terms of the above-mentioned Award.

Kindly take note as follows:

1. I require you to pay to me the sum of £   shown in the account to be payable by you.

2. (a) If within one month of the service of this account on you, you serve on me a notice stating objections to the account, a dispute will be deemed to arise between us, which must be determined by the Surveyors.[3]
   (b) If not, you will be deemed to have no objection to the account, and must pay me the said sum.[4]

3. Until you pay the sum due, the property in the works executed pursuant to the said Award will be vested solely in me.[5]

Signed: [by or on behalf of Building Owner]

Dated:

Notes

1 See s 13(1). The account must be served within 2 months from the completion of the works (see para **11.7**).
2 The adjoining owner's liability for expenses will normally arise from an award.
3 See s 13(2).
4 See s 13(3).
5 See s 14(2) and para **11.8**.

15. Notice of Objections to Account[1]

Party Wall etc Act 1996 ('the 1996 Act')

To: [Name of Building Owner]

of [Address]

From: [Name of Adjoining Owner]

of [Address]

THIS notice is served on you under section 13(2) of the 1996 Act, in response to the account served by you on [me].

I GIVE YOU NOTICE that I object to the said account on the following grounds:

[1. The particulars of the expenses and work are insufficient.

2. No deduction is made [in respect of item   ] for old materials.

3. The work and materials [in respect of items   ] are valued at excessive rates and prices.

etc].

Signed: [by or on behalf of Adjoining Owner]

Dated:

Note

1 See s 13(2). This notice must be served within one month of service of the account. It gives rise to a dispute which must be referred to the surveyors under s 10.

Appendix 5
THE PARTY WALL ETC BILL IN PARLIAMENT

The Bill was introduced as a Private Members Bill into the House of Lords by the Earl of Lytton, himself a chartered surveyor in private practice. In the House of Commons it was sponsored by Sir Sydney Chapman MP. Although the Bill was a Private Members Bill, it received Government support.

The relevant references in Hansard are as follows.

House of Lords
(1) House of Lords Debates 95/96, Vol 568, 31 January 1996, Col 1535 (second reading).
(2) House of Lords Debates 95/96, Vol 572, 22 May 1996, Col 931 (Committee).
(3) House of Lords Debates 95/96, Vol 572, 4 June 1996, Col 1160 (report received).
(4) House of Lords Debates 95/96, Vol 972, 11 June 1996, Col 1575 (third reading).

House of Commons
House of Commons Debates 95/96, Vol 281, 12 July 1996, Col 760 (second reading, Committee stage, report stage, third reading, Royal Assent).

The proceedings in the House of Commons were purely formal, the Act completing its passage in one day without objection (despite a strongly worded Parliamentary Briefing from The Law Society opposing the Bill). In the House of Lords, the report of second reading and Committee stage (references given above) should be consulted.

Appendix 6
ERRORS AND INCONSISTENCIES

1. Section 1(7) (Compensation for work under ss 1(4) and (5): This separate provision is inconsistent with the general provision in s 7(2) for no apparent reason. See **3.4.3**.

2. Section 1(8) (Disputes to be determined under s 10): The words 'or occupier' are inconsistent with the fact that occupiers are given no access to the s 10 procedure. See **3.5**.

3. Sections 2(3)(a), (4)(a), (5) (Conditions affecting certain rights): The word 'furnishings' should be 'finishings'. See **3.7(a)(i)**.

4. Section 7(5) (Deviation from plans): The parenthesis is unnecessary and inappropriate. See **6.3(c)**.

5. Section 9(b) (Restricting prejudicial effect of the Act): The word 'right' should be 'light'. See **15.3.2**.

6. Section 10(10) (Jurisdiction of surveyors): The omission of the words 'from time to time during the continuance of the work' throws undesirable doubt on the jurisdiction to make successive awards. See **8.15**.

7. Section 10(15)(a) (Service of third surveyor's award): The reference to 'the costs of the award' should be to 'his remuneration for making the award'. See **8.11**.

8. Section 20 (Definition of appointing officer): The word 'appointments' is inconsistent with the terminology in s 10, and should be 'selections' (and the same applies to the term 'appointing' officer itself). See **8.4(a)**.

INDEX

References in the right-hand column are to paragraph numbers or Appendix number.

Access orders   15.11
Accounts
  liabilities of adjoining owners
    11.7.1
  notices of objections   11.7.2, App 4
  precedents   App 4
Addresses   13.4.3
Adjacent excavations. *See* Excavations
Adjoining owners
  compensation to   6.6, 6.7
  counternotices, failure to serve
    13.9
  enforcement of rights   6.8
  financial liabilities   11.4
    accounts   11.7.1
    enforcement   11.8
    height reduction   11.4.4
    new walls   11.4.1
    notices of objection   11.7.2, App 4
    recovery   11.7
    repairs   11.4.2, 11.4.3
    requested works   11.4.5
    subsequent use   11.4.6
  meaning   2.5, 4.1, 14.2
  protection   6.2, 6.5
  security for expenses   12.1, 12.6, 12.8.1
  successors in title   14.7.2
  unnecessary inconvenience   6.4, 6.8.1
    compensation   9.5.3
    and nuisance   15.8.1
Adverse possession   2.2.2
Appeals
  Civil Procedure Rules   10.2.2
  court powers   10.2, 10.2.2
  effect   10.6
  fresh evidence   10.2, 10.2.2
  from county court   10.2.2
  generally   10.1–10.8
  jurisdiction   10.3–10.4
  rights   10.1
  time limits   10.5
  to county court
    jurisdiction   10.3
    nature   10.4
    notices   App 4
    particulars of claims   App 4
    precedents   App 4
    preliminary notes   App 4
    procedure   10.2.2
  to Court of Appeal   10.4
  to High Court   10.3
Arbitration, costs   11.5
Arbitrators
  immunity   8.20
  refusal to sign awards   8.9.1
Assignment   14.3, 14.9
Awards
  appeals. *See* Appeals
  effect   1.4, 9.2
  enforcement
    compensation   9.5.2
    damages   9.4.2, 9.4.3
    generally   9.4–9.5
    inconvenience   9.5.3
    injunctions   9.4.4
    interest   9.7
    jurisdiction   9.8
    limitation   9.10
    money payments   9.4.1
    non-monetary terms   9.4.2
    procedure   9.9
    specific performance   9.4.4
    statutory duty   15.10–15.10.2
    unauthorised works   9.5.4
  estoppel   9.3
  fair hearings   10.2.2
  form   8.18
  interest   9.7
  judicial review   10.7
  jurisdiction   8.12–8.14, 9.5.1
  making   8.10
  precedent   App 4
  reasons   10.2.2
  registration as land charges
    14.13.1
  retrospective awards   8.16

Index

Awards *cont*
  service   8.11
  severability   10.8
  successive awards   8.15
  successors in title   14.8–14.10
  surveyors. *See* Surveyors

Bodies corporate, service of notices on   13.4.4
Bonds, security for expenses   12.5
Boundary walls   2.6.4
Bristol   1.7
Building owners
  consent to building
    no consent   3.3.3
    notices   3.3.2
    originating notices   3.3.1
    time limits   3.3.4
  costs and expenses
    generally   11.3, 11.5, 11.6
    recovery from adjoining owners   11.7
  duty to make good   6.9
    payment in lieu   6.10
  entry rights   3.4.4, 7.2
  excavations. *See* Excavations
  existing walls   3.7
  meaning   2.5, 14.2
  new fence walls   3.4
  new walls. *See* New party walls
  party structures   3.8–3.10
  rights   3.1–3.10
  section 2 procedure   3.6–3.7
  section 3 procedure   3.8
  security for expenses   12.1, 12.2–12.5, 12.8.2
  successors in title   14.7.1
Building regulations   15.12
Buildings, meaning   4.5

Cables   4.5.3, 15.11
Cellars   4.4
Common law   3.1, 15.2
Compensation
  adjoining owners   6.6, 6.7
  awards   9.5.2
  enforcement   6.8
  fence walls   3.4.3

  jurisdiction   6.8.1
  law reform   6.6.10, 17.2.2
  no-fault compensation   6.6.9
  occupiers   7.7
Consent notices
  excavations   4.1
  new party walls   3.3.2
  precedent   App 4
Conveyancing
  completion   14.14.3
  consents to party structures   3.8.3
  contracts   14.14.2
  effect of party walls   14.11–14.14
  land charges   14.13, 14.14.4
  pre-contract actions   14.14.1
  purchasers' liabilities   14.12
  registered land   14.14.5
Costs
  arbitration   11.5
  categories   11.5
  fence walls   3.4.3
  general rule   11.5
  meaning   11.2.1
  party walls   3.3.2
  special foundations   5.8
Criminal offences
  entry   16.1, 16.5, 16.7
  generally   16.1–16.8
  occupiers   16.2, 16.6
  reasonable cause   16.4
  refusals   16.3
  summary proceedings   16.8
  time limits   16.8
  vicarious liability   16.2

Damages
  at common law   6.6.3
  enforcement of awards   9.4.2, 9.4.3
  statutory damages   6.6
Demolition
  authorised works   3.7
  making good   6.9
Disputes
  deemed disputes   3.10, 17.2.3
  excavations   4.8
  formal requests   App 4
  meaning   8.2
  multiple parties   8.17
  new party walls   3.5

Disputes *cont*
  notices, precedent   App 4
  party structures   3.10
  precedents   App 4
  registration as land charges
    14.13.1
  resolution procedure   8.1, 8.2
  security for expenses   12.7
  successors in title   14.4–14.8
  surveyors. *See* Surveyors
  third parties   3.5
Disturbance allowance   6.2, 6.5.2
Ditches   15.11
Drains   4.5.3, 15.11

Easements
  generally   15.3, 15.3.1
  light   8.13, 15.3, 15.4
Emergencies, meaning   7.4
Entry rights
  building owners   3.4.4, 7.2
  enforcement   7.6
  generally   7.1–7.8
  hindering   16.7, 17.3
  legal entry   16.5
  new party walls   3.4.4
  notices   7.4, App 4
  occupiers   7.7
  and privacy rights   15.12.3
  refusal of entry   16.1
  registration as land charges
    14.13.3
  successors in title   14.12.2, 14.13.3
  surveyors   7.3
  usual working hours   7.5
Estoppel   9.3
Excavations
  3-metre notices   4.2.1
  6-metre notices   4.2.2
  common law liability   4.12
  consent notices   4.1, App 4
  costs   4.7
  definitions
    adjoining owners   4.1
    bottom of foundations   4.6
    buildings or structures   4.5
    excavations   4.4
  disputes   4.9
  distances   4.1, 4.2

  law reform   17.3
  meaning   4.4
  measurements   4.3, 4.8
  non-apparent structures   4.3.5
  notices   4.1, 4.2, 4.8
    lapse   4.10
    precedent   App 4
  plans   4.8, 4.11
  safeguarding foundations   4.7
  scope   4.3.4
  structures with no foundations
    4.5.2
  subsidence   4.1
  underground services   4.5.3
Expenses
  general rule   11.3
  liabilities of adjoining owners
    accounts   11.7.1, App 4
    enforcement   11.8
    generally   11.4
    height reduction   11.4.4
    new walls   11.4.1
    notices of objection   11.7.2,
      App 4
    recovery   11.7
    repairs   11.4.2, 11.4.3
    requested works   11.4.5
    subsequent use   11.4.6
  meaning   11.2.2
  security. *See* Security for expenses
  successors in title   14.10
External walls   2.6.3

Fair hearings, right to   10.2.2
Family life, respect for   15.12.2,
  15.12.3
Fence walls
  building owners' rights   3.2, 3.4
  compensation   3.4.3
  costs   3.4.3
  entry rights   3.4.4
  footings and foundations   3.4.2
  meaning   2.6.2, 3.2.1
  nature   3.4
  originating notices   3.4.1
Fences   2.6.1
Flats   2.9
Footings   3.4.2, 5.4

Foundations
  bottom   4.6
  excavations   4.7
  fence walls   3.4.2
  special foundations
    consent   5.3, 5.7
    costs   5.8
    generally   5.1–5.8
    meaning   5.2
    notices   5.4
    party structures   5.5–6
  structures with no foundations
    4.5.2

Guarantees   12.5

Hedges   15.10
History   1.2
Hoardings   6.2
Human rights   7.8, 15.12

Inconvenience   6.4, 6.8.1, 9.5.3, 15.8.1
Injunctions, awards   9.4.4
Injurious affection   6.6.4
Inns of Court   1.6
Insurance
  excavations   4.3.5
  surveyors   8.20
Interest, court orders   9.7

Judicial review, awards   10.7

Land charges   14.13, 14.14.4
Law reform
  author's views   17.4
  compensation   6.6.10, 17.2.2
  deemed disputes   17.2.3
  generally   17.1–17.4
  ODPM review   17.2
  Pyramus and Thisbe Club   17.3
  summary procedures   17.2.1
Light, easements   8.13, 15.3, 15.3.1, 15.4

Limitation of actions   9.10
Lines of junction
  meaning   2.6.5
  notices   App 4
Local Acts   1.1, 1.3, 1.7
London   1.2, 1.3, 1.6, 1.7
London Building Acts (Amendment) Act 1939   1.2, 1.3, 1.7, App 2

Making good   6.9–6.10
Measurements, excavations   4.3, 4.8

Negligence
  surveyors   8.20
  works   15.7
Neighbouring land, access to   15.11
New party walls
  application   3.2.1, 3.2.2
  authorised works   3.2.3
  consent notices   3.3.2
    precedent   App 4
    time limits   3.3.4
  contradictions   3.2.1, 3.4
  costs   3.3.2
  disputes   3.5
  entry rights   3.4.4
  fence walls   3.4
  generally   3.2–3.5
  law reform   17.3
  liabilities of adjoining owners   11.4.1
  no consent   3.3
  originating notices
    fence walls   3.4.1
    party walls   3.3.1
  special foundations   5.4
Notices
  amendments   13.3
  checklist   App 3
  consent. *See* Consent notices
  counternotices, failure to serve   13.9
  effect   1.4
    successors in title   14.6
  formalities   13.2
  irregularities   13.10
  notifiable persons   13.7

Notices *cont*
  originating. *See* Originating notices
  service
    addresses   13.4.3
    bodies corporate   13.4.4
    failure to serve   13.9
    generally   13.1–13.10
    joint building owners   13.8
    methods   13.4–13.5
    owners of premises   13.6
    personal delivery   13.4.1
    post   13.4.2, 13.5
  time limits   13.10
Nuisance   6.4, 15.8

Occupiers
  compensation   7.7
  flats   2.9
  meaning   16.6
  party structures   3.8.3
  protection   9.6
  rights   2.5, 7.7
  tenants   7.7
  vicarious liability   16.2
Originating notices
  3-metre notices   4.2.1
  6-metre notices   4.2.2
  excavations   4.1, 4.2, 4.8
    lapse   4.10
    precedent   App 4
  new fence walls   3.4, 3.4.1
  new party walls   3.3.1
  special foundations   5.4
Overhangs   2.2.1, 6.9
Owners
  adjoining owners. *See* Adjoining
    owners
  building owners. *See* Building owners
  common law rights   3.1
  meaning   2.5
  multiple owners   2.8

Party fence walls
  law reform   17.3
  meaning   2.3
  new walls   3.2, 3.2.3
  section 1. *See* New party walls
  works on existing walls   3.7

Party structures
  consents   3.8.3
  counter-notices   3.9
    precedent   App 4
  disputes   3.10
  meaning   2.4
  notices   3.8
    precedent   App 4
  special foundations   5.5–6
  works on existing structures   3.7
Party Wall etc Act 1996
  commencement   1.2, 1.7
  effect on property rights   15.1
  errors and inconsistencies   App 6
  introduction   1.1
  parliamentary references   App 5
  previous legislation   1.2–1.3
  purpose   1.4
  reform. *See* Law reform
  successors in title   14.3, 14.15
  text   App 1
  third parties   15.8.2
Party walls
  boundary walls   2.6.4
  common law rights in   15.2
  external walls   2.6.3
  fence walls   2.6.2
  meaning
    common law   15.2
    statutory meaning   2.2, 2.7
  new walls. *See* New walls
  overhangs   2.2.1
  rights   15.3, 15.3.2
  trespassing buildings   2.2.2
  works on existing walls   3.6–3.7
Pipes   4.5.3, 15.11
Planning permissions   15.12
Plans
  conformity of works to   6.3
  excavations   4.8, 4.11
Postal service   13.4.2, 13.5
Precedents   App 4
Property rights   15.13.2, 15.13.4
Protection of adjoining owners   6.2,
  6.5
Pyramus and Thisbe Club   17.3

Quiet enjoyment   7.7

Receivers 2.5
Reform. *See* Law reform
Repairs
  access orders 15.11
  basic preservation works 15.11
  liabilities of adjoining owners
    11.4.2, 11.4.3
  section 2 rights 3.7

Section 1. *See* New party walls
Section 2. *See* Works
Section 3. *See* Party structures
Section 6. *See* Excavations
Section 9 15.3
Security for expenses
  adjoining owners, by 12.1, 12.6, 12.8.1
  amounts 12.4
  building owners, by 12.1, 12.2–12.5, 12.8.2
  disputes 12.7
  factors 12.3
  generally 12.1–12.8
  methods 12.5
  notices 12.1, 12.2, 12.6
    failure to comply 12.8
    precedent App 4
  time limits 12.7
Services, underground services 4.5.3
Sheds 4.5.1
Specific performance, awards 9.4.4
Structures, meaning 4.5
Subsidence 4.1, 4.5.2
Successors in title
  adoption of proceedings 14.6
  assignment 14.3
  awards 14.8–14.10
  conveyancing 14.11–14.14
  disputes 14.5–14.6
  dissenting successors 14.7
  entry rights 14.13.3
  expenses 14.10
Summary procedures 17.2.1
Summary proceedings 16.8
Support, right to 15.5
Surveyors
  agreed surveyors
    appointment 8.5.1
    incapacity 8.7.1

    meaning 8.1
    refusal and neglect 8.8.1
  appointment 8.4–8.6
    irrevocability 8.4
    precedent App 4
  s 1 disputes 3.5
  as arbitrators 8.19
  awards. *See* Awards
  death 8.7
  entry rights 7.3
  fees 11.2.1, 11.5
  immunity 8.20
  incapacity 8.7
  independence 8.3
  insurance 8.20
  jurisdiction 6.8.1, 8.12–8.14, 9.5.1
  meaning 8.3
  negligence 8.20
  parties' surveyors
    appointment 8.5.2, 8.6.1
    incapacity 8.7.2
    meaning 8.1
    refusal and neglect 8.9
  procedure 8.18
  qualifications 8.3
  refusal and neglect 8.8–8.9
  third surveyors
    appointment 8.5.3, 8.6.2
    incapacity 8.7.3
    meaning 8.1
    precedent App 4
    refusal and neglect 8.8.2
  three surveyors 8.1

Tenants. *See* Occupiers
Terraced buildings 2.9
Third parties 3.5, 15.8.2
Torts, limitation of actions 9.10
Trees 15.10
Trespass 15.9
Trespassing buildings 2.2.2

Underpinnings 5.4, 6.9, 11.3
Unnecessary inconvenience 6.4, 6.8.1, 9.5.3, 15.8.1

Vicarious liability 16.2

Walls, meaning	2.6.1	existing walls, procedure	3.6–3.7
Weather, protection from	15.6	expenses	11.2.2
Weather-proofing	6.9	illegality	15.12
Works		negligence	15.7
access orders	15.11	nuisance	6.4, 15.8
application	3.6	small works	17.2.4
authorised works	3.7, 6.3, 6.6.3	unauthorised works	9.5.4
basic preservation works	15.11	vesting	14.13.4